The Struggle for the Birthright

By Dr. Stephen E. Jones, M.A., Th.D

Table of Contents

The Struggle for the Birthright

by
Dr. Stephen E. Jones, M.A., Th.D

First Printing: 2,000 – 2003
Library of Congress Control Number: 2003108971
I.S.B.N.: 0-8187-0294-X

Additional copies available for $15.00 ($20.00 outside the U.S.) from:

Port Austin Bible Center
P.O. Box 444
Port Austin, Michigan 48467
(USA)

Our Cover Art

Glowing, Jacob's Ladder emerges forward from the depths of space. Weightlessly, Angels ascend and descend steps of light. They are delicate, ghostly, and much resembles translucent butterflies in flight. Below this angelic display, the earth's surface looms. Storms are brewing as clouds swirl in circles of turbulence.

Fists clinched, angry, Esau is aggressively portrayed in the upper left of this painting. His hair was described as a fiery red. Depicted here, it bleeds into a destructive, fiery glow on the earth's horizon. Esau's face is hard to make out – his features obscured by the severe perspective taken here. In fact, viewed from a distance, he almost disappears into the painting. Much neglected in scripture, his identity and birthright taken by his twin Jacob, he also becomes, almost lost here in this depiction. Our focus is clearly on Jacob. With the use of light and shadow, Jacob almost leaps from the painting, demanding the viewer's attention. Every element in the painting frames our focus on his image.

The smarter of the two, and jealous of his twins' status, Jacob sets out to obtain his brother's birthright. He purchases it from Esau when his brother is at his weakest, near starvation. Then he deceives his father into believing he is his older brother and received his twin's birthright, Esau's blessing. Here, shadow obscures half of Jacob's face and left hand. This symbolizes deceit; His face, for faking his brother identity, his hand, for left handedness, sneakiness. His hands are opened, defensive. He is passively aggressive. The left hand also overlaps the angelic display, symbolizing his wrestling with an angel to obtain a blessing. Through God's favored, and selected to father Israel, he used deception to obtain his goals, instead of waiting for God's intervention. It is ironic that while on the run from Esau, Jacob was tricked by his father-in-law, Laban, much the way he tricked his own father, Isaac.

Depicted here, the painting presents the warring bothers clashing from opposite sides of the world; as countries also clash from far ends of the globe. As Jacob and Esau emerged from the same womb, mankind also was born from the same source; oddly, to war with one another with the possibility of destroying their brethren. Jacob and Esau are us. Today, we are living their saga. Their story is ours, and my hopes are that this painting represents this.

Thank you,

Keith Birdsong

CHAPTER 1
The Birthright

The struggle for the birthright and for dominion over the earth is best known to Christians in the story of Jacob and Esau, found in Genesis 27. The history of that struggle, however, is not so well known. For this reason, many Christians do not really understand the current struggle, called in Isaiah 34:8 "the controversy of Zion." If Christians did understand this historic struggle, they would have quite a different view of Bible prophecy than is popular today.

There are two primary areas of study that form the backbone of Bible prophecy. The first is a knowledge of Israel's feast days, which we covered rather thoroughly in our book, The Laws of the Second Coming. The second is a knowledge of the history of the birthright from Adam to the present. It is this second area that we will cover in this book.

The Dominion Mandate

There are two parts to the birthright given to Adam in the beginning. They are the *dominion mandate* and the *fruitfulness mandate*. The dominion mandate is given in Gen. 1:26,

> **26 Then God said, Let us make man in Our image, according to Our likeness; and let them rule** [Heb. *radah*, "to have dominion"] **over the fish of the sea and over the birds of the sky and over the cattle and over all the earth, and over every creeping thing that creeps on the earth.**

In this divine mandate we see that God intended for man to "rule." The Hebrew word is *radah*, which literally means "to have dominion." This, then, is the original dominion mandate. It is what established Adam as the king over all the earth.

Many rivals to this throne have arisen over the centuries, the first notable one being Nimrod, the founder of Babylon (Gen. 10:10). Nimrod literally means "rebel." He revolted against the rulership of Noah and Shem (the builder of Jerusalem) and established a rival city-state, which he called Babel, or Babylon. Since that time, men have dreamed of ruling the world and of making all men the servants of their world-empire. However, all of these rivals to the throne intend to rule by their own laws in rebellion against the divine law and Jesus Christ, God's anointed King.

The dominion mandate given to Adam did not give him any rules or advice that might help him to rule the earth properly. Since Adam was created in the image of God, proper world government was a given. But after Adam sinned and lost the glory of God, it was not long before the leaven of sin gave fallen man the idea that dominion meant enslaving others and forcing them to do the will of the rulers, regardless of what that might be.

It is not until the divine law was given to Moses that we begin to see a clearer idea of the will of God concerning exercising dominion. The first commandment itself, applied to rulers, meant that rulers were to rule their domains *under God*. The fact that the rulers were given divine laws to administer showed that God had not given them a license to rule by their own whims or by their own ideas of right and wrong. They were expected to rule by divine revelation. Perhaps the primary law of rulership was laid down in Deut. 1:16, 17, where Moses said,

> **16 Then I charged your judges at that time, saying, Hear the cases between your fellow countrymen, and judge righteously between a man and his fellow countryman, or the alien who is with him. 17 You shall not show partiality in judgment; you shall hear the small and the great alike. You shall not fear man, for the judgment is God's.**

In the New Testament, this concept of not showing partiality was repeated in James 2:9, where the brother of Jesus wrote,

> **9 But if you show partiality, you are committing sin and are convicted by the law as transgressors.**

By the time we come to the New Testament era, we are given the full revelation of the dominion mandate by the example of Jesus Christ. Though He was born to be the King, yet He came as a servant. He did not come to call a people to a position of privilege. When the disciples disputed over who would have the highest privileges in the Kingdom, Jesus laid down the clearest principle of rulership to date. Luke 22:24-30 says,

> **24 And there arose also a dispute among them as to which one of them was regarded to be greatest. 25 And He said to them, the kings of the Gentiles lord it over them; and those who have authority over them are called Benefactors. 26 But not so with you, but let him who is the greatest among you become as the youngest, and the leader as the servant. 27 For who is greater, the one who reclines at the table, or the one who serves? Is it not the one who reclines at the table? But I am among you as the one who serves. 28 And you are those who have stood by Me in My trials; 29 and just as My Father has granted Me a kingdom, I grant you 30 that you may eat and drink at My table in My kingdom, and you will sit on thrones judging the twelve tribes of Israel.**

Likewise, Jesus said again in Matt. 23:8-12,

> **8 But do not be called Rabbi; for One is your Teacher, and you are all brothers. 9 And do not call anyone on earth your father; for One is your Father, He who is in heaven. 10 And do not be called leaders; for One is your Leader; that is, Christ. 11 But the greatest among you shall be your servant. 12 And whoever exalts himself shall be humbled; and whoever humbles himself shall be exalted.**

In other words, those who are called as rulers in the sight of God are not those that are recognized by men as kings, rabbis, teachers, prophets, or great men. The rulers in God's sight are those who serve God and His people. This is the mind of God. This is how God intended Adam to rule over God's creation. These are the kinds of people who will rule in the Kingdom of God at the first resurrection (Rev. 20:6). They are the ones who have taken Jesus' words seriously and can grasp the concept of serving others, rather than of being served.

This idea of rulers and judges being impartial, ruling as servants, thinking of the good of the people, rather than exploiting the people for their own welfare and comfort, is crucial in the age-long struggle between the kingdom of darkness and the Kingdom of God. Any people who claim to be called to rule the Kingdom will ultimately be disqualified if they do not rule others by these basic standards. As we proceed with this book, we will see just how this principle ought to impact the thinking of the Church.

The Fruitfulness Mandate

The second part of the birthright given to Adam was the fruitfulness mandate. We read of this a few verses later in Gen. 1:28,

> [28] **And God blessed them; and God said to them, Be fruitful and multiply, and fill the earth, and subdue it . . . .**

God's intent was not merely to fill the earth with carnally-minded men. It was His intent to fill the earth with the sons and daughters of God. It was His intent to fill the earth with men and women in His Own Image. In the law of biogenesis, *like begets like*. If Adam and Eve had brought forth children before the original sin, these children would have been begotten in the likeness and image of God. However, they sinned, and their children were born only *after* they had lost the glory and image of God. For this reason, since like begets like, all mankind were born after the flesh, not after the Spirit.

Even so, it is yet God's intent to fulfill this mandate, for Romans 8:19 speaks of the manifestation (unveiling) of the sons of God. This concept of Sonship begins in Gen. 1:26-28.

There are carnally-minded men who attempt, through technology and learning, to achieve the immortality and bodily transformation promised to the sons of God. They believe that if they can find the secret of life and transformation, they will be able to secure forever the dominion over the earth. This is the real motive behind their drive to discover secret technologies that have been acquired in the past century, beginning with the remarkable discoveries of the great scientist, Nikola Tesla.

Such carnally-minded people will not succeed in the long run. In fact, their partial successes indicate only that the true manifestation of the sons of God is near. Then those carnally-minded rebels—successors of Nimrod—will find their power eclipsed by the body of Christ, who are destined to rule and reign with Him in the age to come.

CHAPTER 2
The Story of Esau

Most Christians are familiar with the basic story of Jacob and Esau. Genesis 25 tells us that they were twin sons of Isaac and Rebekah. Gen. 25:22, 23 tells us that even before they were born they seemed to be fighting in their mother's womb:

> **22 But the children struggled together within her; and she said, If it is so, why then am I this way? So she went to inquire of the Lord. 23 And the Lord said to her, Two nations are in your womb; and two peoples shall be separated from your body; and one people shall be stronger than the other; and the older shall serve the younger.**

Esau was born first, so as the oldest son, he normally would have inherited the birthright. However, we learn from subsequent history and from Rom. 9:9-13 that God had predestined Jacob to receive the birthright, rather than Esau. This was the foundation of the controversy between the two brothers.

Why Did Esau Despise the Birthright?

The biblical account in Genesis 25 then continues by telling us that one day Esau returned from hunting and was very hungry. He then sold his birthright for a bowl of soup that Jacob was preparing. Gen. 25:34 concludes, "*Thus, Esau despised his birthright.*"

These few details do not really tell us why Esau would despise his birthright. Normally, such a carnally-minded man would want to keep the birthright, because such people always seem to desire wealth and power. Isaac was quite wealthy, for he had received the birthright from his father, Abraham, who was also wealthy. Abraham, in fact, could field 318 armed men in a battle to retrieve his nephew, Lot, in Gen. 14:14. No one could have had that many servants with families of their own without being very wealthy.

So why would Esau despise all of this wealth? He must have had a reason to think that such wealth was inconsequential, because carnal men do not think like this. If we look outside the Bible to an ancient historical source called the Book of Jasher, we find a possible answer. The Book of Jasher is mentioned in Joshua 10:13 and in 2 Sam. 1:18. After the destruction of Jerusalem in 70 A.D., this book was lost until an old copy was found in a rabbi's office in 1613. It was finally translated into English in 1840. Jasher gives us an interesting account that explains why Esau despised his birthright. Jasher 27:1-13 says,

> 1 And Esau at that time, after the death of Abraham, frequently went in the field to hunt. 2 And Nimrod king of Babel, the same was Amraphel, also frequently went with his mighty men to hunt in the field, and to walk about with his men in the cool of the day. 3 And Nimrod was observing Esau all the days, for a jealousy was formed in the heart of Nimrod against Esau all the days. 4 And on a certain day Esau went in the field to hunt, and he found Nimrod walking in the wilderness with his

> two men. [5] And all his mighty men and his people were with him in the wilderness, but they removed at a distance from him, and they went from him in different directions to hunt, and Esau concealed himself from Nimrod, and he lurked for him in the wilderness. [6] And Nimrod and his men that were with him did not know him, and Nimrod and his men frequently walked about in the field at the cool of the day, and to know where his men were hunting in the field. [7] And Nimrod and his two men that were with him came to the place where they were, when Esau started suddenly from his lurking place, and drew his sword, and hastened and ran to Nimrod and cut off his head. [8] And Esau fought a desperate fight with the two men that were with Nimrod, and when they called out to him, Esau turned to them and smote them to death with his sword. [9] And all the mighty men of Nimrod, who had left him to go to the wilderness, heard the cry at a distance, and they knew the voices of those two men, and they ran to know the cause of it, when they found their king and the two men that were with him lying dead in the wilderness. [10] And when Esau saw the men of Nimrod coming at a distance, he fled, and thereby escaped; and Esau took the valuable garments of Nimrod, which Nimrod's father had bequeathed to Nimrod, and with which Nimrod prevailed over the whole land, and he ran and concealed them in his house. [11] And Esau took those garments and ran into the city on account of Nimrod's men, and he came unto his father's house wearied and exhausted from fight, and he was ready to die through grief when he approached his brother Jacob and sat before him. [12] And he said unto his brother, Jacob, Behold I shall die this day, and wherefore then do I want the birthright? And Jacob acted wisely with Esau in this matter, and Esau sold his birthright to Jacob, for it was brought about by the Lord. [13] And Esau's portion in the cave of the field of Machpelah, which Abraham had bought from the children of Heth for the possession of a burial ground, Esau also sold to Jacob, and Jacob bought all this from his brother Esau for value given.

In this account we find that Esau, like Nimrod (Gen. 10:9), was a hunter. Nimrod was jealous of Esau's hunting ability and was spying on him, or having him watched. Esau apparently knew this, because Jasher was written from Jacob's perspective. One day Esau began to stalk Nimrod and suddenly ambushed him from his hiding place. Esau killed Nimrod and then had to fight for his life against Nimrod's two bodyguards. After killing them as well, he ran for his life, for he could hear the other men in the party running to help Nimrod's men. Because all the men who actually saw Esau were dead, there were apparently no witnesses left alive, leaving the rest of the party guessing who had ambushed their king.

Esau escaped and ran home, taking with him the special garments of Nimrod. These garments are said to be those that God gave to Adam, which signified his right to rule the earth. Garments had great significance in those days. Note that when Jacob himself gave the birthright to his son, Joseph, he gave him a special garment as well—a "*coat of many colors*" (Gen. 37:3, KJV).

The seventh chapter of Jasher explains that Adam's garments had been passed down to Noah, but after the flood, when Noah became drunk on wine, his son Ham stole those garments. Ham apparently never attempted to wear them, but passed them down to his son, Cush, who ultimately gave them to his son, Nimrod. Nimrod was the first to wear them openly at the age of twenty, and by these skins, he laid claim to Adam's dominion mandate over the earth. In this way Nimrod became the first open rebel who usurped the divine authority from Noah and Shem.

Esau stole the garments from Nimrod, and thus seemed to become the heir of the dominion mandate over the earth. With these garments, he thought that he could be like Nimrod and rule the world. What need would he have for the blessing of Isaac? Isaac was allied with Shem, the builder of Jerusalem, whose title was Melchizedek, "King of Righteousness," or Adonizedek, "Lord of Righteousness." In fact, this became the title of all the kings of Jerusalem long after Shem died, and we read of such a king by this name-title in Joshua 10:1.

Shem was Melchizedek

To show that Shem was the Melchizedek of Gen. 14:18, we will quote from Jasher 16:11, 12, which tells us the story of Abram's meeting with Melchizedek after freeing Lot:

> [11] And Adonizedek king of Jerusalem, the same was Shem, went out with his men to meet Abram and his people, with bread and wine, and they remained together in the valley of Melech. [12] And Adonizedek blessed Abram, and Abram gave him a tenth from all that he had brought from the spoil of his enemies, for Adonizedek was a priest before God.

Many people have misunderstood Melchizedek, thinking him to be Jesus Christ incarnate. Their belief is based upon a misreading of Heb. 7:1-8. Verse 3 says of Melchisedec that he was:

> **[3] without father, without mother, without genealogy, having neither beginning of days nor end of life; but made like the Son of God. (NASB)**

This must be taken in the context of verse 6. Heb. 7:6 says in the KJV, "*But he whose descent is not counted from them received tithes of Abraham.*" The NASB reads, "*But the one whose genealogy is not traced from them collected a tenth from Abraham.*" In other words, Melchisedec's genealogy is not counted, traced, or RECORDED by the biblical writer, and in this way is he also a type of Christ. It does NOT say that Melchisedec literally had no parents. It only says that he merely appears out of nowhere in the biblical text, with no explanation of who he was or who were his parents. This divine silence in the biblical text was done purposefully in order to make him a type of Christ, that is, "*one like the Son of God.*"

Shem himself lived to the ripe old age of 600 years. He was a century old when the flood came, and lived 500 years after the flood. If one charts the genealogies of Gen. 11, as we did on page 17 of Secrets of Time, we find that Shem outlived Abraham. In fact, Shem died when Isaac was 50 years old.

Jewish traditions teach that Shem built Jerusalem, and he would therefore be its king. He was still alive during all of Abraham's life. Therefore, it would only stand to reason that Abraham would pay tithes to him, for he was the true king of all the earth and was the birthright holder. In fact, because Shem outlived Abraham, Abraham never did receive the birthright, though he was in line to receive it. Hence, it passed directly from Shem to Isaac, and this is why the biblical narrative does not tell us about the birthright until Isaac's sons fought over it.

Esau is Edom, Idumea, Mount Seir, Teman, and Amalek

Understanding Esau—who he is and how his life has affected modern history—is of utmost importance in the study of Bible prophecy. The descendants of Esau were called various names in the Bible. The first name was Edom, which means "red," as we read in Genesis 25:30 in the NASB,

> [30] **And Esau said to Jacob, Please let me have a swallow of that red stuff there, for I am famished. Therefore his name was called Edom** ["red"].

The Hebrew name, "Edom," sometimes is written in its Greek form, "Idumea." These are the same name, but written in different languages. By marrying the daughter of Seir the Horite, Esau made an alliance with him and then went to live with that Canaanite family, as we read in Genesis 36:8,

> [8] **So Esau lived in the hill country of Seir; Esau is Edom.**

Jasher confirms this, saying that the reason he moved away was due to disputes with the Canaanites over pasture land and water rights. He then intermarried with the family of Seir the Horite and gave his daughters in marriage to the men of that family (Jasher 30:29). Eventually, in a dispute, Esau's family destroyed the family of Seir the Horite and thus inherited all of that land. And so, mount Seir became Esau's inheritance, the "land of Edom," and is so identified in later Scripture. It was located south of the Dead Sea all the way to the Gulf of Akaba on the Red Sea.

In Ezekiel 35 the prophecy against Esau's descendants is directed against "mount Seir and all Edom" (NASB of 35:15). The prophet also directs his anti-Esau prophecies against "Teman" in Ezekiel 20:46 and in 25:13. Teman was Esau's grandson through Eliphaz (Gen. 36:11).

Eliphaz also had a son named Amalek (Gen. 36:12) who established a prominent Edomite tribe that was one of Israel's fiercest enemies. They settled east of Edom between Canaan and Egypt. The Amalekites were the ones who attacked Israel as they came out of Egypt under Moses. Israel won the battle as long as Moses interceded for Israel with his hands raised (Exodus 17:11). In Exodus 17:16, after Israel had defeated Amalek in battle, God told Moses,

> [16] **and he said, The LORD has sworn; the LORD will have war against Amalek from generation to generation.**

From that time forward, the prophets consistently identify the descendants of Esau as being Israel's enemy that would be overthrown in the latter days. The book of Obadiah is only one chapter, but it is entirely devoted to this subject. It says in verse 18 that the house of Esau would be consumed as a field of stubble is consumed by fire.

> [18] **Then the house of Jacob will be a fire and the house of Joseph a flame; but the house of Esau *will be* as stubble. And they will set them on fire and consume them, so that there will be no survivor of the house of Esau, for the LORD has spoken.**

Interestingly enough, the "fire" is said to be first "the house of Jacob" (Israel) and more specifically "the house of Joseph." You recall that Joseph was the birthright holder and carried the name "Israel," ever since Jacob had given that name to the sons of Joseph in Gen. 48:16. This shows a particular conflict between Joseph and Esau. The reason is that both houses were to fight over the birthright. Esau had lost it, and his descendants continually desired to take it back. Joseph had ultimately received it, but was to lose it temporarily in the latter days. The struggle over the birthright is called "the controversy of Zion" in the King James Version of Isaiah 34:8. The NASB reads,

[8] **For the Lord has a day of vengeance, a year of recompense for the cause of Zion.**

In the footnote of the NASB, "the cause" is said to mean "controversy." They rendered it "cause," in the sense of a legal cause. The Hebrew word is *reeb*, and Strong's Concordance renders it "a contest (personal or legal)." In other words, God has a court date set for Edom, because He has a legal cause, or controversy, regarding "Zion," that is, regarding the administration of the Kingdom. Because the original Zion was the place of David's seat of government, Zion became a symbol of the administration of the Kingdom. Of course, this side of the Cross, we believe that the New Jerusalem takes precedence over the Old Jerusalem, and likewise, there is a New Zion that is distinct from the original location. This will be discussed further in Chapter Eight.

Once we understand that the prophecies regarding Esau come under all of these various names, it is apparent that the Bible is full of prophecies against Esau's descendants in the latter days. Many do not realize this, however, because many prophetic statements are directed at one of the other names: Edom, Idumea, Seir, Teman, or Amalek.

The Birthright Sale: Price-Gouging

Of course, Jacob and Esau themselves were rivals for the birthright and blessing (rulership, or dominion). When Esau was extra hungry one day, he sold his birthright to Jacob for a bowl of soup (Gen. 25:29-34). The birthright was the ownership of all the property owned by Isaac. When Jacob purchased the birthright for a bowl of soup, this sale was unlawful, according to Leviticus 25:14, which says,

[14] **If you make a sale, moreover, to your friend** [Heb. *amiyth*, "an associate, neighbor"]**, or buy from your friend's hand, you shall not wrong** [Heb. *anah*, "oppress, mistreat"] **one another.**

In the context of buying or selling, to mistreat or oppress means to take advantage of someone's situation, buying something at a very low price or selling at a very high price. Jacob broke this law when he bought the birthright from Esau for a bowl of soup. Jacob did not have enough money to purchase the birthright for a fair price.

Many years later, at the death of Isaac, Jacob did make the attempt to make this right with Esau. Jasher 47:15-19 tells us the story,

[15] And at the death of Isaac, he left his cattle and his possessions and all belonging to him to his sons; and Esau said unto Jacob, Behold I pray thee, all that our father has left we will divide it in two parts, and I will have the choice, and Jacob said, We will do so. [16] And Jacob took all that Isaac had left in the land of Canaan, the cattle and the property, and he placed them in two parts before Esau and his sons, and he said unto Esau, Behold all this is before thee, choose thou unto thyself the half which thou wilt take. [17] And Jacob said unto Esau, Hear thou I pray thee what I will speak unto thee, saying, The Lord God of heaven and earth spoke unto our fathers Abraham and Isaac, saying, Unto thy seed will I give this land for an inheritance forever. [18] Now therefore all that our father has left is before thee, and behold all the land is before thee; choose thou from them what thou desirest. [19] If thou desirest the whole land, take it for thee and thy children forever, and I will take this riches, and if thou desirest the riches, take it unto thee, and I will take this land for me and for my children to inherit it forever.

So the choice was between the wealth of Isaac and the land of Canaan. Esau, of course, decided to take the wealth and leave the land to Jacob, because the land was already claimed by the Canaanites and might never be inherited. The deal was recorded in a book, signed, and sealed. Esau moved back to his territory south of Canaan, and Jacob remained in Canaan. This settled the dispute, at least temporarily.

What neither Jacob nor Esau understood was that the "land of Canaan" included a great deal more than just a geographical land inheritance. As we showed earlier from Gen. 1:26-28, God had in mind from the beginning that this birthright should be promise of Sonship. In other words, the so-called "land inheritance" was really the manifestation of the Sons of God. How? Because our bodies are made of the dust of the ground. Adam was formed of the dust of the ground and was a "manifested Son" at the beginning. That is, Adam's body was spiritual flesh. His earthly body manifested the glory of God.

The purpose of creation was for God to manifest His glory in the earth that He had created. The highest manifestation of glory was reserved for Adam and man in general. The body, though made from earthly materials, was not evil, but "very good" (Gen. 1:31). God had always been glorified in the heavens, but God created this earth in order to glorify Himself in this dimension as well. But Adam sinned and lost that glorified body. That is, he literally lost his inheritance and found himself in bondage to an earthly body that was devoid of the former glory. The purpose of history is for man to regain the glorified body, where the dust of the ground once again houses and manifests the divine glory.

For this reason, the Sonship is actually man's prime inheritance. It is the real "land of Canaan" that God intended from the beginning to give us. The old land of Canaan was merely a type and shadow of the real inheritance. Yet when Esau chose the wealth, leaving Jacob with the promise of the land inheritance, Esau was despising the true birthright once again. And Jacob obtained the promise of Sonship that was inherent, but disguised, in the land of Canaan.

The point is that Esau was given a fair choice this time. But Esau was not a spiritual man, nor did he discern what was really at stake here. He chose the immediate blessing of wealth and rejected the long-term inheritance of the land inheritance, which the Apostle Paul calls "the redemption of our body" (Rom. 8:23).

But what about the dominion mandate? This, too, was something God gave to Adam in the first chapter of Genesis. Recall that this had been passed down from generation to generation. It resided in Shem, the King of Righteousness, King of Jeru-Salem ("City of Salem"). Abraham had died too soon to receive this mantle of rulership, but Isaac did receive it at the death of Shem, for he was the next prime inheritor in the lineage. How did Jacob get this dominion mandate?

The Dominion Mandate Stolen by Fraud

The conflict between Jacob and Esau came to a head when Isaac was ready to pass on the blessing to Esau. Isaac apparently became quite sick or weak and felt that his life was coming to an end soon. So he decided to bless his oldest son, Esau, with the dominion mandate. The blessing was customary when a patriarch felt like he was coming toward the end of his life. It was done to formally establish his successor as ruler of the estate. It was the moment when the birthright holder was lawfully appointed as RULER.

The difference between the birthright and the rulership was established in the first chapter of Genesis. In Gen. 1:26 God said to Adam and Eve, "*Let them have dominion.*" In verse 28 God said, "*Be fruitful and multiply.*" The blessing of being fruitful and multiplying was the birthright that Esau sold to Jacob for a bowl of soup. The dominion mandate is the blessing that Jacob stole.

Isaac intended to give the dominion "blessing" to his oldest son, Esau. He sent Esau to hunt venison for the occasion, but Rebekah overheard the conversation and remembered the prophecy during her pregnancy that "*the older shall serve the younger.*" She immediately decided to help God secure the blessing for Jacob. Taking advantage of Isaac's blindness (Genesis 27:1), Jacob pretended to be Esau, even dressing in Esau's finest clothing. Genesis 27:15, 16 says,

> [15] **Then Rebekah took the best garments of Esau her elder son, which were with her in the house, and put them on Jacob her younger son.** [16] **And she put the skins of the kids on his hands and on the smooth part of his neck.**

Isaac was suspicious, because he seemed to recognize Jacob's voice. Verse 19 says,

> [19] **And Jacob said to his father, I am Esau your first-born; I have done as you told me. Get up, please, sit and eat of my game** [venison]**, that you may bless me.**

Later, Isaac was still suspicious, so he tried once again to verify Esau's identity. Verse 24 says,

> [24] **And he said, Are you really my son Esau? And he said, I am.**

Isaac then blessed Jacob and proclaimed him as his successor from Adam, divinely appointed to rule the earth. But then Esau returned with the venison and requested the blessing. When he was told that Jacob had already usurped it, he was furious. One can hardly blame him. Isaac, too, was greatly disturbed by Jacob's deceit. We then read in verse 36:

> [36] **Then he said, Is he not rightly named Jacob, for he has supplanted me these two times? He took away my birthright, and behold, now he has taken away my blessing. And he said, Have you not reserved a blessing for me?**

Here we see a clear distinction between the birthright and the blessing. Many years later, Jacob preserved this distinction when he blessed his 12 sons, giving the blessing of the dominion mandate to Judah and the birthright to Joseph. 1 Chronicles 5:1, 2 says,

> [1] **Now the sons of Reuben the first-born of Israel for he was the first-born, but because he defiled his father's bed, his birthright was given to the sons of Joseph the son of Israel; so that he is not enrolled in the genealogy according to the birthright.** [2] **Though Judah prevailed over his brothers, and from him *came* the leader, yet the birthright belonged to Joseph.**

It is clear from this that Judah received the blessing of leadership, and this meant that from him would come the kings of Israel—most importantly, the Messiah. On the other hand, Joseph received the birthright, which was the mandate to "*be fruitful and multiply.*" The birthright included, then, the people of Israel—that is, the Kingdom itself. This was a type and shadow of a greater fulfillment that was yet to come—not merely carnal people who were nationally known by the name of Israel, but the Sons of God manifested in the earth. Remember that when God gave the fruitfulness mandate to Adam, He did not intend to produce mere fleshly children, but the Sons of God. The nation of Israel was certainly called to bring forth the Kingdom and bring forth the Sons of God, but they failed to do so.

The blessing of the dominion mandate was to produce the KING-MESSIAH. Having the birthright was to possess the KINGDOM. Jacob supplanted Esau in both of these. First Jacob took the birthright by price-gouging, taking advantage of Esau's hunger. But by deceit, he simply stole the blessing of the dominion mandate.

There is one thing I have learned about the divine law: it is impartial (James 2:9). That means Esau had lawful cause against Jacob, because Jacob wronged him. Many have attempted to justify Jacob's actions here, but they cannot be justified. The Bible says Jacob lied to his blind father. Jacob was guilty of outright fraud. For this reason, God had to hold Jacob accountable. So he led Isaac to pronounce a very important blessing upon Esau, a blessing which was not fulfilled until the twentieth century, as we shall yet see as we continue our study.

Isaac's Blessing on Esau

Isaac must have been well aware that God would judge Jacob for defrauding Esau. It made no difference that Esau was carnal, not having the character of God (or even of Isaac). Obviously, neither did Jacob. As the victim of deceit himself, Isaac knew that there would be a day of reckoning, when Jacob would have to return the birthright and blessing to Esau and allow God to give it to whomsoever He would—and in His own way. So Isaac gave this blessing to Esau in Gen. 27:39, 40,

> [39] **Then Isaac his father answered and said to him, Behold, away from the fertility of the earth shall be your dwelling, and away from the dew of heaven from above.** [40] **And by your sword you shall live, and your brother you shall serve; but it shall come about when you become restless** [Heb. *rood*, "to trample, to rule"]**, that you shall break his yoke from your neck.**

The key to understanding Esau's blessing is in the meaning of the Hebrew word, *rood*. The NASB translates it "become restless," but this rendering is meaningless. The KJV renders it "have the dominion." Young's Concordance says it means "to rule." Strong's Concordance says it means "to tramp about; i.e., ramble (free or disconsolate)."

It is apparent that the word paints the picture of a man who is free to "tramp" where he wishes—as in the case when a man owns his own land and can tramp where he pleases. In the above verse, where it is used in the blessing to Esau, we may picture Esau breaking free of Jacob's dominion, or rule, so that he is free to tramp about where he pleases. In fact, because Isaac has just prophesied that Esau would live by his sword, the word pictures Esau in a time when he would be free to do according to the dictates of his own violent character.

In other words, the day would come when Esau would receive the dominion mandate by force and be free to trample upon whomsoever he pleased. This is consistent with the character of Esau, and oppressive rule is what we would expect out of his descendants. Because Jacob had stolen this dominion mandate from Esau, Jacob would have to return it to Esau for a season at some point in the future. This was Isaac's righteous judgment in this case.

Yet even so, God will not allow Edom to have the dominion forever. Their time was to end after they had proven to all that they were not called or capable of ruling the earth with impartiality and with love. Their time of dominion would prove to all men that they are tyrants who expect to be treated as a privileged class. But God will have no tyrants ruling His Kingdom.

Esau, the First Zionist

Esau believed that the land of Canaan was rightfully his and that his brother, Jacob, had unlawfully usurped the land. All through history, it was his desire to evict Jacob and to conquer or settle the land in place of Jacob. While Jacob's descendants were in Egypt, the main tribe called Edom settled in the Arabah just south of the Dead Sea all the way to the Gulf of Akaba. The Amalekites, who were another branch from Esau, settled to their west in the Negev, directly south of Canaan. The Amalekites attacked Israel as they were coming out of Egypt under Moses (Ex. 17). In this sense, they were Israel's oldest enemies and probably were determined to prevent them from returning to Canaan.

Centuries later, in the days of Gideon, Israel was in captivity to an alliance of three people: Amalek, Midian, and the children of the East (Judges 6:3). So we find Amalek still the enemy of Israel and desirous of putting them into captivity.

When Judah was taken captive to Babylon, Edom rejoiced at their downfall, for this meant that they might be able to settle the land of Canaan. This is mentioned in Ezekiel 35 in a prophecy directed specifically at Edom.

> [2] **Son of man, set your face <u>against Mount Seir,</u> and prophesy against it.**
>
> [5] **Because you have had everlasting enmity and have delivered the sons of Israel to the power of the sword at the time of their calamity, at the time of the punishment of the end, [6] therefore, as I live, declares the Lord GOD, I will give you over to bloodshed, and bloodshed will pursue you; since you have not hated bloodshed, therefore bloodshed will pursue you.**
>
> [10] **Because you have said, These two nations** [Israel and Judah] **and these two lands will be mine, and we will possess them, although the LORD was there, [11] therefore, as I live, declares the Lord GOD, I will deal *with you* according to your anger and according to your envy which you showed because of your hatred against them; so I will make Myself known among them when I judge you.**

Notice here that Mount Seir, or Edom, was not a peace-loving people. They desired blood and were thus violating the law against "eating blood" (Lev. 17). Today men would describe them as bloodthirsty. Blood is red; Edom means "red." We cannot help but include Edom's name in the prophetic description of national character.

In verse 10 above, we see by the mouth of the prophet that Edom's desire was to possess the two lands of Israel and Judah. Though Isaac had prophesied Esau's eventual dominion—and presumably his claim to the land of Canaan—this return to Canaan was NOT to be done under godly motives. Hence, God says He will judge them according to their envy, hatred, and anger.

Esau wanted to rule the Kingdom of God for his own personal gain and with carnal motives and methods. In Ezekiel 36, the prophet turns to Israel and tells them about Edom in verses 2-5,

> [2] **Thus says the Lord GOD, Because the enemy has spoken against you, Aha! and, The everlasting heights have become our possession, [5] therefore, thus says the Lord GOD, Surely in the fire of My jealousy I have spoken against the rest of the nations, and <u>against all Edom</u>, <u>who appropriated My land for themselves</u>**

as a possession with wholehearted joy *and* with scorn of soul, to drive it out for a prey.

The conflict between Jacob and Esau in this prophecy is very clear. The fight is over the land of Canaan, which both wanted as their possession. When God scattered the House of Israel from 745-721 B.C., only Judah stood in the way of Esau's descendants from possessing the land. When Judah was taken to Babylon from 604-586 B.C., Edom then appropriated God's land for themselves, not to use it for God's will, but for their own selfish motives.

This prophecy was partially fulfilled in the days of Ezekiel, but at that time, not Edom, but Babylon actually possessed the land. The Assyrians before them had settled other people in the land to replace the Israelites that had been deported (2 Kings 17:24). The descendants of these people became known as Samaritans even in Jesus' day.

So even though Edom would have liked to possess the two countries of Israel and Judah, they were prevented from doing so at that time. This means that the fulfillment of Isaac's blessing upon Esau would come at a later time. The same is true of Ezekiel's prophecy of Edom.

Malachi's Prophecy of Esau

The prophet Malachi (about 450-400 B.C.) is probably the clearest statement of Esau's Zionist motivations. In chapter one we read,

1 The oracle of the word of the LORD to Israel through Malachi. 2 I have loved you, says the LORD. But you say, How hast Thou loved us? *Was* not Esau Jacob's brother? declares the LORD. Yet I have loved Jacob; 3 but I have hated Esau, and I have made his mountains a desolation, and *appointed* his inheritance for the jackals of the wilderness. 4 Though Edom says, We have been beaten down, but we will return and build up the ruins; thus says the LORD of hosts, They may build, but I will tear down; and *men* will call them the wicked territory, and the people toward whom the LORD is indignant forever.

Esau's Zionistic motive is in the statement, "*We will return and build.*" God's response is "*They may build, but I will tear down.*" In essence, God is re-affirming Isaac's blessing upon Jacob that they will indeed return and build, but at some point it will all be torn down. At that time the world will learn God's view of Edom and his methods. Men will then "*call them the wicked territory.*"

Even so, the way in which God restored the land and the birthright to the descendants of Esau is largely hidden from most people's view. God deliberately blinded both the world and the Church, lest we oppose His plan and method. But we believe the time has arrived when all may see what God has done to right the wrong done to Esau. To understand this properly, we must look at the historical record and see what actually happened to Esau's descendants, called Edom in Hebrew and Idumea in Greek.

The Maccabee Conquest of Edom: 126 B.C.

The conquest of Edom, or Idumea (as it was then known by its Greek name), began with Judas Maccabeus in 163 B.C., according to 1 Maccabees 5:3-8. Eventually, Edom ceased to be a nation in 126 B.C. when John Hyrcanus of Judah finished his conquest and forcibly converted the remaining Edomites to Judaism. Never again was there a nation called Edom or Idumea. The story is told in great detail by the first-century Jewish historian, Josephus, in his Antiquities of the Jews, XIII, ix, 1. Here we read:

> "Hyrcanus took also Dora and Marissa, cities of Idumea, and subdued all the **Idumeans**; and permitted them to stay in that country, if they would be circumcised, and make use of the laws of the Jews; and they were so desirous of living in the country of their forefathers, that they submitted to the use of circumcision and the rest of the Jews' ways of living; at which time therefore, this befell them, that **they were hereafter no other than Jews**."

Josephus was the first-century Jewish historian who initially fought against the Romans in the war that destroyed Jerusalem. He was himself a descendant of the Maccabees. He was well-acquainted with these things when he wrote of these things, because he was writing about his own family history. The Jewish Encyclopedia, 1925 edition under "Edom," affirms the Edomite absorption into Jewry, saying,

> "Judas Maccabeus conquered their territory for a time (B.C. 163; *Ant.* Xii, 8 par. 1, 2). They were again subdued by John Hyrcanus (c. 125 B.C.) by whom they were forced to observe Jewish rites and laws (*ib.* 9, par. 1; xiv. 4, par. 4). They were then incorporated with the Jewish nation, and their country was called by the Greeks and Romans 'Idumea' (Mark iii. 8; Ptolemy, *Geography* v. 16). With Antipater began the Idumean dynasty that ruled over Judea till its conquest by the Romans. Immediately before the siege of Jerusalem 20,000 Idumeans, under the leadership of John, Simeon, Phinehas, and Jacob, appeared before Jerusalem to fight in behalf of the zealots who were besieged in the Temple (Josephus, *B.J.* iv. 4, par. 5).
>
> "From this time the Idumeans ceased to be a separate people."

Books have been written attempting to prove that Turkey or China or other nations are modern Edom, in the vain effort to identify Edom with the real or imagined enemies of the modern Jewish state. Yet even The Jewish Encyclopedia itself (above) states the truth in plain language. "*The Idumeans* [or Edomites] *ceased to be a separate people*" from the Jews about 125 or 126 B.C.

This is confirmed again by The Jewish Encyclopedia, 1925 edition, Vol. 5, p. 41, which says, "*Edom is in modern Jewry.*"

Edom was absorbed by the Jews and ceased to be a separate people in history. This fact of history is beyond dispute, and no historian has even made the attempt to refute it. It is so well-known to historians that it is incredible how few Christians know this or have incorporated it into their views of Bible prophecy. Only God could have blinded the Church so as to make them lose the entire nation of Edom!

Hence, the Jews—or some branch of them—became the only people remaining to fulfill Isaac's blessing and the Zionist prophecies of Edom. These will be known by their character, manifested by their Zionistic *methods*. We would expect Edom's Zionism to be fulfilled by violence, theft, and bloodshed. In contrast, we would expect the true, godly Zionism of Israel (Joseph) to be fulfilled by peace, righteousness, and justice that would be a blessing to all families of the earth (Gen. 12:3). This is the contrast between the old Jerusalem and the New, between carnal and spiritual, between counterfeit and genuine.

Herod, the Jewish-Edomite Pattern-King

In the first advent of Jesus Christ, King Herod was His rival for the throne, His nemesis. For this reason, Herod attempted to kill Jesus by slaughtering the children of Bethlehem shortly after He was born. In that this past generation has seen the revival of child murder once again in the form of legalized abortion, we cannot help but see the historic parallel to the events preceding the second coming of Christ.

The pattern of King Herod himself has not been fully appreciated today, because few people have thought of this connection, and those who do would rather avoid it. But King Herod was half Idumean and half Judean. His father, Antipater, had been captured by Idumeans while he was still young and had been raised in Idumea. He later married an Idumean girl, Herod's mother.

Antipater rose to power when the Roman government appointed him Procurator of Judea in 47 B.C. Shortly afterward, the Parthians conquered Syria and Judea, setting Antigonus on the throne, for he was of the Maccabean lineage. But ultimately, Antipater's son, Herod, went to Rome and in 40 B.C. obtained their backing as King of Judea. Josephus wrote in his Antiquities of the Jews, XIV, xv, 2,

> "Herod had now a strong army; and . . . went on for Jerusalem . . . . Antigonus, by way of reply to what Herod had caused to be proclaimed . . . said, that they would not do justly if they gave the kingdom to Herod, who was no more than a private man, and an Idumean, i.e., a half Jew . . ."

Herod overthrew Antigonus in 37 B.C. and ultimately executed him in 34 B.C. Herod took the throne as King of the Jews and began the Idumean dynasty, which ruled Judea for a century until its destruction in 70-73 A.D. King Herod represented the Judean nation well, because he, like the nation itself, was half Idumean and half Judean.

In other words, Jewry itself—that is, those who adhere to Judaism and reject Jesus Christ—is the only modern nation that can fulfill the prophecies of Edom. In incorporating Edom into the nation of Judea and its religious system, *the Jews became the heirs of both sets of prophecies*—prophecies of Judah as well as the prophecies about Edom.

So far, we have shown but one side of this issue—that of Edom. Later, we will show how the Jews are fulfilling a portion of the prophecies of Judah as well. In order to understand the full scope of this picture, one must have a good grasp of both sets of prophecies and see how they merge without contradiction.

But before we can make sense of twentieth-century Zionism, and its connection to Edom, we must show also its Judah connection. Then when we have established both branches of this prophecy, all will be abundantly clear.

Chapter 3
Judah's Dominion Mandate

Reuben was the first-born son of Jacob, but he did not receive the birthright because he "defiled his father's bed" (1 Chron. 5:1). This is a reference to the incident recorded in Gen. 35:22,

22 And it came about while Israel was dwelling in that land, that Reuben went and lay with Bilhah his father's concubine; and Israel heard of it.

This disqualified Reuben from receiving the birthright—both the dominion mandate and the Sonship blessing. In Gen. 49:4 Jacob tells Reuben that he was "uncontrolled as water" because he had not had the self-control to refrain from this sexual relationship with Bilhah. Reuben's name means "Behold a son," but he lost the Sonship because of his actions. The Sonship was instead given to his brother Joseph, and the dominion mandate was given to his brother Judah.

Judah was the fourth son of Jacob-Israel. He did not receive the birthright itself, but Jacob did give him the dominion mandate portion. We read of this in 1 Chron. 5:1, 2,

1 Now the sons of Reuben the first-born of Israel (for he was the first-born, but because he defiled his father's bed, his birthright was given to the sons of Joseph the son of Israel; so that he [Reuben] **is not enrolled in the genealogy according to the birthright. 2 Though Judah prevailed over his brothers, and from him came the leader, yet the birthright belonged to Joseph.**

The manner in which Jacob divided the dominion mandate from the fruitfulness mandate is told in the book of Genesis. In Gen. 37:3 we find the first hint that the birthright was given to Joseph, when Jacob gave him the sign of the birthright holder—a special robe:

3 Now Israel loved Joseph more than all his sons, because he was the son of his old age; and he made him a varicolored tunic.

The actual transfer of the birthright, however, was later given to Joseph's sons, particularly Ephraim, whose name means "fruitfulness." His name was therefore prophetic of the fulfillment of the fruitfulness mandate, dating back to Gen. 1:28. When Jacob was old and about to die, he called for Joseph and his sons and gave them a blessing recorded in Genesis 48. Joseph expected that Jacob would give the blessing to Manasseh, his oldest son, so he positioned Manasseh to be near Jacob's right hand. Ephraim was positioned at Jacob's left hand.

But Jacob then crossed his arms, placing his right hand upon the head of Ephraim and his left hand upon the head of Manasseh. Gen. 48:15, 16 says,

15 And he blessed Joseph and said, The God before whom my fathers Abraham and Isaac walked, the God who has been my shepherd all my life to this day, 16 the angel who has redeemed me from all evil, bless the lads; and may my name live on in them, and the names of my fathers Abraham and Isaac; and may they grow into a multitude in the midst of the earth.

The angel who had redeemed Jacob was the angel that Jacob wrestled at Penuel in Gen. 32:24-32. This was the angel that had given Jacob the name "Israel." So in this blessing, Jacob-Israel was passing that name ISRAEL to the sons of Joseph. At the same time he blessed them with a "multitude" of descendants—that is, with the fruitfulness mandate of the birthright.

And so for this reason 1 Chron. 5:1, 2 (above) tells us that Joseph received the birthright. And yet we learn also that the birthright given to Joseph was not the entire birthright as it had existed up to that time. Jacob separated the dominion mandate from the rest of the birthright and gave this portion to Judah.

Jacob's Blessing upon Judah

Judah's blessing is given in Gen. 49:8-12, where we read,

> [8] **Judah, your brothers shall praise you** [Judah means "praise"]; **your hand shall be on the neck of your enemies; your father's sons shall bow down to you.** [9] **Judah is a lion's whelp; from the prey, my son, you have gone up. He couches** [Heb. *rabats*, "to crouch or recline"], **he lies down as a lion, and as a lion, who dares rouse him up?** [10] **<u>The scepter shall not depart from Judah</u>, nor the ruler's staff from between his feet, until Shiloh comes, and to him shall be the obedience of the peoples.** [11] **He ties his foal to the vine, and his donkey's colt to the choice vine; he washes his garments in wine, and his robes in the blood of grapes.** [12] **His eyes are dull** [Heb., *chakleel*, "dark, or blood-shot"] **from wine, and his teeth white from milk.**

We see here that Judah was given the "scepter." He is also compared to a lion, which became Judah's national symbol on its banners. Hence also we read of Christ in Rev. 5:5 pictured as "*the Lion that is from the tribe of Judah.*" We also see that the lion would crouch or lie down. This pictures prophetically the death of the Jesus Christ. The only One "*who dares to rouse him up*" is the Spirit of Him that raised Jesus from the dead (Rom. 8:11).

Samson's Riddle of the Dead Lion

This same theme of the dead lion being raised from the dead is set forth in the riddle of Samson in Judges 14. Samson killed a lion with his bare hands by the power of God (Judges 14:5, 6), and later some bees made a hive in the lion's dead carcass. Samson took honey from that hive, ate some and gave some to his parents. Soon afterward, he went to Timnah to his seven-day wedding feast, because he intended to marry a Philistine woman who lived in Timnah. At the beginning of the feast, he proposed a riddle to the Philistines. If they could solve it, he would give each of his thirty friends a new garment. But if they could not solve the riddle, they each were to give Samson a new garment.

The riddle is given in Judges 14:14,

> [14] **Out of the eater came something to eat, and out of the strong came something sweet.**

The Philistines could not figure out the meaning of the riddle, because they had not seen the dead lion, out of whose death came honey. Nor did they know its meaning—that the secret of the Promised Land flowing with milk and *honey* was by seeing the dead Lion of Judah, "*who was delivered up because of our transgressions, and was raised because of our justification*" (Rom. 4:25). The revelation of the riddle would bring the reward of new garments, the "garments of salvation" (Isaiah 61:10). Paul speaks of these garments as a "tabernacle" with which we desire to be clothed, so that we might obtain immortality (2 Cor. 5:1-4).

This story, then, is another prophecy of how to be saved and to be granted immortality, clothed with a new and glorified body. This is actually the purpose of the Feast of Tabernacles, which we described in Chapter Seven of our book, The Laws of the Second Coming.

Samson's riddle tells us how to interpret Jacob's blessing upon Judah. Judah was to bring forth the King-Messiah, the Lion of the Tribe of Judah, who would die and be raised from the dead. That was Judah's calling, and Jesus was indeed born of the tribe of Judah. Hence, Judah fulfilled its calling. But we cannot expect Judah to bring forth the message of Sonship, for that is reserved for Joseph.

We cannot expect Judah to fulfill the calling of the birthright, for that was given to Ephraim, the son of Joseph.

Nor did Judah have the right to use the birthright name of ISRAEL that was given to the sons of Joseph.

The Breach in the Kingdom

The separation of the dominion mandate from the fruitfulness mandate sowed the seeds of the breach that was to come upon the nation of Israel after the death of Solomon. Solomon may have been the wisest man that ever lived, but he was not mature enough in his character to use his wisdom wisely. For this reason he became very corrupt, and with this came utter foolishness. He loved to build, but he overtaxed the people to support his building projects.

After Solomon died, the people came to his son, Rehoboam, and asked that he reduce the tax burden upon the people. Rehoboam inquired of his advisors. The wise ones advised him to reduce the tax load; the young advisors, however, advised him to increase the taxes and not allow the people to dictate his policies. This caused a breach in the Kingdom, where ten tribes revolted against Rehoboam and set up their own nation with their own king, an Ephraimite named Jeroboam.

This had been prophesied in 1 Kings 11:28-39 by the prophet Ahijah,

> **[30] Then Ahijah took hold of the new cloak which was on him, and tore it into twelve pieces. [31] And he said to Jeroboam, Take for yourself ten pieces; for thus says the Lord, the God of Israel, Behold, I will tear THE KINGDOM out of the hand of Solomon and give you ten tribes. . . . [34] Nevertheless, I will not take THE WHOLE KINGDOM out of his hand, but I will make him ruler all the days of his life, for the sake of My servant David whom I chose, who observed My commandments and My statutes; [35] But I will take THE KINGDOM from his son's hand and give it to you, even ten tribes.**

Take note especially that it was "the Kingdom" that God removed from the king of Judah. This constituted a separation of the King from the Kingdom. This was the great breach in the land. Because the ten tribes included the tribes of Joseph (Ephraim and Manasseh), who were the custodians of the name ISRAEL, the ten-tribed nation of the north were the ones who were legally allowed to use this birthright name. Hence, they were called "The House of Israel," while the southern two tribes (Judah and Benjamin) could only be called "The House of Judah."

This is very important. From this point on, the prophets speak of these distinct nations by their official names. When they speak of the northern tribes, they refer to them as "The House of Israel." When they speak of the southern two tribes, they refer to them as "The House of Judah." The prophets never confuse the two when prophesying of the separate destinies of these two nations.

Historically speaking, the other foreign nations also considered Israel and Judah to be distinct nations and also referred to them under different names. Most nations knew the northern House of Israel, NOT by the name of Israel, but by the name of the builder of Samaria, King Omri. In those days, this king's name was actually pronounced "Gomer" or "Ghomri." The Assyrians, who later deported Israel, called them officially Beth-Ghomri, or Beth-Khumri, "house of Omri." This is the name as it appears on the Black Obelisk of Shalmanezer, the Assyrian king who conquered Samaria (2 Kings 18:9). These Khumri later migrated into the largely uninhabited forests of Europe, where they were known as the Celts, Saxons, and by other names as well. They formed the bulk of the European population.

For a more complete study of the names of Israel in their captivity, and how they migrated under those names into Europe, see William Bennett's book, The Story of Celto-Saxon Israel. The Black Obelisk of Shalmanezer is discussed, complete with pictures and text, in Appendix Two of that book.

Israel went into an Assyrian captivity and never returned to the old land; Judah was to go into a Babylonian captivity for just 70 years and then return so that the Messiah could be born at the appointed place in Bethlehem of Judea (Micah 5:2).

The destiny of the House of Israel was to fulfill the birthright. The destiny of the southern House of Judah was to bring forth the King-Messiah. In Christ's first coming, He came of the tribe of Judah, born in Bethlehem, the city of David, in order to fulfill Judah's calling as the Messiah. But in His second coming, He must come in a different manner to fulfill the birthright calling of the House of Israel and bring many sons into glory. We have already discussed this in full in chapters ten and eleven of our book, The Laws of the Second Coming, so we will not pursue this further.

The Two Fig Trees of Judah

The tribe of Judah consisted of two types of Judahites: good and bad. The good side of Judah was to receive the dominion mandate, while the bad side was to be rejected by God. This picture fully emerges in the prophecies of Jeremiah. The main portrait of these two "trees" is found in Jeremiah 24, which speaks of the nation of Judah being like two baskets of figs. One basket contained very good figs; the other contained very rotten figs that could not be eaten. Jeremiah tells us of these in the first verses of Jeremiah 24,

> **1 After Nebuchadnezzar king of Babylon had carried away captive Jeconiah the son of Jehoiakim, king of Judah, and the officials of Judah with the craftsmen and smiths from Jerusalem and had brought them to Babylon, the Lord showed me: behold, two baskets of figs set before the temple of the Lord! 2 One basket had very good figs, like first-ripe figs; and the other basket had very bad figs, which could not be eaten due to rottenness.**

God then told the prophet the explanation of this revelation. The basket of good figs were those men of Judah who submitted to the judgment of God and who went to Babylon into captivity. God said that He would bring them back to the land and "*give them a heart to know Me*" (24:7).

The basket of bad figs, however, represented those men of Judah who refused to submit to the king of Babylon—that is, they refused to submit to the judgment of God. God said of these figs,

> [8] **But like the bad figs which cannot be eaten due to rottenness—indeed, thus says the Lord—so I will abandon Zedekiah king of Judah and his officials, and the remnant of Jerusalem who remain in this land, and the ones who dwell in the land of Egypt. [9] And I will make them a terror and an evil for all the kingdoms of the earth, as a reproach and a proverb, a taunt and a curse in all places where I shall scatter them. [10] And I will send the sword, the famine, and the pestilence upon them until they are destroyed from the land which I gave to them and to their forefathers.**

What a contrast! The fig tree was, of course, the symbol of the nation of Judah. But it is apparent that the two baskets of figs came from two different fig trees. Jesus clearly saw both types of Judahites in His day, for He said in Matt. 7:17-20,

> [17] **Even so, every good tree bears good fruit; but the bad tree bears bad fruit. [18] A good tree cannot produce bad fruit, nor can a bad tree produce good fruit. [19] Every tree that does not bear good fruit is cut down and thrown into the fire. [20] So then, you will know them by their fruits.**

The good tree brought forth good fruit; the bad tree bore bad fruit. Both are of Judah, but there was a clear division between the people represented by these trees. The good figs were those who accepted Him as the Messiah; the bad figs rejected Him. Jeremiah said that the good figs submitted to the judgment of God against the nation by willingly going to Babylon for 70 years. The bad figs disagreed with God's judgment for their sin and decided to fight the army of King Nebuchadnezzar. This is clear from a simple reading of Jeremiah 24-30.

Divine Judgment for Disobedience

The divine law said in Deut. 17:9-12 that the people were to obey the verdict of the priests when they stood to judge the people according to God's law. Verse 12 says,

> [12] **And the man who acts presumptuously by not listening to the priest who stands there to serve the LORD your God, nor to the judge, that man shall die** [for unrepentance and contempt of court]**; thus you shall purge the evil from Israel.**

Jeremiah was one of the priests of Anathoth (Jer. 1:1). God used him to pronounce judgment upon the nation of Judah in 7:9-15, with these words:

> [9] **Will you steal, murder, and commit adultery, and swear falsely, and offer sacrifices to Baal, and walk after other gods that you have not known, [10] then come and stand before Me in this house, which is called by My name, and say, We are delivered!—that you may do all these abominations? [11] Has this house, which is called by My name, become a den of robbers in your sight? Behold, I, even I, have seen *it*, declares the LORD.**

[12] But go now to My place which was in Shiloh, where I made My name dwell at the first, and see what I did to it because of the wickedness of My people Israel. [13] And now, because you have done all these things . . . [14] therefore, I will do to the house which is called by My name, in which you trust, and to the place which I gave you and your fathers, as I did to Shiloh. [15] And I will cast you out of My sight, as I have cast out all your brothers, all the offspring of Ephraim.

In this lawful sentence against Judah, God says that He was to cast Judah and Jerusalem out of His sight—even as He did Shiloh and Ephraim. Shiloh was the place where God put His name at the beginning, after Joshua conquered Canaan (Josh. 18:1; Ps. 78:60). Because of Eli's sons, God removed His presence (ark) from Shiloh and placed it in Jerusalem.

God never returned to Shiloh but permanently forsook that place and ultimately cast Ephraim out of His sight into the Assyrian captivity. Even so, God said He was about to do the same with Judah and Jerusalem, because they were as corrupt as the Eli priesthood and the people of Ephraim. There were some Judahites who had sense enough to submit to God's judgment, but the majority did not. They chose to fight it, and so God pronounced the death penalty upon the bad fig tree in accordance with Deut. 17:12.

In order to understand more fully the judgment that God was pronouncing upon Judah and Jerusalem, we must first pause to study the divine law of tribulation. This will give us a better understanding of the "yoke" of captivity that God brought upon Judah. We must also trace the history of where God has placed His name, in light of the reference to Shiloh quoted in the passage above.

CHAPTER 4
The Laws of Tribulation

Deuteronomy 28 shows the blessings of obedience and the curses of the law for disobedience to God. When a nation discards God's laws and substitutes man's imperfect laws, sin and injustice begins to increase in the land until the nation finally disintegrates from within or is destroyed by invading armies. We will begin our study with Deut. 28:48, for this is the final, maximum judgment in the law of tribulation.

The Iron Yoke

Deut. 28:48 reads,

> [48] **Therefore you shall serve your enemies whom the LORD shall send against you, in hunger, in thirst, in nakedness, and in the lack of all things; and He will put AN IRON YOKE on your neck until He has destroyed you.**

A yoke is what the farmers used to place on the neck of the ox in order to plow a field. An ox is man's servant. So a yoke upon a man signifies his coming into servitude. While Jesus' yoke is light (Matt. 11:30), man's yoke is heavy, for man's rule is always oppressive in some manner.

In the next verses (Deut. 28:49-57) God gives us His definition of an *iron* yoke. It is the most severe form of servitude. It means being put under an unjust and tyrannical master who does not follow God's laws, but makes his own and enforces them rigorously. When God puts an iron yoke upon the neck of the nation, He brings a foreign nation to lay siege to them until they destroy the whole infrastructure of the nation. Verse 64 says,

> [64] **Moreover, the LORD will scatter you among all peoples, from one end of the earth to the other end of the earth; and there you shall serve other gods, wood and stone, which you or your fathers have not known.**

It is clear from the Scriptures that when Israel or Judah continues in sin and refuses to repent, God promises to destroy the nation and scatter the people. God does not refrain from judgment just because Israel is "chosen." In fact, God requires more of a "chosen" people, because "*from everyone who has been given much shall much be required; and to whom they entrusted much, of him they will ask all the more*" (Luke 12:48).

The iron yoke is the discipline of last resort. It means the destruction of the nation and its cities. It means many of the people are killed without mercy. It also involves the deportation of the surviving citizens into other countries, either to be sold as individual slaves or to be resettled as a group to be subservient to foreign rulers and man-made laws. Any nation that experiences such devastation will certainly know that they are in great tribulation.

When Assyria destroyed *Israel* and deported the remaining citizens to the area around the Caspian Sea (2 Kings 17:6, 18-23), it was because God had imposed the iron yoke upon Israel. A century later when Babylon destroyed Jerusalem and deported the nation of *Judah* for a 70-year captivity, it was an iron yoke that God put upon them. This iron yoke was imposed upon Judah a second time in 70 A.D. when the Romans destroyed Jerusalem and scattered the remaining Jews, selling hundreds of thousands into slavery.

These are brief examples of the iron yoke that God has employed in the past. But as we stated earlier, this is the discipline of last resort. There is a milder judgment that God has placed upon His people in the past. The most important is what Jeremiah calls the *wooden yoke.*

The Wooden Yoke

Long before the days of Jeremiah, during the time of the Judges, God put Israel into captivity to various nations a number of times. Each time, these captivities occurred within the borders of Israel. That is, the nations came to Israel and put them into servitude, making them pay tribute. Even so, the Israelites were allowed to remain in the land God had given them.

In each case the book of Judges tells us that God put Israel into servitude in order to judge them for their sin. If Israel had not become lawless, God would not have allowed the foreign nations to put them into servitude. About the first captivity, Judges 3:5-8 says,

> **5 And the sons of Israel lived among the Canaanites, the Hittites, the Amorites, the Perizzites, the Hivites, and the Jebusites; 6 and they took their daughters for themselves as wives, and gave their own daughters to their sons, and served their gods. 7 And the sons of Israel did what was evil in the sight of the LORD, and forgot the LORD their God, and served the Baals and the Asheroth. 8 Then the anger of the LORD was kindled against Israel, so that He sold them into the hands of Cushan-rishathaim king of Mesopotamia; and the sons of Israel served Cushan-rishathaim eight years.**

God sold Israel into this captivity. It was NOT because the king of Mesopotamia was so powerful that they were able to defeat God's people by force of arms. It was because Israel had cast aside the laws of God and had begun to follow the precepts and laws of other gods. God then sold Israel into the hands of the king of Mesopotamia.

After an eight-year captivity, the people repented, and God sent Othniel to deliver them and throw off the yoke. This yoke was not the iron yoke that Deut. 28 threatened, because the nation was not destroyed, nor were the people deported to another land. It was merely a wooden yoke, as Jeremiah later described. It was a yoke where the people were allowed to remain in their land, grow their crops, do business as usual—but they were required to pay tribute (taxes) to the foreign conqueror.

But the next generation again forsook the divine law, so after a forty-year period of peace, God raised up the Moabites to put Israel into the wooden yoke once again. Judges 3:12 read,

> **12 Now the sons of Israel again did evil in the sight of the Lord. So the Lord strengthened Eglon the king of Moab against Israel, because they had done evil in the sight of the Lord.**

Once again, God took the credit for doing this. It was not the devil who strengthened Eglon. The king of Moab would have had no power to put Israel into captivity had it not been that God strengthened him. Nor did God strengthen him because Eglon was such a righteous man. No, God strengthened Eglon to judge Israel for their sin. And when Israel finally repented, God sent a judge named Ehud to deliver them from the wooden yoke of Moab (Judges 3:15).

The same type of story is repeated each time Israel forsook God and His law. Judges 4 speaks of Israel's third captivity, this time to Jabin, king of Canaan, who reigned in Hazor, a northern fortress. The fourth captivity was to the Midianites for seven years (Judges 6:1). When the people cried out to the Lord, God sent them Gideon to deliver them—but this time the deliverer was sent only after God had sent a prophet to give them a history lesson. We see here the first sign of reluctance on God's part to set Israel free. He wanted them to repent, not merely to cry out to Him.

The fifth and sixth captivities are recorded in Judges 10, first to the Ammonites and then to the Philistines. Each time the cause of captivity was the same—the people had forsaken God and His law. Judges 10:10 then tells us,

> **[10] Then the sons of Israel cried out to the Lord, saying, We have sinned against Thee, for indeed, we have forsaken our God and served the Baals.**

But this time God seems to have had enough of their temporary repentance and emotion-based revivals that had no depth or substance. His reply is very significant:

> **[11] And the Lord said to the sons of Israel, Did I not deliver you from the Egyptians, the Amorites, the sons of Ammon, and the Philistines? [12] Also when the Sidonians, the Amalekites, and the Maonites oppressed you, you cried out to Me, and I delivered you from their hands. [13] Yet you have forsaken Me and served other gods; therefore I will deliver you no more. [14] Go and cry out to the gods which you have chosen; let them deliver you in the time of your distress.**

The people put away their false gods and confessed their sin, so God did deliver them by the hand of a judge named Jephthah. However, it was not long before they again fell into sin, and God delivered them once again into the hands of the Philistines for forty years (Judges 13:1). During this time God raised up Samson as a judge, but God did not permit him to actually deliver Israel from their captivity. Samson, in fact, finally was captivated by Philistines, who put out his eyes and forced him to grind at the mill.

Meanwhile, Eli was the high priest at the tabernacle in Shiloh. Eli's sons were corrupt, and the future of the priesthood looked bleak. The people attempted to free themselves from the yoke of the Philistines, but without success, for they did not repent of their lawlessness and did not receive any help from God. The corrupt sons of Eli then came up with the idea of bringing the Ark of the Covenant into battle to fight the Philistines. Instead of simply repenting of their lawlessness, they thought they could use God to their advantage. They remembered Num. 10:35, which said:

> **[35] Then it came about when the ark set out that Moses said, Rise up, O Lord! And let Thine enemies be scattered, and let those who hate Thee flee before Thee.**

They thought that they could follow the same formula. After all, it was a "proven" tactic, and it was certainly biblical. And so we read of a battle between Israel and the Philistines in 1 Sam. 4:2-4,

> **[2] And the Philistines drew up in battle array to meet Israel. When the battle spread, Israel was defeated before the Philistines who killed about four thousand men on the battlefield. [3] When the people came into the camp, the**

elders of Israel said, Why has the Lord defeated us today before the Philistines? Let us take to ourselves from Shiloh the ark of the covenant of the Lord, that it may come among us and deliver us from the power of our enemies.
[4] **So the people sent to Shiloh and from there they carried the ark of the covenant of the Lord of hosts who sits above the cherubim; and the two sons of Eli, Hophni and Phinehas, were there with the ark of the covenant.**

No doubt, when they took the Ark from Shiloh, the two sons of Eli shouted, "*Rise up, O Lord! And let Thine enemies be scattered. And let those who hate Thee flee before Thee.*"

Their prayer was answered. 1 Sam. 4:10 says, ". . . *So the Philistines fought, and Israel was defeated, and every man fled to his tent.*" What they did not realize in their blindness was that God considered Israel to be His enemy, as long as they were in rebellion against His law! Ex. 23:22 says,

[22] **But if you will truly obey My voice and do all that I say, then I will be an enemy to your enemies and an adversary to your adversaries.**

On the other hand, whenever Israel was in rebellion against God, the reverse would be true, as we read in Is. 63:10,

[10] **But they** [Israel] **rebelled and grieved His Holy Spirit; therefore, He turned Himself to become their enemy; He fought against them** [Israel].

This was the moral and political situation when God raised up Samuel as a prophet and judge. The Philistines had defeated Israel in battle and had captured the Ark of the Covenant. They had killed the priests (Ps. 78:60-64) and destroyed the city of Shiloh. The priests who survived had to move to the town of Nob (1 Sam. 21:1) just north of Jerusalem.

The Philistines held the Ark for just seven months before returning it (1 Sam. 6). But the Ark could not return to Shiloh, where it had been since the days of Joshua, because that city had been destroyed. It was kept, instead, at Kirjath-jearim for about twenty years (1 Sam. 7:2). After the Ark was returned, Samuel led the people into a prayer of repentance (1 Sam. 7:3-6). Only then did Israel defeat the Philistines in battle (1 Sam. 7:13).

So ended the final "wooden yoke" of that historical period in Israel's history.

Israel Asks for a King

It is important to note that from God's perspective, *Israel does not have an inherent right to be free.* Their freedom is a privilege under God and is given only when they are obedient to His law and refuse to follow other gods. This is as true today as it was in biblical days.

The people of Israel finally began to recognize this in the days of Samuel. After all, in the three centuries of their existence since the days of Joshua, the people had spent over a third of that time under the wooden yoke of foreign domination. Yet, instead of deciding once and for all to remain obedient to the divine law, they reasoned that God was too strict with them. They decided that they really did not want to be ruled by God, for He seemed to be a tyrant to them. They needed to be ruled (they thought) by a man who was more like them, one who would be more tolerant of their sin, one who would not put them into captivity every time they began to worship other gods. So they came to Samuel and asked for a change of government. 1 Sam. 8:4-7 says,

[4] Then all the elders of Israel gathered together and came to Samuel at Ramah; [5] and they said to him, Behold, you have grown old, and your sons do not walk in your ways. Now appoint a king for us to judge us like all the nations. [6] But the thing was displeasing in the sight of Samuel when they said, Give us a king to judge us. And Samuel prayed to the Lord.

The people did not understand that there is no freedom apart from God. And there is no true justice or mercy in the land apart from the divine law. They thought that men could substitute for God, and that men would be more just and more merciful than God. So God gave them Saul to be their king. He was the best in the land, but he became Israel's oppressor, little better than the foreign kings who had put Israel into bondage.

So now, instead of being ruled by *foreign* oppressors, they were ruled by their own *Israelite* oppressor.

Saul reigned forty years, and then David reigned another forty years. When David died, his son Solomon ruled another forty years, and during his reign, the great temple was built. The Ark of the Covenant had found a home once again, and God placed His name upon Jerusalem.

Where God Establishes His Name

The divine law says in Deut. 16 that the only lawful place where one can keep the feast days is at the place where God has put His name. It says nothing about any particular location, because God knew that He would change the location of His name from time to time. Deut. 16:1, 2 speaks about the place where the people were to observe the Passover:

[1] Observe the month of Abib and celebrate the Passover to the Lord your God, for in the month of Abib the Lord your God brought you out of Egypt by night. [2] And <u>you shall sacrifice the Passover</u> to the Lord your God from the flock and the herd, <u>in the place where the Lord chooses to establish His name</u>. . . . [5] You are not allowed to sacrifice the Passover in any of your towns which the Lord your God is giving you; [6] but <u>at the place where the Lord your God chooses to establish His name</u>.

We find the same is true with Pentecost, called the "feast of weeks" in the law. Deut. 16:10, 11 says,

[10] Then you shall celebrate the <u>Feast of Weeks</u> to the Lord your God . . . [11] . . . <u>in the place where the Lord your God chooses to establish His name</u>.

Finally, the same is true with the Feast of Booths, or Tabernacles, for we read in Deut. 16:13,

[13] You shall celebrate the <u>Feast of Booths</u> seven days after you have gathered in from your threshing floor and your wine vat; [15] . . . Seven days you shall celebrate a feast to the Lord your God <u>in the place which the Lord chooses</u>.

God first placed His name at Shiloh, where Joshua set up the tabernacle of Moses within the territory of his own tribe of Ephraim. But because the priesthood of that place—Eli's priesthood—became corrupt, God removed His name (and the Ark) from that place and moved it to Jerusalem in the days of Solomon. Psalm 78 tells of this:

[58] For they provoked Him with their high places, and aroused His jealousy with their graven images. [59] When God heard, He was filled with wrath, and greatly abhorred Israel; [60] So that He abandoned the dwelling place at Shiloh, the tent which He had pitched among men. . . . [67] He also rejected the tent of Joseph, and did not choose the tribe of Ephraim, [68] But chose the tribe of Judah, Mount Zion which He loved. [69] And He built His sanctuary like the heights, like the earth which He has founded forever.

So we see that God first placed His name at Shiloh, but later abandoned that location because of its corrupt priests. The Ark of the Covenant later was placed in the new temple that Solomon built in Jerusalem under a new dynasty of priests who were of the family of Zadok (1 Kings 2:27, 35). This means that God established His name in a new location—Jerusalem. But even this place was not the final place where He would place His name, for Jerusalem, too, became corrupted, and God's presence left that place as well. Jeremiah told the people of Judah and Jerusalem that because they had continually violated the divine law, God would forsake Solomon's temple and destroy it. After listing the reasons for this, Jer. 7:12-16 says,

[12] But go now to My place which was in Shiloh, where I made My name dwell at the first, and see what I did to it because of the wickedness of My people Israel. [13] And now, because you have done all these things, declares the LORD, and I spoke to you, rising up early and speaking, but you did not hear, and I called you but you did not answer, [14] therefore, I will do to the house which is called by My name, in which you trust, and to the place which I gave you and your fathers, as I did to Shiloh. [15] And I will cast you out of My sight, as I have cast out all your brothers, all the offspring of Ephraim. [16] As for you, do not pray for this people, and do not lift up cry or prayer for them, and do not intercede with Me; for I do not hear you.

This sentence upon Jerusalem was repeated in Jer. 26:4-6, where we read:

[4] And you will say to them, Thus says the LORD, If you will not listen to Me, to walk in My law, which I have set before you, [5] to listen to the words of My servants the prophets, whom I have been sending to you again and again, but you have not listened; [6] then I will make this house like Shiloh, and this city I will make a curse to all the nations of the earth.

The people did not repent. In fact, *the priests* condemned the prophet to death (Jer. 26:11) and would have killed him as a false prophet. But the people and the princes saved the prophet's life (26:16). The Word of the Lord through Jeremiah was not popular theology. Neither in his day, nor in ours. And so God has indeed made Jerusalem "*a curse to all the nations of the earth.*" This is virtually the OPPOSITE of the Abrahamic promise, whereby his seed would be a BLESSING to all the families of the earth.

When Jeremiah received this Word, it was God's verdict being rendered in the courts of heaven. From this point on, Jeremiah was not allowed to pray that judgment might be averted or that God's name might remain in Jerusalem. Even repentance could not set aside the judgment of God, once the verdict had been handed down. From this time on, Jeremiah had to pray in a different manner. He could only pray that the judgment might be *lessened* by repentance, but not cancelled.

Jeremiah himself did not see God's glory depart from the temple. This vision was given to Ezekiel. We read in Ez. 10:4, 18 and 19 say,

4 Then the glory of the Lord went up from the cherub to the threshold of the temple, and the temple was filled with the cloud, and the court was filled with the brightness of the glory of the Lord.

18 Then the glory of the Lord departed from the threshold of the temple and stood over the cherubim. 19 When the cherubim departed, they lifted their wings and rose up from the earth in my sight with the wheels beside them; and they stood still at the entrance of the east gate of the Lord's house. And the glory of the God of Israel hovered over them.

The final mention of the departure of God's glory is found in Ez. 11:23, which says,

23 And the glory of the Lord went up from the midst of the city, which stood over the mountain which is east of the city.

The mountain where the glory went was the Mount of Olives, situated east of Jerusalem. The glory departed no further than the Mount of Olives at that time, because Jesus was yet to come. Jesus Christ is the glory of God. When He was born about 600 years later, He lived, He died on the cross, and He rose again from the dead. Then He taught the disciples for forty days before finally ascending on the fortieth day (Acts 1:3). At that point, Jesus brought His disciples to the Mount of Olives and ascended to heaven. Acts 1:12 says of the disciples,

12 Then they returned to Jerusalem from the mount called Olivet, which is near Jerusalem, a Sabbath day's journey away.

Jesus Christ is the glory of God. That glory was last seen in the days of Ezekiel on the top of the Mount of Olives in a partial removal from Jerusalem. Jesus' ascension to heaven from the Mount of Olives completed that departure. The glory had now fully departed from the old city of Jerusalem. Ten days later, the glory returned on the day of Pentecost (Acts 2:1). But this time it did not fill the second temple, but rather it filled the 120 disciples in the upper room. They were filled with the Spirit, and the glory of God appeared as tongues of fire upon their heads. The glory of God had found a new location. *God had chosen a new place in which to place His name*. This is confirmed in 1 Cor. 6:19,

19 Or do you not know that your body is a temple of the Holy Spirit who is in you, whom you have from God, and that you are not your own?

And again, we read in Rev. 22:4,

4 And they shall see His face, and His name shall be upon their foreheads.

The progression is clear, then, where God has chosen to place His name. He first placed His name at Shiloh, then at Jerusalem, and now in the Christian believers, who are the temple of God. If any man attempts to keep a feast in any other location than where He has placed His name, he is being unlawful. Many Christians today travel to the old city of Jerusalem for various feast days, thinking that God's glory is soon to return to that old city. They do not understand that the glory departed from that place even as it departed from Shiloh. "Ichabod" has been written on that place, even as it was written on the place called Shiloh (1 Sam. 4:21).

God said through Jeremiah that He would make the old Jerusalem "a curse" to all families of the earth. If someone wants to find the city of blessing, he must find the New Jerusalem. That city is not the old city. The New Jerusalem—like its temple—is made of PEOPLE, not wood and stone. The Old Jerusalem has become a cursed city—not cursed by men, but under God's curse (Jer. 26:6, quoted earlier).

Worse yet, those who go to the old Jerusalem in an attempt to keep the feast may be violating the divine law, for the feast is not to be kept in any other location other than the place where He has placed His name. If anyone says, "I went to Jerusalem to keep the feast," he may be violating the divine law. However, it is not a sin simply to go to Jerusalem (or to any other location) at the time of the feasts. It should be clear, though, that one does not KEEP the feasts by going to some geographical location on earth.

The Feast of Passover must be KEPT in one's own temple by faith, for one is justified by faith in the blood of the only Lamb of God who can take away sin. The Feast of Pentecost must also be kept in one's own temple by being filled with the Spirit, even as we see in Acts 2. The Feast of Tabernacles (Booths) must also be kept in one's own temple by being changed fully into His likeness and image, a bodily change into the immortal, incorruptible body ("house") which is currently reserved for us in the heavens (2 Cor. 5:1-4). For a complete study of this, see The Laws of the Second Coming.

Some people believe that the glory of God is going to be manifested in Jerusalem. This is contradicted by Jer. 7:14. If God's glory never returned to Shiloh, then it will never return to Jerusalem. "Ichabod" has been written on both cities. The glory has found a new resting place in a New Jerusalem temple made of living stones. This was the desire of God from the beginning. This will be discussed more thoroughly in Chapter Eight.

CHAPTER 5
The Captivities of Judah

In Jeremiah 23-30 the prophet told the people that if they would submit to God's just verdict, He would allow them to remain on the land under the wooden yoke only. But if they refused to submit to God's verdict, then they would come under the iron yoke and be deported to Babylon. In Jer. 27:2 the prophet spoke of this wooden yoke,

> **[2] Thus says the LORD to me—Make for yourself bonds and yokes and put them on your neck, [3] and send word to the king of Edom, to the king of Moab, to the king of the sons of Ammon, to the king of Tyre, and to the king of Sidon by the messengers who come to Jerusalem to Zedekiah king of Judah.**

This was a message not only to the king of Judah, but also to the neighboring nations. God was giving all these nations to Nebuchadnezzar, king of Babylon, to be his servants. All those nations were admonished to submit to the wooden yoke of Babylon. In Jer. 27:5-7, God told the prophet,

> **[5] I have made the earth, the men and the beasts which are on the face of the earth by My great power and by My outstretched arm, and I will give it to the one who is pleasing in My sight. [6] And now I have given all these lands into the hand of Nebuchadnezzar king of Babylon, My servant, and I have given him also the wild animals of the field to serve him. [7] And all the nations shall serve him, and his son, and his grandson, until the time of his own land comes; then many nations and great kings will make him their servant. [8] And it will be, *that* the nation or the kingdom which will not serve him, Nebuchadnezzar king of Babylon, and which will not put its neck under the yoke of the king of Babylon, I will punish that nation with the sword, with famine, and with pestilence, declares the LORD, until I have destroyed it by his hand.**

In other words, God said that He had given all these nations to the king of Babylon, Nebuchadnezzar, "*MY servant.*" God claims the right to do this by right of creation. God declares His right to do this in verse 5. Thus we see that God Himself claimed the credit for bringing the king of Babylon to Jerusalem to destroy the temple and to deport the people to another land. God had, in effect, hired the king of Babylon to execute His verdict upon the sinful nation of Judah. But Jeremiah also made it clear in verse 11 that if the people of Judah would submit to God's verdict, they would be allowed a lesser form of judgment—the wooden yoke.

> **[11] But the nation which will bring its neck under the yoke of the king of Babylon and serve him, I will let remain on its land, declares the LORD, and they will till it and dwell in it.**

The next chapter, Jeremiah 28, we are told the decision of the people through their primary spokesman, the prophet Hananiah. Here we also learn that God had actually told Jeremiah to walk around Jerusalem with a wooden yoke around his neck to let people know what he himself had decided to do. Jeremiah's decision was to submit to the king of Babylon and serve him as unto the Lord, knowing that Nebuchadnezzar was God's servant, or employee.

Judah Rejects the Wooden Yoke

The prophet Hananiah was offended at the yoke around Jeremiah's neck, so he forcibly removed it from Jeremiah's neck and broke it. We read in Jer. 28:10, 11,

> [10] **Then Hananiah the prophet took the yoke from the neck of Jeremiah the prophet and broke it.** [11] **And Hananiah spoke in the presence of all the people, saying, Thus says the Lord, Even so will I break within two full years, the yoke of Nebuchadnezzar king of Babylon from the neck of all the nations. Then the prophet Jeremiah went his way.**

Jeremiah made no resistance, knowing that this was simply the people's answer before God. They had no intention of submitting to Nebuchadnezzar, for they thought God was on their side and would help them defeat the Babylonian army. Jer. 2:35 says about them,

> [35] **Yet you** [Judahites] **said, I am innocent; surely His anger is turned away from me.**

They did not believe they were guilty of rebellion against God, because they were continuing to worship Him with all the religious forms and rituals in God's temple. They did not believe that God would allow His beautiful house (temple) to be desecrated or destroyed. In Jer. 7:4 the prophet answers them,

> [4] **Do not trust in deceptive words, saying, This is the temple of the LORD, the temple of the LORD, the temple of the LORD.**

God called two prophets, Jeremiah and Hananiah, to polarize the people and make manifest the hearts of the people. Those who had rebellion in their hearts naturally followed the prophecies of Hananiah, and these believed in *the theology of rebellion*. In rebelling against Nebuchadnezzar, they unknowingly rebelled against God Himself.

Those who believed Jeremiah's message were those who knew and understood the law of tribulation—that God would judge Israel and Judah for casting aside His law. These believers were willing to submit to the wooden yoke, even as Jeremiah did. The rebellious majority, however, decided that God would never want them to be slaves to the king of Babylon. Apparently, they forgot their own history in the book of Judges. They certainly did not believe the laws of tribulation found in Deuteronomy 28. And so they fought and died. The city, temple, and the entire land was devastated. The survivors were forcibly taken to Babylon to serve their 70-year sentence (Jer. 25:11) under a yoke of iron, even as Deut. 28:48 had warned.

Judah Sentenced to an Iron Yoke

In Jeremiah 28:12-14 we read,

> [12] **And the word of the LORD came to Jeremiah, after Hananiah the prophet had broken the yoke from off the neck of the prophet Jeremiah, saying,** [13] **Go and speak to Hananiah, saying, Thus says the LORD, <u>You have broken the yokes of wood, but you have made instead of them yokes of iron</u>.** [14] **For thus says the LORD of hosts, the God of Israel, <u>I have put a yoke of iron on the neck</u>**

<u>of all these nations,</u> that they may serve Nebuchadnezzar king of Babylon; and they shall serve him. And I have also given him the beasts of the field.

The nation of Judah could have avoided the absolute desolation and destruction if they had taken heed to the word of the Lord from Jeremiah. However, they were far too patriotic to submit to the judgment of God. There is nothing wrong with patriotism, but when one chooses patriotism over submission to God's judgment for sin, such patriots do a great disservice to their own people. This is why it is so important even today to recognize the judgments of God, rather than merely to assume that all national enemies or oppressors are "of the devil."

In the days of Jeremiah, it was the religious patriots who led the people like lambs to the slaughter at the hands of Babylon.

Jeremiah's Advice to the Good Figs

There were two men named Hananiah. One represented the good figs; one represented the bad figs. The Hananiah who opposed Jeremiah was the prophet of the bad figs, for he thought that God would bless Judah even in their rebellion. He thought that being "chosen" meant that they were a people of privilege, and that God therefore would never put them into captivity or slavery.

The other Hananiah was one of Daniel's friends who submitted to God and was carried to Babylon as a captive. We read of him in Dan. 1:6. He represented the good figs as described in Jer. 24:7.

Jeremiah then wrote a letter to the captives in Babylon—that is, to the Judahites who were the "good figs," including the good Hananiah. He told them how to live in Babylon while in captivity. His advice was NOT to organize a revolt or even a general strike. He did NOT command them to assassinate any of their captors, nor plot against the king. His advice is found in Jer. 29:4-7,

4 Thus says the Lord of hosts, the God of Israel, to all the exiles whom I have sent into exile from Jerusalem to Babylon. 5 Build houses and live in them; and plant gardens, and eat their produce. 6 Take wives and become the fathers of sons and daughters, and take wives for your sons and give your daughters to husbands, that they may bear sons and daughters, and multiply there and do not decrease. 7 And <u>seek the welfare of the city where I have sent you into exile, and pray to the Lord on its behalf, for in its welfare you will have welfare</u>.

In other words, Jeremiah told the captives to pray for Babylon's well-being, its peace. Do not pray that Babylon would be destroyed, for it was only the executioner of God's righteous judgment upon Judah. Do not work to overthrow king Nebuchadnezzar, for he was God's servant. Do not attempt to assassinate the king, for God had given Judah into his hands. Peter gave the same advice to servants, saying in 1 Pet. 2:18,

18 Servants, be submissive to your masters with all respect, not only to those who are good and gentle, but <u>also to those who are unreasonable</u>.

The bad figs would have scoffed at Jeremiah's advice, but the good figs took heed. Neither Daniel or his friends ever made any attempt to plot against the king of Babylon. They lived to bring forth children, who then were able to return to the old land after 70 years of captivity. Jer. 29:10 says,

> [10] **For thus says the Lord, When seventy years have been completed for Babylon, I will visit you and fulfill My good word to you, to bring you back to this place.**

For a complete study that explains why Judah was sentenced to seventy years in Babylon, see Secrets of Time, Chapter Seven.

The Return from Exile

In previous years Babylon had been one of the provinces of the Assyrian empire. But Babylon was able to revolt and overthrow Assyria, capturing the capital city of Nineveh in 607 B.C. Three years later they conquered Jerusalem and Judah in 604 B.C. Yet the Babylonian Empire only lasted seventy years (607 – 537 B.C.), and Jerusalem's captivity was likewise just seventy years (604-534 B.C.). These dates are proven in Chapter Eight of our book, Secrets of Time.

About 50,000 people of Judah, Benjamin, and Levi returned to the old land to begin the long and difficult task of rebuilding a nation under the leadership of Zerubbabel, the governor, with the help of Ezra. They also had the inspiration of the prophets, Habakkuk, Haggai, Zechariah, and Malachi. But during the next 450 years the people had no known prophets to guide them prior to the birth of Jesus. Many of them forgot the law of tribulation, and soon the bad figs again began to multiply in the land.

Their situation was as follows: Babylon fell to the Medes and Persians in 537 B.C. This event is recorded in Daniel 5. Darius the Mede took the city of Babylon and ruled it for a few years and organized the new empire into 120 provinces (Dan. 6:1). Later, King Cyrus the Persian arrived, and Darius returned to his nation of Media. Cyrus then issued his famous edict in 534 B.C. that allowed the Judean exiles to return to their land.

The Continuing Wooden Yoke Captivity

Cyrus the Persian did not give Judah independence. Zerubbabel was made governor in Judea, but he remained under the authority of the Persian monarchs. In fact, many years earlier Daniel had already foreseen a series of four main world-wide empires in Daniel 2, which would control the world until the coming of the great Stone Kingdom—the Kingdom of God under Jesus Christ and His overcomers (Dan. 2:44, 45).

In Daniel 7 we are given further details, learning that these "beast" empires (lion, bear, leopard, and the nameless beast) would remain in power until "*the time arrived when the saints took possession of the kingdom*" (Dan. 7:22). These beast empires were Babylon, Medo-Persia, Greece, and the Roman Empire. Daniel also saw a "little horn" that would take up the reins of authority at the fall of the Roman Empire in 476 A.D. This was fulfilled in Papal Rome, which then ruled until recently. Thus, we see that the captivity was for a long duration, and the Edict of Cyrus merely exchanged the iron yoke for a yoke of wood.

So Judah simply became one of the provinces of the Medo-Persian Empire. Whereas Judah had been under an iron yoke for seventy years, now they were put under the milder wooden yoke. God allowed them to remain in their land as servants of the Medes and Persians. This Empire was pictured in Daniel 2 as the two arms of silver and in Daniel 7 as the bear.

This changed again about 200 years later, when Alexander the Great conquered Persia and formed the Grecian Empire. The domination of the Grecian Empire was pictured in Daniel 2 as the belly and thighs of brass (bronze) on the great image. This empire was also pictured in Daniel 7 as the leopard. In the change from Persia to Greece, Judah's wooden yoke remained. They merely changed masters.

When Alexander died, his Grecian Empire was divided among his four generals. Ptolemy received Egypt, and Seleucid received Syria. Palestine was caught in the middle and became the battleground of these two empires, sometimes being controlled by Syria, and at other times by Egypt. Finally, about 163 B.C., after some particularly obnoxious things that the Syrian king did to the temple in Jerusalem, the Maccabees rose up and threw off the yoke of Syria. For one century the nation of Judah (or Judea, as it was called in Greek) became independent. It is apparent that God allowed the wooden yoke to be removed temporarily because of the Syrian king's blasphemy.

Then in 63 B.C. the Roman army under Pompey captured Syria and Judea, and once again Judea came under a wooden yoke. The Roman Empire was pictured in Daniel 2 as the two legs of iron. In Daniel 7 it is pictured as a nameless beast with iron teeth.

Many of the Judeans grumbled and complained under the rule of Rome, not accepting them as God's servant. They did not want to be under the wooden yoke. Many false messiahs arose, promising to deliver them and bring in the Kingdom of God, but they all failed. Rome's great iron teeth and bronze claws trampled all resistance under its feet (Dan. 7:19). If the people had understood the Scriptures, they would have realized that they themselves needed to repent and pray for Rome, even as Jeremiah had said to pray for the welfare of Babylon. But as time passed, their rebellion against God grew, and God responded by increasing the oppression of Rome.

If the people had decided to be friendly to Rome, the Romans would have treated them much more kindly—like they did with other nations. But Judea was a difficult country to govern because they were the most rebellious of all Rome's provinces. Rome did not take kindly to rebellion. They believed in crushing all rebellion thoroughly in order to make it clear to all that rebellion was futile. They believed that only by removing all hope of success could they discourage further revolt.

The Judeans, however, believed that God was on their side, that their temple was the house of God, and that God wanted them to be free and independent. They saw pagan Rome as an ungodly, idolatrous oppressor—not as God's servant to scourge them until they repented and believed Jeremiah's message. They did not want to submit to the wooden yoke of Rome any more than their forefathers had wanted to submit to the wooden yoke of Babylon. And so Judean history moved steadily toward that final showdown in 70 A.D. when it would become known to all once and for all on whose side God would fight. God fought for Rome. Jerusalem was once again destroyed, and God put the people under the iron yoke once again.

The Revolt Against Rome (and God): 66-73 A.D.

In Abram Leon Sachar's 1930 book, A History of the Jews, page 117, this Jewish author writes,

> "Ultimately, Roman patience was thoroughly exhausted and the procurators introduced measures of barbarous severity. Soldiers slew on the slightest provocation. Eminent Jewish leaders were crucified, while whole villages were razed. All in vain. A

> fever of martyrdom seemed to seize upon the harassed people. Fanatics went up and down the country, wild-eyed and frantic, prophesying the end of the world, and the advent of the Messiah. Multitudes were ready to follow every impossible visionary who claimed inspiration from heaven. Zealots rushed to their deaths crying in hysterical exaltation. What was one to do with such a nation? The Romans were frankly bewildered. They had dealt with many turbulent peoples, but with none so contrary—so insanely intractable."

The war began in 66 A.D. while Florus was the Roman procurator in Judea. Judea was seething with unrest and with hatred for the Romans. The Romans believed that yet another revolt could break out at any time. They had tried diplomacy in their own way, but it had failed. Now they instructed Florus to be firm and even ruthless, if necessary. Josephus, the Judean historian of that time, wrote in his Wars of the Jews, II, xiv, 3, 4,

> "He, [Florus] therefore, every day augmented their calamities in order to induce them to a rebellion. . . At the same time began the war in the twelfth year of the reign of Nero and the seventeeth of the reign of Agrippa in the month Artemisius or Jyar."

In our modern way of reckoning, the beginning of the war occurred in the spring of 66 A.D. If we read history through the eyes of God, we see that history is simply fulfilled prophecy. Thus, without some knowledge of history, one cannot really understand what the prophets foretold by the inspiration of God. Those who do not know history are doomed to repeat it. In the case of Judah in the first century, they had forgotten the laws of tribulation, and they did not believe Jeremiah's message. They forgot the reason for the iron yoke of Babylon, and so they were doomed to return to its heavy judgment.

God intended to judge Jerusalem and the people for their hypocritical religion (as Isaiah put it), which they had demonstrated fully by their leaders' rejection of John the Baptist and of Jesus Himself. John had been executed at Passover of 30 A.D., and Jesus had been crucified at Passover of 33 A.D. Now their forty years of grace (obtained by Ezekiel in Ez. 4:6) was coming to an end from 70-73 A.D.

God moved upon the heart of Rome to appoint Florus over Jerusalem, knowing that his fear-based policy would only provoke Jewish rebellion, and that rebellion would in turn provoke a response from Rome in the final judgment. Florus did not know that he was but a pawn in the hands of God, for he could not see the bigger picture. The same was true for the people of Judea.

Around that time a band of Jewish extremists called Sicarii (Jewish "assassins") were expelled from Jerusalem where they had caused much havoc. They managed to take the fortress of Masada by stealth and to kill the Roman soldiers who were there—after the Sicarii had promised to spare their lives if they would surrender. Josephus says, "*and thus were all these men barbarously murdered, excepting Metilius,*" who was spared only because he agreed to become a Jew. (These assassins, or "terrorists," as we would call them today, remained at Masada until the Romans conquered them in 73 A.D.)

At the same time the governor of the temple in Jerusalem began to refuse to make sacrifices for any foreigners, and they even rejected the customary sacrifice of Caesar. Josephus then tells us in his Wars of the Jews, II, xvii, 2, "*this was the true beginning of our war with the Romans.*"

Within a few months, as the people were traveling to Jerusalem for the Feast of Tabernacles, open hostilities broke out (Wars, II, xix, 1). Rome's 12th Legion from Antioch was destroyed under the leadership of Cestius Gallus. Five thousand three hundred footmen and 380 horsemen were killed. Rome was not pleased with this and prepared to send a greater army to put down the revolt. It became apparent at that point that Jesus' words in Luke 21:20-22 were about to be fulfilled:

> **20 But when you see Jerusalem surrounded by armies, then recognize that her desolation is at hand. 21 Then let those who are in Judea flee to the mountains, and let those who are in the midst of the city depart, and let not those who are in the country enter the city. 22 because these are days of vengeance, in order that all things which are written may be fulfilled.**

Jesus was speaking of the destruction of Jerusalem prophesied in Jeremiah 19. He was also speaking of the "days of vengeance" prophesied in Is. 34:8. While these prophecies have yet to see their final fulfillment, they were at least partially fulfilled in the Babylonian war and again in the Roman war.

The destruction of Rome's 12th Legion was the final act that sealed the fate of Jerusalem. Josephus says in Wars, II, xx, 1,

> "After this calamity had befallen Cestius, many of the most eminent of the Jews swam away from the city, as from a ship when it was going to sink."

Eusebius, the fourth-century Christian historian who was the bishop of Caesarea, writes about this in Eccl. Hist., III, 5:

> "Furthermore, the members of the Jerusalem church, by means of an oracle given by revelation to acceptable persons there, were ordered to leave the City before the war began and settle in a town in Perea called Pella. To Pella, those who believed in Christ migrated from Jerusalem."

The Christians in Jerusalem moved to Pella, a city east of the Jordan River many miles north of the Dead Sea. In other words, the tribulation did not decimate the Jerusalem Church, who represented the good figs of Judah. God brought tribulation to judge the bad figs—those who remained in Judaism, those who supported the lawless, hypocritical religious system that had rejected Jesus as the Christ. Rome surrounded Jerusalem on the morning of Passover in 70 A.D. The siege lasted until August, when the temple was destroyed on Ab 10, the same day that the Babylonians had burnt the first temple in 586 B.C. Josephus again tells us in Wars, VI, iv, 5,

> "So Titus [the Roman general] retired into the tower of Antonia and resolved to storm the temple the next morning with his whole army, and to encamp round about the holy house. But as for that house, God had for certain long ago doomed it to fire. And now that fatal day was come according to the revolution of ages; it was the tenth day of the month Lous, or Ab, upon which it was formerly burnt by the king of Babylon."

The Iron Yoke Re-imposed upon the Evil Figs of Judah

Jerusalem was destroyed in 70 A.D. and the final devastation of the land was completed with the capture of Masada in 73 A.D. During this entire time, the Judahites adopted the same attitude as their forefathers in the days of Jeremiah. They could not believe that God would actually fight against them. They could not believe that God was judging them for their sin. They could not believe that it was the will of God for them to submit to their hated conquerors. And so once again, the religious zealots and patriots among them brought the nation into utter disaster.

It is clear from history that in 70 A.D. the Jews came under the iron yoke as defined in the laws of tribulation. Deut. 28:48-50 says,

> **48 Therefore you shall serve your enemies whom the LORD shall send against you, in hunger, in thirst, in nakedness, and in the lack of all things; and He will put an iron yoke on your neck until He has destroyed you. 49 The LORD will bring a nation against you from afar, from the end of the earth, as the eagle swoops down, a nation whose language you shall not understand, 50 a nation of fierce countenance who shall have no respect for the old, nor show favor to the young.**

Rome's national symbol was the eagle. The Roman Empire was also the fourth beast kingdom in Daniel, which the prophet describes as having legs of IRON. So this prophecy of the *iron* yoke and an *eagle* nation seems particularly descriptive of Rome.

> **52 And it shall besiege you in all your towns until your high and fortified walls in which you trusted come down throughout your land, and it shall besiege you in all your towns throughout your land which the LORD your God has given you.**

The Roman army besieged Jerusalem and all the towns of Judea until it had subdued all of them, even as Moses specified.

> **62 Then you shall be left few in number, whereas you were as the stars of heaven for multitude, because you did not obey the LORD your God. 63 And it shall come about that as the LORD delighted over you to prosper you, and multiply you, so the LORD will delight over you to make you perish and destroy you; and you shall be torn from the land where you are entering to possess it. 64 Moreover, the LORD will scatter you among all peoples, from one end of the earth to the other end of the earth; and there you shall serve other gods, wood and stone, which you or your fathers have not known. 65 And among those nations you shall find no rest, and there shall be no resting place for the sole of your foot; but there the LORD will give you a trembling heart, failing of eyes, and despair of soul.**

Take note that Moses said this would happen to the people *because of their disobedience to God.* Those who do not believe the words of Moses may blame the Romans for this calamity in 70 A.D. Others will blame circumstances. Some Christians blame the devil. But Moses gives God the credit for bringing this tribulation. Jesus said of them in John 5:45-47,

> **45 Do not think that I will accuse you before the Father; the one who accuses you is Moses, in whom you have set your hope. 46 For if you believed Moses, you would believe Me; for he wrote of Me. 47 But if you do not believe his writings, how will you believe My words?**

The iron yoke as defined by Moses meant that the Judeans would be dispossessed from the land. Over a million Judeans were killed in this war. Many more were sold into slavery into other lands. But they were not yet fully dispossessed from the land. That is, they were not yet forbidden to set foot on that land. This order was given later after yet another revolt known as the Bar Kochba revolt from 132-135 A.D.

In spite of all their protests to the contrary, the Jews did not believe Moses any more than they believed Jesus. If they had believed Moses, they would have understood that it was not the Romans, but God who was bringing judgment and tribulation upon them. If they had believed Jeremiah, they would have submitted to the Romans and prospered under the wooden yoke, even as their forefathers had prospered in Babylon. But their reaction to the Roman army was identical to the reaction of the bad figs toward the army of Babylon many years earlier.

They did not understand that God was judging them. Instead, they continued to fight to the death, thinking that God would always be on their side. It seems to be a fact of history that those who are lawless are also blind to their own lawlessness. For this reason, they fight the ones that God raises up to judge the nation. They fight the stick, rather than repent before the One who wields it. Deut. 28:64 prophesies that they would serve other gods in their captivity in other lands. Judaism fulfills this prophecy as well, for they do not worship the God of the Bible, except with their lips.

And so Jewish history books are full of complaints about how other people have treated them badly. As Christians, let us not be among those who purposely mistreat anyone, including Jews. And yet let us also recognize that God raised up people of ungodly character against them in order to judge them according to the law of Moses. God uses evil men for His purposes as much as He uses men of good character—but in different ways.

The Timing of the Judgment on Jerusalem

This judgment from God came as a direct result of their rejection and execution of John the Baptist and Jesus Christ. God gave them forty years of grace in which to repent, but they refused. In their blind religious zeal, they fought until the whole land was devastated and millions dead or sold into slavery.

John the Baptist was executed at Passover of 30 A.D., about six months after he had baptized Jesus. Matthew 14:1-12 tells us that after John was executed, his disciples came and told Jesus. Jesus then fed the 5,000 with five barley loaves and two fish. (The same story is told in John 6, where we learn in verse 4 that this miracle was done near Passover.) John died at Passover of 30 A.D.

Forty years later at Passover of 70 A.D., the Romans began to lay siege to the city of Jerusalem. Josephus, one of the Judean generals who had fought against the Romans until his capture, wrote of the 115,880 casualties carried through just one gate of Jerusalem. In his Wars of the Jews, V, xiii, 7 he wrote:

> "No fewer than a hundred and fifteen thousand eight hundred and eighty dead bodies, in the interval between the fourteenth day of the month Xanthicus, or Nisan [i.e., Passover], when the Romans pitched their camp by the city, and the first day of the month Panemus, or Tamuz."

Josephus recorded that the Romans pitched their camp around Jerusalem to begin the siege at Passover in 70 A.D. This was precisely forty years after the execution of John the Baptist. The city was destroyed by late August of the same year. The temple was burned. All the gold melted from the heat. Later, in the scramble for gold, the people pried every stone from the other to salvage the gold that had collected like water between the rocks. By the time the destruction was finished, not one stone stood upon the other, as Jesus foretold in Matt. 24:1, 2,

> [1] **And Jesus came out from the temple and was going away when His disciples came up to point out the temple building to Him. [2] And He answered and said to them, Do you not see all these things? Truly I say to you, not one stone here shall be left upon another, which will not be torn down.**

So the words of Jesus were fulfilled.

The Capture of Masada: 73 A.D.

The Zealots were the Jewish extremists of the day. They were called *Sicarii*, which means "people of the daggers." They were assassins and terrorists. Everyone was their enemy that did not help them try to overthrow the Roman authorities. One of Jesus' disciples, Simon Zelotes, had been one of them (Luke 6:15) before Jesus showed him a better way. Zelotes means "the Zealot."

In 73 A.D. a man named Eleazar was the commander of the Sicarii. Before going to Masada, he and his men killed thousands of people in Jerusalem, terrorizing the people so they would join the revolt against the Romans. Anyone who was peaceable among them was assassinated. When the Sicarii were finally expelled from Jerusalem, they took over a fortress mountain called Masada.

Three years after the destruction of Jerusalem, the Romans finally captured Masada. The Romans had to build a ramp up to the fortress in order to take it. They finished the ramp on the fourteenth day of the first month in 73 A.D. This was the day the people would normally have killed their lambs for Passover to be eaten that evening. The Romans then decided to storm Masada the following morning. But that night the Sicarii in Masada assisted each other in committing suicide instead of keeping the Passover. Only one elderly woman and five children hid themselves and survived the ordeal. The fact that they had to hide in order to survive the night shows that this was more than a voluntary suicide. It was also murder in the guise of "assisted suicide." There is no way to tell how many of those people were actually murdered. Josephus tells us in Wars of the Jews, VII, ix, 1,

> "This calamitous slaughter was made on the fifteenth day of the month [Xanthicus] Nisan."

One cannot help but be reminded of the slaughter of the firstborn in Egypt which occurred at the original Passover night. The only reason the Israelites were spared was because they had placed the blood of the lamb on their door posts and lintels. Ex. 12:12, 13 says,

> [12] **For I will go through the land of Egypt on that night, and will strike down all the first-born in the land of Egypt, both man and beast; and against all the gods of Egypt I will execute judgments—I am the Lord. [13] And the blood shall be a sign for you on the houses where you live; and when I see the blood, I will pass over you, and no plague will befall you to destroy you when I strike the land of Egypt.**

The Sicarii did not celebrate Passover in the spring of 73 A.D. Instead, they helped each other commit suicide on the night commemorating the slaughter of the first-born of Egypt. This event identifies the Sicarii, not with righteous Israelites, but with the Egyptians who died on that first Passover. It is also significant that the Sicarii terrorists who died at Masada are memorialized by the Israelis today as heroes. They ought rather to be memorialized as examples of bad figs whose attitudes and actions are to be abhorred by all future generations.

Josephus makes it clear that these religious zealots (the Sicarii) were among the ones most responsible for the disasters that came upon Jerusalem and the whole nation. Their doctrine of rebellion was "*to look upon God as their only Lord and Master*" (Wars, VII, x, 1). They did not believe that God wanted them to be ruled by any foreigner. By this they meant that they were duty-bound by God Himself to make war on any nation that had conquered them. They did not comprehend the law of tribulation in Deut. 28. They did not understand the book of Judges, where God makes it very clear that He would not allow them to be free, as long they were in rebellion against His law and remained in an unrepentant condition. Neither did they learn anything from the writings of Jeremiah and the destruction of Jerusalem at the hand of Babylon.

Thus, the bad figs of Judah, in attempting to throw off the wooden yoke, succeeded only in securing for themselves the iron yoke. Many were slaughtered, the land was devastated, the nation itself destroyed, and the people sent into foreign lands as captives and slaves. Everything that Moses prophesied in the law of tribulation came upon them.

This iron yoke continued until the twentieth century, when modern Zionism was born. Zionism was the attempt to throw off the iron yoke and to return to the old land without first repenting of their hostility against Jesus Christ, as the law demands. The movement itself, therefore, is lawless. But many Jews became tired of waiting, yet remained blinded to the causes of their dispersion.

The question is, why did Zionism succeed in establishing the Israeli state, even though the law of tribulation seemed to make this impossible? There is no biblical precedent for throwing off a yoke of either wood or iron until the people had repented. The answer is found in the fact that Judaism is fulfilling two sets of prophecies, one for Judah, and one for Edom. Under the banner of Judah, the people were banned by divine legislation from throwing off the yoke of iron.

But under the banner of Edom, the Jews had a genuine case to present before the divine court. God had promised Esau-Edom that he would be given the land of Canaan. Jacob-Israel was obligated by law to give the land back to his brother, because he had taken it by fraudulent means. And so, in 1948 the "Union Jack" flag of Great Britain was removed from Palestine, and a new nation was born, calling itself Israel. The name "Jack" is short for Jacob. In 1948 Jacob was forced to return the land to the Zionist Jews, not because they were descended from the northern House of Israel, nor yet because of their descent from the southern House of Judah, but because of their descent from Edom.

But before we can make sense of these more recent events in the twentieth century, we must explain the significance of the rejection of Jesus Christ at His first appearance.

CHAPTER 6
The Rejection of Jesus

It is common knowledge that the people of Judah rejected Jesus as the Messiah. Most people also know that Judas betrayed Jesus, siding with Jesus' avowed enemies, even though he was Jesus' disciple and friend. But not many understand that this entire story of Jesus' rejection was foreshadowed and prophesied in the Old Testament story of Absalom, who usurped his father's throne with the help of Ahithophel

In order to understand fully why and how the Jews rejected Jesus as the Messiah, one must see the corresponding prophetic story in the Old Testament. Unless we study the types and shadows of the Old Testament, we will not have an accurate understanding of the New Testament.

Absalom: Temporary Usurper of David's Throne

David had family problems that stemmed from his affair with Bathsheba. In 2 Samuel 13 we read the story of David's son, Amnon, and how he raped his half-sister, Tamar. Tamar and Absalom were brother and sister. Their mother was Maacah, a foreign princess, as we read in 2 Sam. 3:3,

> [3] **And his second, Chileab, by Abigail the widow of Nabal and Carmelite; and the third, Absalom the son of Maacah the daughter of Talmai, king of Geshur.**

Absalom hated Amnon for raping his sister (2 Sam. 13:22). His hatred simmered for two years, and during that time, his father (King David) appeared to do nothing to bring Amnon to justice. In studying the mind of David, we can be sure that he had prayed earnestly about the situation to know what to do. The law applicable to this crime was found in Lev. 18:9, which reads,

> [9] **The nakedness of your sister, either your father's daughter or your mother's daughter, whether born at home or born outside, their nakedness you shall not uncover.**

Such lawless behavior was one of the reasons God cast the Canaanites out of the land when their iniquity was full. The judgment of the law is found in Lev. 18:24-29, which reads,

> [24] **Do not defile yourselves by any of these things; for <u>by all these the nations which I am casting out before you have become defiled</u> . . . [27] For the men of the land who have been before you have done all these abominations, and the land has become defiled; [28] so that the land may not spew you out, should you defile it, <u>as it has spewed out the nation which has been before you</u>. [29] For whoever does any of these abominations, those persons who do so <u>shall be cut off from among their people</u>.**

Thus, there is no question that David must have prayed about sending Amnon into exile, cutting him off from Judah and revoking his citizenship rights, as the law prescribed. Yet he remembered his own sin with Bathsheba. David himself was guilty of both adultery with Bathsheba and the murder of Uriah, her husband. In that situation, God had been merciful to David, not requiring that David be executed for his sin, but that his son, the son of Bathsheba would die. That entire story is told in 2 Samuel 12, the chapter immediately preceding Amnon's rape of Tamar.

When Nathan the prophet confronted David with his sin, he first told David a story about a rich man who had taken his poor neighbor's only lamb to feed his guest. David was angered by this injustice and pronounced judgment upon the rich man. He said to Nathan in 2 Sam. 12:5, 6,

> [5] **. . . As the Lord lives, surely the man who has done this deserves to die.** [6] **and he must make restitution for the lamb fourfold, because he did this thing and had no compassion.**

David's son was called as a substitute to die for his sin. That son of David was a type of Christ, called to die for our sin. But the second part of this judgment was that David was to make fourfold restitution, according to the law (Ex. 22:1-4). And so we find that David lost four sons in the years to come: the nameless child, Amnon, Absalom, Adonijah.

David was "very angry" with Amnon (2 Sam. 13:21), but he knew better than to judge the situation in the heat of anger. He also personally knew the mercy of God. In studying the law, David understood that being a judge was not as easy as it might appear to a legalist. And so he remained in prayer to know how to handle Amnon's rape of Tamar according to the mind of God with the proper balance of justice and mercy. David's delay in judging Amnon was not due to neglect, for no father could just forget about such a situation.

The delay was divinely inspired, and, as we shall see shortly, it was imperative in order to fulfill the prophetic types and shadows of events yet to come.

Absalom, however, did not understand the delay. Though David was very angry, Absalom burned with hatred (2 Sam. 13:22). There is a difference. His hatred finally consumed him, and he took matters into his own hands, and as a legalist he himself became lawless. Legalism is the worst form of lawlessness, for it is also blind.

Absalom called for a family feast, and told his servants to kill Amnon at the feast. The plot was successful (2 Sam. 13:28-33). Amnon was killed. Absalom then fled to Geshur, where he lived with Talmai, his mother's father. We read in 2 Sam. 13:37-39,

> [37] **Now Absalom fled and went to Talmai the son of Ammihud, the king of Geshur. And David mourned for his son every day.** [38] **So Absalom had fled and gone to Geshur, and was there three years.** [39] **And the heart of King David longed to go out to Absalom; for he was comforted concerning Amnon, since he was dead.**

So Absalom found asylum in Geshur and remained there three years. During that time, David longed to see his son, but did nothing and said nothing that would cause Absalom to return to Jerusalem. David knew that Absalom had acted lawlessly, and that exile was his judgment. But from Absalom's point of view, he felt that he was justified in killing Amnon and thought that his exile, though necessary, was unjust. He wanted to return to the land.

Finally, Absalom asked David's general, Joab, to intercede for him. Only then did David allow Absalom to return in peace to Jerusalem. But another two years went by, and David still refused to see Absalom in person (2 Sam. 14:28).

Finally, Absalom again called for Joab, but Joab refused to come. Absalom then told his servants to set fire to Joab's barley field, and they did so. This got Joab's attention, and he came immediately, demanding to know why Absalom had burned his barley. Absalom then insisted that Joab go to David and intercede on his behalf. The plan worked. Absalom was brought back into the presence of his father, David. We read in 2 Sam. 14:33,

> [33] **So when Joab came to the king and told him, he called for Absalom. Thus he came to the king and prostrated himself on his face to the ground before the king, and <u>the king kissed Absalom</u>.**

Soon afterward, Absalom decided that his father was not worthy to be the king, and he plotted to overthrow him and usurp the throne. So he asked permission from David to go south to Hebron to "*pay my vow*" (2 Sam. 15:7). David granted this, but when Absalom arrived in Hebron, he proclaimed himself king in place of David (2 Sam. 15:10). He also sent messengers to Ahithophel, David's counselor and friend, to come and take his side. Ahithophel came and sided with Absalom. In this way he betrayed David by helping Absalom usurp the throne. 2 Sam. 15:12 says,

> [12] **And Absalom sent for Ahithophel the Gilonite, David's counselor, from his city Giloh; while he was offering the sacrifices. And the conspiracy was strong, for the people increased continually with Absalom.**

One may ask why Ahithophel sided with Absalom. But when we see that Ahithophel was Bathsheba's grandfather, the motive becomes clear. 2 Sam. 11:3 tells us,

> [3] **. . . Is this not Bathsheba, the daughter of Eliam, the wife of Uriah the Hittite?**

In 2 Sam. 23:34 we read in the genealogical record of "*Eliam the son of Ahithophel the Gilonite.*" In other words, Ahithophel had a son named Eliam, who had a daughter named Bathsheba, the woman with whom David committed adultery (2 Samuel 11). A genealogical table would look like this:

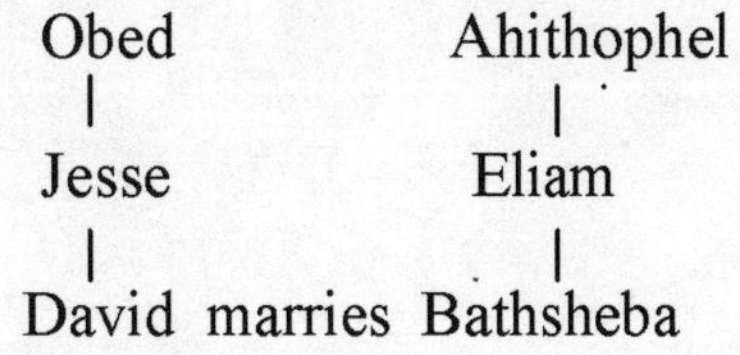

Ahithophel never forgave David for this sin, and this made him vulnerable to the temptation to betray David, even though he was David's counselor and friend. David wrote about Ahithophel later in Psalm 41:9, saying of him,

> [9] **Even my close friend, in whom I trusted, who ate my bread, has lifted up his heel against me.**

Jesus quoted this verse in John 13:18, applying it prophetically to Judas, the betrayer:

18 I do not speak of all of you. I know the ones I have chosen, but it is that the Scripture may be fulfilled, He who eats My bread has lifted up His heel against Me.

David had trusted Ahithophel, but in quoting Ps. 41:9 Jesus left out "*in whom I trusted*," because He knew that Judas would betray Him. In not trusting his friend Judas, Jesus differed from David, who did trust Ahithophel. Nonetheless, we see from this that Ahithophel was a type and shadow of Judas. Ahithophel betrayed David. Judas betrayed the Son of David.

By extending the type, we see that Absalom's role in usurping the throne of David was later played by the nation of Judah itself, specifically represented by the chief priests.

Crucified on the "Skull" of the Mount of Olives

David refused to fight against Absalom and his men over the throne. Instead, he meekly left Jerusalem, knowing that God would establish His throne. In this, he showed the attitude of Jesus Christ, who also refused to fight for His throne rights, even though He was the rightful Heir to the throne. 2 Sam. 15:30, 31 says,

30 And David went up the ascent of the *Mount of* Olives, and wept as he went, and his head was covered and he walked barefoot. Then all the people who were with him each covered his head and went up weeping as they went.

This is the same path Jesus took when He bore the cross to the place of crucifixion. Can we not see in David's experience a prophetic pattern of the crucifixion?

31 Now someone told David, saying, Ahithophel is among the conspirators with Absalom. And David said, O LORD, I pray, make the counsel of Ahithophel foolishness.

This is a Hebrew play on words. Ahithophel's name means "my brother is foolish." I believe his name is prophetic of Judas' attitude toward Jesus, his "brother." Judas thought Jesus was foolish not to use his power to authenticate his calling as the Messiah and to establish his authority in Jerusalem. Judas also disagreed with Jesus' refusal to force the chief priests into declaring Him the Messiah. But if Jesus had forced the issue, where would the force end? The people would then expect Him to use violence against the Romans and take the Kingdom by force. But Jesus would have nothing of the kind, for He intended to wait and win the hearts of the people by love. He had no intention of destroying Roman people, for He loved the Romans as much as the Judeans.

Quoting from The Interlinear Bible, 2 Sam. 15:32 says,

32 It happened as David had come to the top [Heb. *Rosh*, "head"]**, there where he bowed** [Heb. *shachah*, "bow or worship"] **to God.**

The Hebrew word translated "top" above is *rosh*, which means "head." For example, *Rosh Hashana* is the "head" of the year, that is, the first day of the year, marked by the Feast of Trumpets. John 19:17 says Jesus was crucified at the place of the skull (Greek: *kranion*, from which we get our word "cranium," head, or skull). Even as David walked up to the summit, or "head" of the Mount of Olives, so also did Jesus carry His cross to the same place where David worshiped God.

This was the ancient location of the sacrificial altar where the red heifers were burned "outside the camp," whose ashes were used to purify people as they came to worship at the temple. Jesus, of course, fulfilled this burnt offering, as He did all the offerings. He was crucified outside the camp (Heb. 13:11-13), and this was defined in those days as 2,000 cubits outside the walls of Jerusalem. The top of the Mount of Olives was precisely that distance. The place today that is presumed to be the place of the skull in Jerusalem is not located outside the camp. That hill now looks like a skull, but archeologists tell us that this is the result of erosion only in the past thousand years.

The story of Absalom's usurping the throne and David's path to the top of the Mount of Olives shows clearly and conclusively that the story of Absalom's rebellion and Ahithophel's betrayal is a prophetic pattern of Jesus' crucifixion and Judas' betrayal.

Later, when Absalom did not follow Ahithophel's advice to pursue David immediately, Ahithophel was wise enough to know that David would eventually return to the throne. He knew that Absalom's kingship would end, and he himself would then have to face David's justice for the betrayal. So we read in 2 Sam. 17:23,

> **23 Now when Ahithophel saw that his counsel was not followed, he saddled his donkey and arose and went to his home, to his city, and set his house in order, and strangled himself; thus he died and was buried in the grave of his father.**

Ahithophel hanged ("strangled") himself, even as Judas did later, as we read in Matt. 27:3-5,

> **3 Then when Judas, who had betrayed Him, saw that He had been condemned, he felt remorse and returned the thirty pieces of silver to the chief priests and elders, 4 saying, I have sinned by betraying innocent blood. But they said, What is that to us? See to that yourself! 5 And he threw the pieces of silver into the sanctuary and departed; and he went away and hanged himself.**

David later returned to the throne, and Absalom was killed (2 Sam. 18:15).Thus, the revolt of Absalom, though immediately successful, ultimately failed. This story is prophetic of the story of Jesus. The chief priests were immediately successful in their plot to overthrow King Jesus, but their effort ultimately will fail.

Judah's Rebellion Against King Jesus

The entire conflict between Absalom and David was prophetic of the conflict between the bad figs of Judah and Jesus, the Son of David. Absalom represented the bad figs; David represented the good figs, particularly Jesus Christ. Amnon, the rapist, represented the lawlessness of the nation's leadership in general. Strong's Concordance gives the meaning of his name as "faithful," tracing its root to the Hebrew word *aman*, "to build up or support; to *foster* as a parent or nurse." Young's Concordance says Amnon means "tutelage or upbringing." In other words, Amnon's name appears to indicate the idea of rearing children, building them up, supporting them, or fostering them in order to bring them into maturity.

The children of Judah were being reared and taught to know the mind of God through the divine law. The law itself is the tutor by which children are brought into the maturity of the mind of Christ (Gal. 3:24; 4:2). Yet when the law is applied legalistically, apart from the mind of Christ, it has the effect of raping the bride of Christ.

Tamar's name means "erect, upright, or a palm tree." She represented the true believers in Judah—that is, the good figs. As a woman, she also represents the true bride of Christ.

There are at least two ways of looking at this prophetic parable. First, the story of Amnon shows how the leaders of Judah would rape the bride of Christ. Their religious traditions nullified the divine law (Matt. 15:6) and made them lawless. In the centuries from Judah's return from Babylon to the birth of Jesus, the Pharisees and Sadducees of Judah slid steadily into a hypocritical form of religious lawlessness.

A second way of looking at Amnon is that he represented the divine law itself. Because of the lawlessness of Judah, God's law had decreed that they would be given an iron yoke under Babylonian masters in a 70-year captivity, followed by a longer period of time under a wooden yoke. They were still under a Roman wooden yoke at the time that Jesus was born. In essence, the divine law was their tutor, and by these judgments, God was teaching them obedience. He was also hiring other nations as tutors—first Babylon, then Medo-Persia, then Greece, and now Rome.

In an extended sense, then, Amnon (tutelage) was prophetic of these other empires that were lawless and oppressive. They had raped the bride of Christ, Tamar. There were many injustices perpetrated upon the people of Judah during those centuries. They longed for freedom and for justice. They did not comprehend that the yokes of iron and wood were God's lawful judgment upon the nation for their sin. Hence, like Absalom, they became dissatisfied, thinking that God (David) was unfit to rule them, for He seemed to do nothing, in spite of all their religious activity.

And so, like Absalom, they did unlawful things to force God's hand. Absalom burned Joab's barley field. In our book, The Barley Overcomers, we show that the barley represents the overcomers—applicable here to the good figs of Judah. Specifically, it prophesies of the prophets who were all killed at Jerusalem, culminating with the last of the Old Testament prophets, John the Baptist, whom Herod imprisoned and ultimately executed. This was the final act of "barley burning" that brought Absalom into the presence of David. John's rejection and imprisonment was the event that began Jesus' public ministry. It brought the Absalom people into the presence of King Jesus, son of David.

2 Sam. 14:33 says, "*the king kissed Absalom.*" This speaks of Jesus coming face to face with the Chief Priests in Jerusalem. Jesus blessed ("kissed") the nation with many good works and miracles of healing. But, as Ps. 109:3-5 says, they repaid His goodness and love with evil and with hatred:

> **3 They have also surrounded me with words of hatred, and fought against me without cause. 4 In return for my love they act as my accusers; but I am in prayer. 5 Thus they have repaid me evil for good, and hatred for my love.**

The bad figs of Judah, led by their religious leaders in the temple, wanted a Messiah who would be a great military leader, so that He could overthrow the hated Romans and make slaves out of the rest of the world. They believed in world peace—after the world was subdued by military conquest. This was their concept of the Messiah, and so when Jesus came as the Prince of Peace, they utterly disagreed with His methods. In their estimation, He simply was not the Messiah type.

There are two princes of peace in the prophetic story of David. Absalom was the first. His name is Ab-salom, "father of peace." The second is Solomon, which also means "peace." Both of these men were sons of David; hence they both were princes. But Absalom was a prince of violence who was hypocritically named "father of peace." Solomon, on the other hand, established true peace in Israel and in that way was a type of Christ, the true "Prince of Peace."

Absalom disagreed with David for apparently doing nothing after Amnon raped Tamar. He demanded "justice," and when none was forthcoming, he overthrew David and usurped his throne. Likewise, in Jesus' day the people disagreed with God for seeming to do nothing about Rome's "rape" of people of Judah. The people prayed to God to do them "justice," and when none was forthcoming, they overthrew King Jesus and usurped His throne.

Jesus was the God of the Old Testament, known first as El Shaddai and later as Yahweh. He was the Lawgiver that Moses knew face to face. In His pre-incarnate existence as God in heaven, Jesus did nothing to free the people from their wooden yoke under Medo-Persia, Greece, or Rome. When Jesus was born in Bethlehem, coming to earth, He again did nothing to set the people free of the wooden yoke of Rome—even though He had the power to do so. Why? The people could not comprehend it. But Jesus understood the law of tribulation. And so, like David, He appeared to do nothing.

Like Absalom, the bad figs totally disagreed with this do-nothing policy. And like Ahithophel, even Judas, the disciple of Jesus, agreed with the bad figs.

One would think, then, that Absalom would have learned not to commit the crime of rape. But Absalom himself ended up raping all of David's concubines at the advice of Ahithophel! This story is told in 2 Sam. 16:20-23,

> **[20] Then Absalom said to Ahithophel, Give your advice, What shall we do? [21] And Ahithophel said to Absalom, Go in to your father's concubines, whom he has left to keep the house; then all Israel will hear that you have made yourself odious to your father. The hands of all who are with you will also be strengthened. [22] So they pitched a tent for Absalom on the roof, and Absalom went in to his father's concubines in the sight of all Israel. [23] And the advice of Ahithophel, which he gave in those days, was as if one inquired of the word of God; so was all the advice of Ahithophel regarded by both David and Absalom.**

It is peculiar that so many people who accuse others of injustice are guilty of the same things. In this case it speaks prophetically of the abuse of Israel, the wife of God. The Chief Priests thought God was unjust in allowing Rome to rule them, but yet they themselves abused the people even more than the Romans ever did. Jesus said in Matt. 23:2-15,

> **[2] The Scribes and the Pharisees have seated themselves in the chair of Moses... [4] And <u>they tie up heavy loads and lay them on men's shoulders</u>, but they themselves are unwilling to move them with so much as a finger. . . [13] But woe to you, scribes and Pharisees, hypocrites, because <u>you shut off the kingdom of heaven from men</u>; for you do not enter in yourselves, nor do you allow those who are entering to go in. [14] Woe to you, scribes and Pharisees, hypocrites, because <u>you devour widows' houses</u>, even while for a pretense you make long prayers; therefore you shall receive greater condemnation. [15] Woe to you, scribes and Pharisees, hypocrites, because you travel about on sea and land to**

make one proselyte; and when he becomes one, you make him twice as much a son of hell as yourselves.

In raping the wife of God, they made themselves "odious" to the Father (2 Sam. 16:21), precisely as Ahithophel had said.

In Matthew 21 Jesus told a parable of the Kingdom, in which He described the Jewish leaders of the day plotting to usurp the Messiah's throne. The vine-growers, or farmers, in God's vineyard had been given authority over the vineyard in order to render to the Owner (God) the fruits in their seasons. When the Owner of the vineyard sent servants to collect the fruits, the farmers beat them, stoned them, and sometimes killed them (Matt. 21:35, 36). Finally He sent His Son, thinking they would surely reverence His Son. But verse 38 says,

> [38] **But when the vine-growers saw the son, they said among themselves, This is the heir; come, let us kill him, and seize his inheritance.** [39] **And they took him, and threw him out of the vineyard, and killed him.**

Absalom knew that his father was the king, and for that reason he usurped the throne. Likewise, so also did the chief priests know that Jesus was the Heir. They killed Him because they knew who He was. It was a deliberate revolt and rebellion to seize His inheritance. Take note also that the Romans were not the vine-growers. They had not been given custody of the Kingdom of God, nor had they killed the prophets, who were the king's servants in the same parable. The Romans did not crucify Jesus. In fact, Pilate wanted to release Jesus. (Acts 3:13). John 19:15-18 tells us who did the crucifying:

> [15] **They therefore cried out, Away with *Him*, away with *Him*, crucify Him! Pilate said to them, Shall I crucify your King? The chief priests answered, "We have no king but Caesar.** [16] **So he** [Pilate] **then delivered Him to THEM** [the chief priests] **to be crucified.** [17] **THEY took Jesus therefore, and He went out, bearing His own cross, to the place called the Place of a Skull, which is called in Hebrew, Golgotha.** [18] **There THEY** [the Chief Priests] **crucified Him, and with Him two other men, one on either side, and Jesus in between.**

In the days following Pentecost, the Jewish leaders of the Sanhedrin objected to Peter's preaching, saying he intended "*to bring this Man's blood upon us*" (Acts 5:28). In other words, the Jewish leaders accused Peter of holding them accountable for Jesus' crucifixion. Peter responded in Acts 5:30, saying,

> [30] **The God of our fathers raised up Jesus, whom YOU had put to death by hanging Him on a cross.**

But perhaps the most important passage showing the connection between the chief priests of the Sanhedrin and Absalom's usurpation of David's throne is found in Acts 7:51-53, where Stephen gives his sermon rehearsing the story of God's Kingdom. His sermon ended with this:

> [51] **You men who are stiff-necked and uncircumcised in heart and ears are always resisting the Holy Spirit; you are doing just as your fathers did.** [52] **Which one of the prophets did your fathers not persecute? And they killed those who had previously announced the coming of the Righteous One, whose betrayers and murderers YOU have now become;** [53] **YOU who received the law as ordained by angels, and *yet* did not keep it.**

In Matthew 22:1-7 Jesus told another parable that was directed against the Chief Priests. Those who had first been called to the wedding feast refused to come. In fact, they abused the messengers (prophets) who had invited them to the wedding. We read,

> 5 **But they paid no attention and went their way, one to his own farm, another to his business.** 6 **and the rest seized his slaves** [God's prophets] **and mistreated them and killed them.** 7 **But the king was enraged and sent his armies, and destroyed those murderers, and set their city on fire.**

This was obviously fulfilled in 70 A.D. when God sent the Roman army to set Jerusalem on fire and to destroy "*those murderers.*" In other words, God used the Romans to execute judgment upon Jerusalem. God did NOT send His armies to destroy Rome, because they were NOT the murderers mentioned in verse seven. To blame the Romans for Jesus' crucifixion would be a *false accusation* that is certainly prohibited in the divine law (Deut. 19:16-20).

Many today prefer to blame the Romans, because it is more politically correct and because it makes it easier to convert Jews to Christianity. In doing this, however, we dishonor God by disagreeing with His Word. We believe the Word to be inspired Scripture, and our purpose is to teach what it says, for only the truth sets people free. So let us not be found as false witnesses.

We also admonish our Christian brethren to rid themselves of any emotional hatred that they might have toward Jews or any other people. Such things are unbecoming in those who profess the name of Jesus Christ. It is one thing to believe and teach what is written in the Scriptural record; it is quite another to harbor hatred and bitterness in one's heart. While we certainly affirm that the Aaronic priests crucified Jesus, we must also understand the necessity of this sacrifice at their hands. They were, after all, the only ones qualified to offer this great Sacrifice. Without them, Jesus' sacrifice would have been unacceptable by the divine law. These priests could not have been Roman, Edomite, or of any other descent, for that would have violated the law of sacrifice. Hence, in the bigger picture of the plan of God, they unintentionally did us all a great service.

Judas: The Son of Perdition

In 2 Thess. 2:3 (KJV) Paul speaks of "the man of sin" as being also the "son of perdition." The NASB uses slightly different terms:

> 3 **Let no one in any way deceive you, for it will not come unless the apostasy comes first, and the man of lawlessness is revealed, the son of destruction** [Greek: *apoleia*].

Jesus uses the same term of Judas, "*the son of perdition*" in John 17:12,

> 12 **While I was with them, I was keeping them in Thy name which Thou hast given Me; and I guarded them, and not one of them perished but the son of perdition** [Greek: *apoleia*]**, that the Scripture might be fulfilled.**

Jesus appointed Judas to be the treasurer of the ministry even though He knew that Judas was helping himself to some of the money and was a thief. John 12:6 says,

> 6 **Now he** [Judas] **said this, not because he was concerned about the poor, but because he was a thief, and as he had the money box, he used to pilfer what was put into it.**

Later, during the last supper before the crucifixion, we read in John 13:27,

> 27 **And after the morsel, Satan then entered into him** [Judas]. **Jesus therefore said to him, What you do, do quickly.**

Judas then left the room to betray Jesus. Only then did Jesus give His special instructions and teaching to the other disciples, beginning in John 14, telling them that He was going to leave them shortly, but that He would send them the Holy Spirit to guide them into all truth. John 16:13 says,

> 13 **But when He, the Spirit of truth, comes, He will guide** [Greek: *hodegos*] **you into all the truth; for He will not speak on His own initiative, but whatever He hears, He will speak; and He will disclose to you what is to come.**

This is important because Judas was a "guide" to those who came to arrest Him and crucify Him. Acts 1:16 says,

> 16 **Brethren, the Scripture had to be fulfilled, which the Holy Spirit foretold by the mouth of David concerning Judas, who became a guide** [Greek: *hodegos*] **to those who arrested Jesus.**

As we will see as we proceed in our study, Judas must be viewed in contrast to the Holy Spirit, who is the true Guide, who leads into truth. Judas is the guide who leads people into the deceptive spirit of betrayal, and in this sense is like a counterfeit of the Holy Spirit. This is evident from 2 Thessalonians, where Paul speaks of the man of sin sitting in the temple of God, where the Holy Spirit is supposed to dwell.

It is also significant that Judas was replaced in Acts 1:20-26 just before the coming of the Holy Spirit on the day of Pentecost. The disciples had discerned from Psalm 69:25 and Psalm 109:8 that Judas was destined to be replaced. So Acts 1:20 tells us,

> 20 **For it is written in the book of Psalms, Let his homestead be made desolate, and let no man dwell in it;** [quoted from Ps. 69:25] **and, His office let another man take** [quoted from Ps. 109:8].

Psalms 69 and 109 are prophetic about Judas and the chief priests. These are too lengthy to quote here. Many of these verses were later quoted in the New Testament, applicable to the circumstances surrounding Jesus' crucifixion.

The disciples drew lots and chose Matthias to replace Judas, but on the higher level, the Holy Spirit was the only One who could guide us into all truth. On the day of Pentecost the Holy Spirit replaced the man of sin (Judas) in the temple. On still another level, God Himself called the Apostle Paul to replace Judas.

Betrayed in the House of Friends

Judas Iscariot (Ish-Kerioth) was from a town called Kerioth, or Kerjath. Iscariot means "Man of Kerioth." In other words, Judas' home town was Keriath-arba, which is Hebron, as we read in Gen. 35:27,

> 27 **And Jacob came to his father Isaac at Mamre of Kiriath-arba (that is, Hebron), where Abraham and Isaac had sojourned.**

In order for Judas to play the part of Ahithophel in Absalom's revolt, he had to be a man of Hebron, for that was where Absalom's conspiracy began. Furthermore, in order for Judas to betray Jesus, he had to be Jesus' "friend," for Zech. 13:6 prophesied that He would be betrayed in the house of His friends:

> [6] **And one will say to him, What are these wounds between your arms** [hands]**? Then he will say, *Those* with which I was wounded in the house of my FRIENDS.**

Hebron means "friendship." Judas betrayed Jesus with a kiss of friendship, and Jesus called him "friend" in Matthew 26:49, 50.

> [49] **And immediately he** [Judas] **went to Jesus and said, Hail, Rabbi! and kissed Him.** [50] **And Jesus said to him, Friend, *do* what you have come for. Then they came and laid hands on Jesus and seized Him.**

Anyone can treat another person unjustly, but it takes a friend to betray.

In conclusion, then, we see that in David was a type of Christ; Absalom was a type of the chief priests; and Ahithophel was a type of Judas. It is a story of those who would kill the Heir and usurp the dominion mandate from the Servant of Servants, because certain violent men wanted to lord it over others. It is also a story of how the disciple and friend of the King betrayed Him because he disagreed with His methods. Finally, we see the tragic end, not only of the usurpers, but also of the betrayer, the man of lawlessness.

All of this gives us an understanding of the son of perdition and his prophetic role. It was written for our learning, so that we do not find ourselves, as Jesus' disciples and friends, playing the role of Judas today.

CHAPTER 7
The Conflict

So far we have focused upon the bad figs described in Jeremiah 24. We must now look at the other tree of Judah, for this is of utmost importance in understanding the relationship of the Church with Judah and Israel. There are some who teach that a "Gentile Church" replaced Israel. Others teach that Christians ought to unite with the bad figs in order to fulfill Bible prophecy. Neither view is true.

Classic "replacement theology" as taught traditionally in the Roman Catholic Church and some Protestant denominations is not biblically accurate. But neither is the view of their main opponents who advocate Messianic Judaism. We will show in this chapter that the good figs of Judah—namely, those Judahites who followed Jesus—formed the trunk of the "tree" of New Testament Christianity. This fig tree producing good fruits, following the King of Judah, retained the right to be called by the tribal name of Judah. They are the "true Jews," as it were.

We saw in Chapter Five that God saw the nation of Judah as a fig tree in Jer. 24. We saw also that the nation was actually divided into two groups of people—those whose fruits were very good, and those whose fruits were very bad. This is really no different from any other nation, for there is not a nation in the world that has all righteous people or all unrighteous people. But in the case of Judah it is a matter of divine separation into two distinct fig trees, because God intended to treat them differently. He intended to give Judah's dominion mandate to those who produced good fruit, and at the same time He intended to disinherit those who produced bad fruit.

Jesus Himself produced good fruit. He was born of a Judahite mother, as proven in the genealogies of Matthew 1 and Luke 3. But as the King of Judah, He was more than just a fig branch that was producing good fruit. He was the tree itself. He was the trunk of the tree, to which were attached various branches that bore good fruit. Jesus said as much when He used a slightly different motif of the vine and branches. John 15:1-6 says,

> **1 I am the true vine, and My Father is the vinedresser. 2 Every branch in Me that does not bear fruit, He takes away; and every branch that bears fruit, He prunes it, that it may bear more fruit. . . 5 I am the vine, you are the branches; he who abides in Me, and I in him, he bears much fruit; for apart from Me you can do nothing. 6 If anyone does not abide in Me, he is thrown away as a branch and dries up; and they gather them, and cast them into the fire, and they are burned.**

It is clear from this that only those who abide in Christ will bear the type of fruit that God is seeking. If one claims to be in Christ, but does not produce these fruits of the Kingdom, he is cut off. And "*if anyone does not abide in Me*," Jesus says, "*he is thrown away as a branch and dries up.*" Surely He had in mind those Judahites who had rejected Him as Messiah. Only a few days earlier, Jesus had cursed the fig tree, and the disciples had marveled that it had dried up by the following morning. He was saying, then, that the people who produced no fruit—or, as Jeremiah put it, those who produced only bad figs that could not be eaten—would be cut off.

This is precisely what happened. Judah split into two factions, or two "trees." Those who accepted Jesus as Messiah became the branches of the good fig tree. These were the inheritors of the dominion mandate given to Judah. Of these, Jesus said He would prune them in order that they would bring forth even more fruit.

Those who refused to accept Jesus as Messiah were cut off and are no longer inheritors of the dominion mandate. Jesus clearly said that there is no way that anyone can bear fruit apart from being attached to Christ.

Replacement Theology

A "Gentile Church" did NOT replace a "Jewish Church." The bad figs were simply cut off, and the good figs of Judah, who followed Jesus, the King of Judah, were left to carry the banner of the Judah Church. There was *no replacement* here, as Classic Roman Catholic theology has taught in the past. The promises to Abraham were never transferred from one people to another. The promises simply continued through the unbroken line of the good fig tree of Judah.

Replacement Theology teaches that the fig tree was rooted out and replaced by an apple tree. This did not happen. The truth is that there were two fig trees, one good and one bad. Both were of Judah. The bad fig tree was rooted out, and the good fig tree remained to carry on the Kingdom of God upon the earth. The good fig tree did not replace anything, because *it was always there*.

Likewise, it is not a "Jewish" Church, at least not in the way that people mean when they make that claim. It is certainly a Judahite fig tree; but those who make the claim that this is a "Jewish" Church usually say also that Christian believers are supposed to re-unite with Jews who are still cut off from Christ. In other words, they are attempting to re-unite the good fig tree with the bad fig tree. Nearly always, this movement teaches that the bad fig tree is still God's chosen nation.

The problem with this view is that it is a move to engraft the branches of good figs to the bad fig tree, rather than the other way around. That teaching would ultimately bring all Christians into Judaism, rather than bringing Jews to Christ. The fact is, the bad fig tree will NEVER bring forth fruit, for that was the nature of Jesus' curse (Matt. 21:19). The only solution is for the individual branches to be cut off from that dead fig tree and grafted to the only Tree that can give them life—Jesus Christ, the trunk of the good fig tree. As long as conversion to Christ is repugnant to a Jew, he is not a partaker of the dominion mandate of Judah, nor is he of that tribe in the sight of God, as we will prove shortly from Scripture.

The Good Fig Tree was "the Church"

The good fig tree attempted to remain in the old land for a time, but conflict soon forced most of them to flee for their lives into other parts of the Roman Empire. The book of Acts tells the story of this persecution. Even so, the fig tree grew rapidly. There were 3,000 converted on the day of Pentecost (Acts 2:41). Acts 2:47 says,

> [47] **And the Lord was adding to their number day by day those who were being saved.**

Again, in Acts 4:4, we read,

[4] But many of those who had heard the message believed; and the number of the men came to be about five thousand.

Again, in Acts 5:14, we read,

[14] And all the more believers in the Lord, multitudes of men and women, were constantly added to their number.

Acts 6:7 says further,

[7] And the word of God kept on spreading; and the number of the disciples continued to increase greatly in Jerusalem, and a great many of the priests were becoming obedient to the faith.

Each time other Judahites were converted, the good fig tree grew in strength. The disciples had great success, even though they did not hesitate to place responsibility for the crucifixion of Jesus upon their own nation. The apostles did not believe that they ought to tread softly on this controversial issue. They preached boldly, and multitudes repented and followed Jesus Christ.

These multitudes of Judahites were "natural branches" of the fig tree. Yet they were cut off from the Kingdom tree, whose trunk was Jesus Christ, until they repented and placed their faith in Jesus as the Messiah. The good fig tree continued to grow, and soon the opposition in the temple became so alarmed that they began to seriously persecute the Church.

Yes, this good fig tree was THE CHURCH.

It was the inheritor of the dominion mandate given to Judah. It was not a "Gentile Church," as is often taught. It was a Judah Church and will always be a Judah Church.

The good figs from the Judah fig tree were soon scattered by persecution into all parts of the Roman Empire and beyond it. Wherever they went, they told the good news to those who would listen. They fed all nations with the good fruit from the tree and made many converts among non-Judahites. As these new converts came to Christ, they were then "grafted" as branches into that fig tree of Judah. Within a century, the Church (fig tree) began to bear many different types of fruit from all nations, with each branch obtaining its life from Jesus Christ. In fact, soon, the figs were outnumbered by the apples, pears, and apricots from the engrafted branches of other nations.

But in spite of the great variety of branches and fruit that the tree was bearing, it was still a Judah tree in its trunk. It never was a "Gentile Church," nor did a "Gentile Church" replace Judah. Judah simply divided into good and bad trees, with the good tree of Judah becoming the heir of the dominion mandate—and then this good Judah tree was opened up to receive branches from all other trees of the world.

God did NOT plant a new tree and call it the "Gentile Church." Instead, God took His fig tree and engrafted branches of apples, pears, apricots, and so on. Those new branches, though part of the fig tree, continue to bear other fruits. When people of other races are engrafted into this fig tree, they do not change their race or their genetics. They simply produce different types of fruit. God loves variety. And in the end, this tree will bear twelve kinds of fruit, as we read in Rev. 22:2,

> [2] **. . . And on either side of the river was the tree of life, bearing twelve kinds of fruit, yielding its fruit every month; and the leaves of the tree were for the healing of the nations.**

The Tree of Life is Jesus Christ, and it is made up of many branches—those who are in Christ, or part of His Body.

Those who rejected Jesus were, collectively, the corrupt fig tree that could only produce figs that were so bad that they could not be eaten. That corrupt fig tree lost its legal status as the tribe of Judah when they rejected the Messiah and usurped His throne, even as Absalom usurped the throne of his father, David. Even so, for the past 2,000 years a steady stream of Jews have repented and followed Jesus Christ. These have been grafted back into the good fig tree and—with the other believers—are joint heirs with Christ in the dominion mandate.

It is NOT the case, however, that Christian Jews have some special status toward God which allows them to rule above any others. Figs are not better than apples; they just have a different flavor. Neither are apples better than figs; they just have a different flavor.

But in order to understand this, we must look at the divine law to see what actually happened.

The Law of Pruning Trees

Deuteronomy 29 tells us that there were certain conditions by which individuals and even entire tribes of Israel might be cut off, or pruned from the Kingdom Tree. Deut. 29:18-21 says,

> [18] **Lest there shall be among you a man or a woman, or family OR TRIBE, whose heart turns away today from the Lord our God, to go and serve the gods of those nations; lest there shall be among you a root bearing poisonous fruit and wormwood.** [19] **And it shall be when he hears the words of this curse, that he will boast, saying, *I have peace, though I walk in the stubbornness of my heart* in order to destroy the watered land with the dry.** [20] **The Lord shall never be willing to forgive him, but rather the anger of the Lord and His jealousy will burn against that man, and every curse which is written in this book will rest on him, and the Lord will blot out his name from under heaven.** [21] **Then the Lord will single him out for adversity from all the tribes of Israel, according to all the curses of the covenant which are written in this book of the law.**

The idea that God might blot out one of the tribes of Israel is not new. There have been many Bible teachers who have suggested this is why the tribe of Dan is not mentioned in the listing of the tribes sealed in Revelation 7. While I do not believe that this was the reason for Dan's omission, that view does show that Bible teachers recognize the possibility that a tribe or a large portion of a tribe might be cut off from the Kingdom.

In fact, we will show that the fig tree bearing bad figs was cut off in this manner and for the reason stated above. The other fig tree bearing good figs was the portion of Judah that accepted Jesus as the Messiah and adopted His attitude of submission to the Roman yoke that God had decreed for Judah. The reason given in Deut. 29:19 is: "*he will boast, saying, I have peace, though I walk in the stubbornness of my heart.*" In other words, such a person (or family, or tribe) will think that they are reconciled (at peace) with God, even though their hearts continue to be rebellious and stubborn.

This is a very accurate description of the bad fig tree, both in Jeremiah's day and in Jesus' day. They thought that they were doing the will of God by being zealous for their traditions and by performing all the rituals of the temple faithfully. They believed that to be rebellious against Rome was an act of obedience to God. They did not understand the laws of captivity or the laws of tribulation. Jesus did understand, and so he acted much like a friend to the Romans and never challenged their authority or right under God to rule over Judea.

The Laws of Sacrifice

The priests were most proud of their knowledge of the laws of sacrifice. They knew every detail about sacrificing sheep and oxen, but they did not know the Author of the laws of sacrifice. And so they violated this law in the worst way possible in that final Sacrifice of the Lamb of God. Lev. 17:3-5 says:

> [3] **Any man from the house of Israel who slaughters an ox, or a lamb, or a goat in the camp, or who slaughters it outside the camp, [4] and has not brought it to the doorway of the tent of meeting to present it as an offering to the Lord before the tabernacle of the Lord, bloodguiltiness is to be reckoned to that man. He has shed blood and <u>that man shall be cut off from among his people</u>. [5] The reason is so that the sons of Israel may bring their SACRIFICES which they were sacrificing in the open field, that they may bring them in to the Lord, at the doorway of the tent of meeting to the priest, and sacrifice them as sacrifices of peace offerings to the Lord.**

Jesus was the Passover Lamb of God that was sacrificed for the sin of the world. He was crucified "*outside the camp*" (Lev. 17:3; Heb. 13:13) in order that He might also fulfill the law of the red heifer (Num. 19:3). The priests took Jesus to the top (skull, head) of the Mount of Olives, where David had made his sacrifice (2 Sam. 15:30-32). They even crucified Him on the right day—Passover— and He died at precisely the right hour of the day—the ninth hour—as the law specified (Ex. 12:6). So far, the priests did precisely what forms of the law commanded.

But the priests failed to apply the blood of that Sacrifice in the lawfully-prescribed manner. Insofar as Jesus was the Passover Lamb, they failed to apply His blood to their lintels (foreheads) and door posts (ears) of their "houses." Hence, God did not see the blood and "pass over" them (Ex. 12:13). They were not justified by faith in the blood of the Lamb.

Secondly, they did not sprinkle His blood upon the altars of their hearts, for they had no faith in His blood. For these people the sentence of the law applies, as written in Lev. 17:4, "*He has shed blood and <u>that man shall be cut off from among his people</u>.*" In other words, that man shall be pruned from the fig tree of Judah for he has forfeited his legal status as a member of the tribe. Lev. 17:6 says,

> [6] **And <u>the priest shall sprinkle the blood on the altar of the Lord</u> at the doorway of the tent of meeting, and offer up the fat in smoke as a soothing aroma to the Lord.**

Even as our bodies are the temples of God, so also our hearts are the altar of the Lord. And so Heb. 10:22 explains this, saying,

> [22] **Let us draw near with a sincere heart in full assurance of faith, having our hearts sprinkled clean from an evil conscience and our bodies washed with pure water.**

It was necessary in the plan of God that Jesus Christ be crucified and that He die as a Sacrifice for sin once for all. However, both the people and the priests were required to do something with the blood of every sacrifice. In Jesus' case, they were required to sprinkle His blood (figuratively) upon the altars of their hearts for their justification. This they did not do—except for those priests who accepted Him as the Messiah and came to see Him as the great Sacrifice for sin. Those who did accept Him remained on the Kingdom fig tree that bears good fruit unto God.

Who is a "Jew"?

The Church and Judah are the same entity. The Church is the "called-out" body of people, called out of the bad fig tree of Judaism to be grafted into the good fig tree of Jesus Christ. Although there are non-Judahites who have been grafted into this Judah Church, the Church itself is the legitimate tribe of Judah. The Apostle Paul makes this very clear in Rom. 2:28, 29,

> [28] **For he is not a Jew who is one outwardly** [Greek: *en phaneros*, "in manifestation, or what is apparent"]**; neither is circumcision that which is outward in the flesh.** [29] **But he is a Jew who is one inwardly** [Greek: *kruptos*, "hidden"]**; and circumcision is that which is of the heart, by the Spirit, not by the letter; and his praise is not from men, but from God.**

Here is Paul's definition of a Jew, and he defines it both negatively and positively. He tells us that there are two groups of people, each laying claim to being a Jew (Judean). The bad figs are "apparent" Jews (The Concordant Version), for they were recognized by men as Jews.

The good figs were the real Jews, though their identity was hidden, or not so well known to the general public. The apparent Jews were those who followed the Judaism of the day. The hidden Jews were those whose hearts were right with God. The apparent Jews laid claim to their tribal status and covenant status with God by means of physical circumcision. The hidden Jews laid claim to their tribal status and covenant status with God by means of the heart circumcision.

In other words, just because unbelieving Jews were able to retain the name of Judah (usually in its shortened form, "Jew"), this did not mean that they were really Jews at all. From the perspective of the Christians (including Paul) the unbelieving Jews had been cut off from their people and no longer had the right before God to call themselves Jews. Only those Judahites who accepted the Mediator of the New Covenant, the King of Judah, the Custodian of the tribal name, could lawfully claim to be Judahites (i.e., Judeans, or Jews).

The "tribeship" was resident in the prince of the tribe. If a member of a tribe decided to go to another part of the world and establish his own tribe or nation, he could not legally claim to be the legitimate representative of the tribe from which he came. Likewise, if a man of, say, the tribe of Judah were "cut off from among his people," or exiled for some major violation of the law, he could not claim to be the legitimate representative of the tribe of Judah.

Even so, Jesus was the King of Judah, not only by right of lineage, but also by right of His actions. And thus, the tribal name went with Jesus and those who followed Him. It did not remain with those who revolted against Him and killed Him in order to seize upon His inheritance. It was the majority of the people, led by the chief priests, who were in revolt and who lost their status in the tribe of Judah. But because they had usurped the throne, they were able to convince the world that they were still the "true Jews." And thus, the name "Jew" has continued to be applied—in the eyes of men—to the bad fig tree that rejected the King of Judah and usurped the throne and the name of Judah.

By the end of the first century, John the Revelator says in Rev. 2:9,

> 9 **I know your tribulation and your poverty (but you are rich), and the blasphemy by <u>those who say they are Jews and are not</u>, but are a synagogue of Satan.**

He repeats this idea in Rev. 3:9, saying,

> 9 **Behold, I will cause those of the synagogue of Satan, <u>who say that they are Jews, and are not</u>, but lie—behold, I will make them to come and bow down at your feet, and to know that I have loved you.**

It is strange that in the past few decades Messianic Judaism has promoted this idea that the true Jews (followers of Jesus, King of Judah) ought to be grafted to the dead fig tree that God cut off nearly 2,000 years ago for its lawlessness. The basic error of Messianic Judaism is that they want to replace the good figs with the bad figs. *This is their brand of replacement theology.* They call the bad figs "God's chosen people," and then attempt to identify with their religious practices as a ploy to induce some of them to accept Christ.

That is like drinking with drunkards in order to induce them to stop drinking.

The apostles would have rolled over in their graves. Never did they attempt to get Christians to return to the old brand of Judaism. In fact, the Apostle Paul wrote entire gospels refuting such an idea. There is no life in the religion of Judaism, for it has rejected—and continues to reject—the only One in whom is Life. One cannot force it to become Christianized by converting to Judaism. To try to bring Judaism back to life by swarming its ranks with Christians is a fallacy of the first order.

The book of Hebrews was written to show that, as Christians, we have something better than Judaism has to offer. We have a better covenant, a better priesthood, a better temple, and better sacrifices. To revert back to the old rabbinic traditions of Judaism, by which they made void the law of God, is an apostasy for which there is no excuse.

As we have already shown, the glory of God departed first from Shiloh, and later from Jerusalem. On the day of Pentecost in Acts 2, the glory of God came to rest upon a new temple in a New Jerusalem. Whether the Jewish Zionists succeed or not in their plan to build the third temple in Jerusalem, it makes no difference. The glory of God has already been there—and has departed. Ichabod has already been written on that place. He has already forsaken it "as Shiloh" (Jer. 7:14). Furthermore, the glory of God has moved to a better temple made up of living stones and built upon the foundation of the apostles and prophets (Eph. 2:20).

He does NOT intend to move again into buildings made of wood and stone, no matter how great its architecture might be.

The Early Church

The temple leaders in Jerusalem began to persecute the Christian believers very soon after they crucified Jesus. In Acts 4:1-3 we read of the beginnings of persecution, after Peter and John had healed the lame man at the very gate of the temple. We read,

> **[1] And as they were speaking to the people, the priests and the captain of the temple guard, and the Sadducees, came upon them, [2] being greatly disturbed because they were teaching the people and proclaiming in Jesus the resurrection from the dead. [3] And they laid hands on them and put them in jail until the next day, for it was already evening.**

The next day Peter gave testimony before the high priest that the man had been healed by the power of the risen Christ. His testimony is the foundation of a Christian's testimony before all Jews even today. We read in Acts 4:8-12,

> **[8] Then Peter, filled with the Holy Spirit, said to them, Rulers and elders of the people, [9] if we are on trial today for the benefit done to a sick man, as to how this man has been made well, [10] let it be known to all of you and to all the people of Israel, that by the name of Jesus Christ the Nazarene, whom you crucified, whom God raised from the dead—by this name this man stands here before you in good health. [11] He is the Stone which was rejected by you, the builders, but which became the very corner stone. [12] And there is salvation in no one else; for there is no other name under heaven that has been given among men, by which we must be saved.**

Few people questioned Peter's words until recently. Then, in the name of having better relations with Judaism, various Christian leaders first began to blame the Romans for the crucifixion, denying the Scriptures that the Sacrifice had to be made by the Levitical priests alone in order to be acceptable to God. Then more recently, various Christian leaders began to think that Jews are actually saved apart from faith in Jesus Christ. I myself first saw this view written in Billy Graham's "My Answer" column in the 1960's, although I doubt that this was written by Mr. Graham himself. It was too far out of character for him to have written it personally.

The article said that gentiles are saved by grace through faith in Christ, while Jews are saved by the law. But if that were the case, then no Jew could ever be saved, for there is none righteous, no not one (Rom. 3:10). Not a single Jew has ever been perfect before the law his entire life, unless, perhaps, he died very early in life. I myself would never make salvation for a Jew to be such a hopeless cause. At any rate, when we read the book of Acts, we find Jews everywhere being saved by faith in Jesus Christ. I would like to ask these other so-called Bible teachers to tell me the date that this requirement for salvation changed.

Just for the record, let me state that I believe what Peter said is still true: "*There is no other name under heaven that has been given among men, by which we must be saved.*"

The reaction of the Jewish leaders to Peter's statement set the pattern for Judaism that has been followed to this day. We find it in Acts 4:14-18,

> **[14] And seeing the man who had been healed standing with them, they had nothing to say in reply. [15] But when they had ordered them to go aside out of the Council, they began to confer with one another, [16] saying, What shall we do**

with these men? For the fact that a noteworthy miracle has taken place through them is apparent to all who live in Jerusalem, and we cannot deny it. [17] But in order that it may not spread any further among the people, let us warn them to speak no more to any man in this name. [18] And when they had summoned them, they commanded them not to speak or teach at all in the name of Jesus.

In other words, they were fully aware of the miracle of healing that had taken place in front of the temple. This was undeniable. But they did not want to believe that Jesus was the Messiah, and so they resorted to "damage control." These same leaders were also fully aware that Jesus Christ had been raised from the dead—but they did not want to follow Him anyway. They preferred a lie. Matt. 28:11-15 says,

[11] Now while they were on their way, behold, some of the guard came into the city and reported to the chief priests all that had happened. [12] And when they had assembled with the elders and counseled together, they gave a large sum of money to the soldiers, [13] and said, You are to say, His disciples came by night and stole Him away while we were asleep. [14] And if this should come to the governor's ears, we will win him over and keep you out of trouble. [15] And they took the money and did as they had been instructed, and this story was widely spread among the Jews and is to this day.

Thus, it is no surprise that the leaders of the people continued to reject Jesus Christ even though a lame man had been healed by His power at the very gate of the temple. Their reaction to this good deed was to command the disciples to stop teaching in the name of Jesus. They refused to stop, and many sick were healed (Acts 5:15, 16). The high priest, then, filled with jealousy, put the apostles into the jail (Acts 5:18). But the angel released them, and the apostles continued preaching boldly.

It really began to alarm them when they found that they could not even keep the apostles in prison, because the angels would release them. I mean, who was God to go against their legal decisions? So they arrested the apostles again. But Peter told them in no uncertain terms the problem and the solution to that problem. Acts 5:30-32 says,

[30] The God of our fathers raised up Jesus, whom YOU had put to death by hanging Him on a cross. [31] He is the one whom God exalted to His right hand as a Prince and a Savior, to grant repentance to Israel, and forgiveness of sins. [32] And we are witnesses of these things; and so is the Holy Spirit, whom God has given to those who obey Him.

This made them really angry, and they would have attempted to kill the apostles, except that Gamaliel counseled against it. Even so, Acts 5:40 says,

[40] And they took his advice; and after calling the apostles in, they flogged them and ordered them to speak no more in the name of Jesus, and then released them.

In Acts 6 and 7 the conflict intensified with the stoning of Stephen. This marked the day of the formal outbreak of persecution against the Christian company of good figs. We read in Acts 8:1-5,

> [1] **And Saul was in hearty agreement with putting him** [Stephen] **to death. And on that day a great persecution arose against the church in Jerusalem; and they were all scattered throughout the regions of Judea and Samaria, except the apostles. . .** [4] **Therefore, those who had been scattered went about preaching the word.** [5] **And Philip went down to the city of Samaria and began proclaiming Christ to them.**

Soon most were driven from the land of Judea into other parts of the Roman Empire. In this manner they fulfilled Jeremiah's description of the basket of good figs, who were the people who submitted to God and who went into captivity—originally to Babylon, but now into the Roman Empire.

This is the history of the early Church. It was a Church of good figs, not of bad figs. The bad figs were jealous of the good figs and refused to believe that Jesus was the Messiah, even though great signs and miracles were done among them. Yet in the eyes of God, these believers carried the dominion mandate of Judah. They were the true Jews, for they carried the tribal name of Judah and its calling.

The good figs did not consider anyone—Jew or otherwise—to be in a saving covenant with God apart from Jesus Christ. They boldly preached repentance, telling the people that they had to repent of the rejection and crucifixion of the Messiah in order to be saved. That message has not changed, even if modern theologians say it has. The Bible is still the Word of God, even if the traditions of men contradict it.

Furthermore, let it be clearly understood that the conflict did not begin with Jesus persecuting the bad figs. It began with the bad figs persecuting and crucifying Jesus. After the day of Pentecost, the conflict did not begin with the Christians persecuting the Jews. It began with the chief priests of the temple persecuting the Christians. It was only later, as Christians lost the glow of Pentecost, that carnally-minded Christians began to fight back and to persecute the Jews. They were wrong in doing this. Christians ought to have a higher standard than that. While we might expect the Jewish leaders to be "*cut to the quick*" (Acts 5:33) by the call to repentance, and we might expect them to react with anger, we ought not to see this same carnality manifested in those who claim to follow Jesus' example. Christians, too, have much repentance to do.

CHAPTER 8
The New Jerusalem

It was necessary for Jesus to leave the earth and ascend to heaven in order to establish the final removal of God's glory from earthly temples and cities. Once this had been completed, then the glory of God returned and rested upon the disciples in the upper room ten days later on the day of Pentecost.

From this point on, as the Apostle Paul explains, we as individuals are the temples of God (1 Cor. 3:16). Speaking corporately, the Church is also a temple, having Jesus Christ as its chief cornerstone and the apostles and prophets as the foundation stones (Eph. 2:20-22). Others are living stones in this temple (1 Peter 2:5). Most importantly, perhaps, is the fact that God's name now rests upon us as *people*, not upon an external ark of the covenant in a temple made of wood and stone in a carnal city in Palestine.

One cannot understand the fulfillment of prophecy without seeing that there are two Jerusalems: the old Jerusalem and the New Jerusalem. This distinction makes it possible to understand the *seeming contradiction* between biblical statements of blessings and curses upon Jerusalem.

Isaiah Prophesies of the New Jerusalem "Bride"

In Isaiah we read a prime example of "Jerusalem," which John says is to be interpreted as the New Jerusalem. Is. 62:1, 2 says,

> **1 For Zion's sake I will not keep silent, and for Jerusalem's sake I will not keep quiet, until her righteousness goes forth like brightness, and her salvation like a torch that is burning. 2 And the nations will see <u>your righteousness</u>, and all kings <u>your glory</u>; and <u>you will be called by a new name</u>, which the mouth of the LORD will designate.**

At first glance one may think that Isaiah was speaking of the original city of Jerusalem. But John applies the prophecy, not to the old Jerusalem, but to the New Jerusalem. Rev. 3:12 makes reference to Is. 62:1 above, saying this new name is <u>New Jerusalem</u>:

> **12 He who overcomes, I will make him a pillar in the temple of My God, and he will not go out from it anymore; and I will write upon him the name of My God, and <u>the name of the city of My God, the new Jerusalem</u>, which comes down out of heaven from My God, and My new name.**

It is plain from John's prophecy that Isaiah was speaking of the New Jerusalem, not the old city. This temple in the New Jerusalem is the place where God has placed His name. It is a place of blessing, not an accursed place. Is. 62:4 and 5 prophesy Jerusalem to be a "diadem of glory" in God's hand. She would no longer be called "Forsaken" or "Desolate," but instead, "Married."

> [4] **It will no longer be said to you, Forsaken, nor to your land will it any longer be said, Desolate; but you will be called, My delight is in her, and your land, Married; for the LORD delights in you, and *to Him* your land will be married.** [5] **For *as* a young man marries a virgin, *so* your sons will marry you; and *as* the bridegroom rejoices over the bride, *so* your God will rejoice over you.**

John refers to this prophecy in Rev. 21:2, where we read that the holy city which God marries is not the old Jerusalem. The Bride is the New Jerusalem—even though Isaiah merely calls it "Jerusalem."

> [2] **And I saw the holy city, New Jerusalem, coming down out of heaven from God, made ready as a bride adorned for her husband.**

In Rev. 21:9, 10 an angel again identifies the Bride as the Jerusalem that descends from heaven, as opposed to the Jerusalem that originated in the earth:

> [9] **And one of the seven angels who had the seven bowls full of the seven last plagues, came and spoke with me, saying, Come here, I shall show you the bride, the wife of the Lamb.** [10] **And he carried me away in the Spirit to a great and high mountain, and showed me the holy city, Jerusalem, coming down out of heaven from God.**

As we can see, just because Isaiah says nothing about a NEW Jerusalem, John tells us that this is what God meant. In other words, John tells us *which* Jerusalem God meant when He gave the prophecy to Isaiah.

The Walls of the New Jerusalem

John describes the "walls" and "gates" of this city in physical terms, but it is quite obvious that these are symbolic things. The wall is said to be 144 cubits high (21:17) which is the biblical number denoting the elect. The numeric value of the letters in the name Lazarus is precisely 144. This connects the number to those elect who are raised from the dead and saved from death. (See John 11.)

Walls of a city are for its protection and act as a boundary to keep out those who are not authorized to enter the city. In that the walls are called "Salvation," it indicates that only the saved may enter this city. Zech. 2:5 (quoted below) describes the walls as "*a wall of fire*." Why is it described as a fire? Deut. 33:2 tells us that He gave Israel a "fiery law" at Sinai. The law is the "fire" of God that judges all men. A law is a moral boundary. Sin is transgression of the law (1 John 3:4). And so the wall of fire in Zechariah's prophecy is the boundary of the law.

We read that all those who enter this city are righteous. One cannot be lawless and enter this city. Nor do the saved transgress the law when they enter.

This city is more than a single location upon the earth. Zech. 2:1-5 prophesies,

> [1] **Then I lifted up my eyes and looked, and behold, *there was* a man with a measuring line in his hand.** [2] **So I said, Where are you going? And he said to me, To measure Jerusalem, to see how wide it is and how long it is.** [3] **And behold, the angel who was speaking with me was going out, and another angel was coming out to meet him,** [4] **and said to him, Run, speak to that young man, saying, Jerusalem will be inhabited without walls, because of the multitude of**

men and cattle within it. [5] For I, declares the LORD, will be a wall of fire around her, and I will be the glory in her midst.

On the one hand, Zechariah prophesies the city will be "*without walls,*" and then in the next verse he says there will be a "*wall of fire around her.*" Yes, there is a "wall" around this Jerusalem, but it is not a physical wall around a group of buildings called a "city." It is a wall of Salvation and a wall of Fire (Law). No one passes through this wall by physically walking through one of its gates. One may qualify only by "Salvation."

The Gates of the New Jerusalem

It also is said to have twelve gates with the names of the twelve tribes of Israel written on them. These are also said to be twelve pearls (Rev. 21:21). These descriptions of the gates are obviously not literal. The prophet gives us the basic definition of the gates when he says in Is. 60:18,

[18] Violence will not be heard again in your land, nor devastation or destruction within your borders; but you will call your walls salvation, and your gates praise.

John says in Rev. 21:12 that the twelve tribes of Israel are written on the twelve gates of the city. Later in verse 21 the twelve gates are called "pearls," because the twelve tribes taken collectively are the "pearl of great price." Jesus came to purchase this pearl by His death on the cross, but in doing this, He ended up purchasing the whole world. Jesus spoke of these things in two short parables in Matt. 13:44-46, where He said,

[44] The kingdom of heaven is like a TREASURE hidden in the field, which a man found and hid; and from joy over it he goes and sells all that he has, and buys that field. [45] Again, the kingdom of heaven is like a merchant seeking fine PEARLS, [46] and upon finding one pearl of great value, he went and sold all that he had, and bought it.

Jesus took the themes of His parables from the Scriptures themselves, so they are not difficult to interpret. God called Israel His peculiar treasure in Ex. 19:5. Israel was dispersed into Assyria and into the world. Jesus said in Matt. 13:38, "*the field is the world.*" Hence, Jesus came and found the lost tribes of Israel hidden in the world in their dispersion. So He purchased the entire field (the world) in order to obtain the treasure. Thus, the whole world has benefited from the fall of Israel.

The second parable is like the first, but this time Jesus compares Israel to a "pearl of great value." Comparing the two parables above shows us that both the treasure and the pearl is Israel. And John confirms this by telling us that the twelve gates of New Jerusalem are the twelve tribes of Israel—and they are called "*twelve pearls.*" The only difference is that Jesus lumped them all together into a single "pearl of great value," while John speaks of each tribe as being a pearl.

Is. 60:18, quoted earlier, tells us that the gates are "praise." This is a play on words, because Judah means "praise." Judah was to be the leading tribe of Israel. And so in this case Judah represents all the tribes, for in that day the King of Judah—Jesus Christ—will rule over all the tribes in one nation, as well as over the entire earth.

Is. 60:19, 20 tells us that Jerusalem will have no need for the sun or moon to give it light, because God Himself will be its light:

> **[19] No longer will you have the sun for light by day, nor for brightness will the moon give you light; but you will have the LORD for an everlasting light, and your God for your glory. [20] Your sun will set no more, neither will your moon wane; for you will have the LORD for an everlasting light, and the days of your mourning will be finished.**

In Rev. 21:23 John prophesies the same for the New Jerusalem,

> **[23] the city has no need of the sun or the moon to shine upon it, for the glory of God has illumined it, and its lamp is the Lamb.**

Again, Isaiah 60:21 says of Jerusalem,

> **[21] Then all your people *will be* righteous; they will possess the land forever, the branch of My planting, the work of My hands, that I may be glorified.**

John echoes in Rev. 21:27 that only the righteous will inhabit the New Jerusalem:

> **[27] And nothing unclean and no one who practices abomination and lying shall ever come into it, but only those whose names are written in the Lamb's book of life.**

A simple comparison of Is. 60:18-21 with Rev. 21 makes it clear that this is not the old Jerusalem restored and made glorious. Both speak of the light of the sun and moon as being replaced by light from a divine source. Both speak of sinners being excluded from the city.

This is the New Jerusalem whose origin is in heaven, not on the earth. It must also be noted that at no time does the Bible state that the New Jerusalem will come down and overlay itself upon the piece of real estate that presently is called Jerusalem. I am often amused by the way men depict the New Jerusalem as a physical city coming down from outer space with a system of cranes and pulleys as if it were a physical city weighing billions of tons.

Christians need to learn that the New Jerusalem is a spiritual, heavenly "city" that will cover the whole earth in the restoration of all things. The purpose of the physical creation was to manifest the glory of God, and this purpose will at last be fulfilled. Though Adam lost this glory when he sinned, the Last Adam will restore this glory to the earth. Jesus prayed the Father's will be done in earth as it is in heaven. That prayer will be answered when the New Jerusalem has fully come down from heaven, for the New Jerusalem is the will of God for creation. But at the present time all of creation is yet groaning as they await the manifestation of the sons of God (Rom. 8:19), for we do not yet see all things put in subjection to Christ (Heb. 2:8).

Zion and Jerusalem Prophecies

We have shown thus far that the favorable prophecies of "Jerusalem" in Isaiah 60 are essentially the same as those of the "New Jerusalem" found in Revelation 21. It is plain from this comparison that the New Testament interprets the "Jerusalem" of Isaiah 60 to mean the New Jerusalem, rather than the old Jerusalem. Jews, of course, who do not agree with the New Testament, will dispute John's revelation. But as Christians, we believe that John's revelation is divinely inspired, so we conclude that God is building a new city unlike the old.

Besides "Jerusalem," the Bible often uses another term, "Zion" and the prophetic end-time "daughter of Zion" (Isaiah 62:11). Zion in the Old Testament was the place from which David ruled Jerusalem and the rest of Israel. It became a symbol of rulership. Because the Bible speaks of Zion as well as Jerusalem in the prophets, many have assumed that the Zion of Bible prophecy is the physical location within the old city of Jerusalem. Hence, we have "Zionists" today who are those who have placed their faith in the old Jerusalem, thinking this is the fulfillment of the promises to Abraham. But Hebrews 12:22-24 says,

> [22] **But you have come to Mount Zion and to the city of the living God, the heavenly Jerusalem, and to myriads of angels, [23] to the general assembly and church of the first-born who are enrolled in heaven, and to God, the Judge of all, and to the spirits of righteous men made perfect, [24] and to Jesus, the mediator of a new covenant.**

The book of Hebrews makes it clear that our hope is in a greater High Priest (Jesus Christ), who ministers in a greater temple (our hearts) in a heavenly Jerusalem and its greater "Mount Zion" by means of a better covenant. In other words, there is a new Mount Zion just as there is a New Jerusalem. The New Zion has all the characteristics of the New Jerusalem, but it symbolizes the place of Jesus' rule, for He is the Son of David.

The book of Hebrews was written after the destruction of Jerusalem in 70 A.D. in order to explain why God would allow the old city and its temple to be destroyed. Many early Christians (especially those of Judean descent) were devastated at that event, because they still did not understand that God had cast out that "bondwoman" with her son (the Levitical priesthood and Judaism itself).

Prophecies of the "Rebuilt" Temple

Ezekiel 40-48 speaks of a "rebuilt" temple. It is common for prophecy teachers to take these chapters in a literal sense, even to the point where they believe God will revert back to animal sacrifices. This is based upon Ezekiel 43:18-27 and other passages. Of course, we must admit that if God intended to build a physical temple in the old Jerusalem and re-consecrate the Levitical priesthood, then we would have to believe that Judaism is to become the true religion once again, and animal sacrifices must be made to God in the days ahead.

But let it be known that I myself do not believe this. As a Christian, I have come to know better things. As I see it, such adherence or reversion to Judaism is precisely the bondage of which the Apostle Paul warned in the book of Galatians. How many times does Paul have to tell us that we are the temple of God before we actually believe this?

Ezekiel's temple, no doubt, would have been built as a literal building with wood and stone—if Israel and Judah had repented and had returned to the old land long ago. But they did not. A portion of the House of Judah returned, but Israel did not return. And so Jesus came to establish a new and better temple, the temple of our bodies. This was, of course, what God had in mind from the beginning. For this reason, the prophecy of Ezekiel's temple must be interpreted according to the New Testament model. The temple made of wood and stone is replaced by a new temple made of living stones. The Levitical priesthood is replaced by a Melchizedek priesthood. The sacrificial system is replaced by the one true Sacrifice for sin—Jesus Christ—who is the fulfillment of all the sacrifices.

Jesus is the *only* Foundation Stone, or Cornerstone, that could be laid in this New Temple, according to 1 Cor. 3:11,

> [11] **For no man can lay a foundation other than the one which is laid, which is Jesus Christ.**

If any man attempts to build a carnal temple at Jerusalem, it is a direct violation of the will of God, for there is no way that they can build a physical temple and still lay Jesus Christ as its Foundation.

In that He died and was laid in the earth, His burial laid the foundation stone of the New Temple. He later indwelt the individual believers on the day of Pentecost in order to begin building this Temple with living stones. Paul told the Ephesians in Eph. 2:19-22,

> [19] **So then you are no longer strangers and aliens, but you are fellow citizens with the saints, and are of God's household,** [20] **having been built upon the foundation of the apostles and prophets, Christ Jesus Himself being the corner** ***stone,*** [21] **in whom the whole building, being fitted together is growing into a holy temple in the Lord;** [22] **in whom you also are being built together into a dwelling of God in the Spirit.**

Two Jerusalems with Different Destinies

Jeremiah was the primary prophet of the old city of Jerusalem. He was there when the Babylonian army came and destroyed the city and the temple. He was the prophet that the priests of the old temple persecuted. Thus, Jeremiah is the most important prophet whose writings reveal the ultimate fate of that city.

In Jer. 18:1-6 God told the prophet to go to the potter's house, where he was to observe the potter making a clay vessel. Verses 3-6 tell us,

> [3] **Then I went down to the potter's house, and there he was, making something on the wheel.** [4] **But the vessel that he was making of clay was spoiled in the hand of the potter; so he remade it into another vessel, as it pleased the potter to make.** [5] **Then the word of the Lord came to me saying,** [6] **Can I not, O house of Israel, deal with you as this potter does? declares the Lord. Behold, like the clay in the potter's hand, so are you in My hand, O house of Israel.**

This prophecy was directed at the House of Israel—not at the House of Judah. It was directed at the ten lost tribes, the nation that God had destroyed from 745-721 B.C. in the days of Hoshea, their last king (2 Kings 17:3). During his days, the Assyrian king Shalmanezer came and put Israel into bondage. Shortly after that, the Assyrian army came and conquered Israel and its capital, Samaria, deporting the survivors to "*Halah and Habor, on the river of Gozan, and in the cities of the Medes*" (2 Kings 17:6). A century later, this is where the prophet Ezekiel prophesied to them. Ez. 1:1 says,

> [1] **Now it came about in the thirtieth year, on the fifth day of the fourth month, while I was by the river Chebar** [or, "Habor"], **among the exiles, the heavens were opened and I saw visions of God.**

It is important to understand then, that Jeremiah's revelation at the potter's house was NOT about Judah, but about Israel. Since many are unaware that Israel and Judah were two different nations, we find it necessary to clarify this. God promised that He would rebuild the House of Israel, even as the potter made a new vessel of clay.

But Jeremiah only spends ten verses on the House of Israel, because he was not sent to them, but to Judah. The rest of Jeremiah 18 and all of chapter 19 focus exclusively upon Judah and Jerusalem. The only reason Jeremiah even spent ten verses on Israel was to show the contrast between the destinies of the two nations. Beginning in Jer. 18:11 and 12, the prophet turns to Judah and Jerusalem:

> **[11] So now then, <u>speak to the men of Judah and against the inhabitants of Jerusalem</u>, saying, Thus says the Lord, Behold, I am fashioning calamity against you and devising a plan against you. Oh turn back, each of you from his evil way, and reform your ways and your deeds. [12] But they will say, It's hopeless! For we are going to follow our own plans, and each of us will act according to the stubbornness of his evil heart.**

The rest of this chapter outlines the rebellion of Judah and Jerusalem against God and gives the reasons for the judgment to come. Finally, in Jer. 19:1-3 we read,

> **[1] Thus says the Lord, Go and buy a potter's earthenware jar, and take some of the elders of the people and some of the priests. [2] Then go out to the valley of Ben-hinnom, which is by the entrance of the potsherd gate; and proclaim there the words that I shall tell you, [3] and say, <u>Hear the word of the Lord, O kings of Judah and inhabitants of Jerusalem</u>: thus says the Lord of hosts, the God of Israel, Behold I am about to bring a calamity upon this place, at which the ears of everyone that hears of it will tingle.**

The prophet then gives God's indictment upon Judah and Jerusalem in verses 4 and 5 for their rebellion against Him. For these reasons, God says, the nation and the city will be destroyed and the people brought to slaughter. When the prophet finished with his indictment upon them, God told him to give the people an object lesson in verses 10-12,

> **[10] Then you are to break the jar in the sight of the men who accompany you [11] and say to them, Thus says the Lord of hosts, Just so shall I break this people and this city, even as one breaks a potter's vessel, which cannot again be repaired; and they will bury in Topheth, because there is no other place for burial. [12] This is how I shall treat this place and its inhabitants, declares the Lord, so as to make this city like Topheth.**

One may continue reading to the end of the chapter, but there is not a single word of comfort for Jerusalem. Not once does he say that in the end of days the city would be restored. In fact, Jeremiah says precisely the opposite. Unlike the wet clay jar that represented the House of Israel—which was beaten down, but then made into a new vessel—<u>this old earthenware jar was smashed</u>. *Once broken, old jars could not be repaired.* Men simply brought them out of the city through the "potsherd gate" (19:2) and cast them into the *gehenna*, the city dump.

Jeremiah makes it clear that the day would come when the old city of Jerusalem would be destroyed like this old earthenware jar in the hands of the prophet. Many cannot believe God would actually do this, and so they interpret this, saying that this destruction was fulfilled when Babylon destroyed Jerusalem. The problem is that seventy years later, the people returned and REBUILT Jerusalem. First King Cyrus allowed the people to return and rebuild their homes in 534 B.C. Then in 458 B.C. King Artaxerxes issued a second decree allowing the city itself to be rebuilt. This fulfilled the prophecy of Dan. 9:24, 25, saying,

> [24] **Seventy weeks have been decreed for your people and your holy city, to finish the transgression, to make an end of sin, to make atonement for iniquity, to bring in everlasting righteousness, to seal up vision and prophecy, and to anoint the most holy place.** [25] **So you are to know and discern that from the issuing of a decree to restore and rebuild Jerusalem until Messiah the Prince there will be seven weeks and sixty-two weeks; it will be built again, with plaza and moat, even in times of distress.**

God told Jeremiah that the city would be destroyed like a jar that could never again be repaired. But then Daniel was told about "*a decree to restore and rebuild Jerusalem.*" In fact, it really was rebuilt. This seems to be an inherent contradiction. Many years later in 70 A.D. the Romans again destroyed the city, but it was rebuilt by later generations. In fact the city has been destroyed and rebuilt about nine times.

This tells us that Jeremiah's prophecy has been only PARTIALLY fulfilled in the past destructions of Jerusalem. The day is coming when Jerusalem will be destroyed in such a way that it will NEVER AGAIN BE REBUILT. The Word of God cannot be broken, but Jerusalem will be broken as the jar in the hand of Jeremiah was broken and never repaired.

This is, in fact, why God has established a New Jerusalem. The old city is under the curse of God and will not be the seat of Christ's government.

When we view this prophecy of Jerusalem's destruction in the light of Jeremiah's statement about the glory departing from that place—as Shiloh—the plan of God begins to clarify. Shiloh was destroyed after the glory had departed. Its priests had been killed as well, because God intended to replace the corrupt lineage of Eli with a new line of priests descended from Zadok. This prophesies of a bigger picture, for Zadok is a type and shadow of the Melchi-Zadok, or Melchizedek Order. It is clear, then, that God intended in the bigger picture to replace the Levitical Order with the Melchizedek Order, with Jesus Christ as its High Priest.

Hagar is Replaced by Sarah

In Galatians 4:22-31 Paul speaks of the old and new covenants and how they are allegorically pictured as Hagar and Sarah. Hagar was the bondwoman from Egypt, while Sarah was the freewoman and the one through whom the promises were to come. Hagar, however, was the first to give birth to a son of Abraham. His name was Ishmael. When Ishmael was 13 years old, God finally told Abraham that he would have a son through Sarah. That son was Isaac, born when Abraham was 100 years old.

There was conflict, of course, between Abraham's two wives over whose son would inherit the birthright. Ishmael was the firstborn from Hagar, but God chose Isaac, who was born of Sarah. Likewise, the old covenant came first under Moses, but God chose the New Covenant under Jesus Christ to bring forth the promise. Then Paul makes a very remarkable statement in 4:25 and 26,

> [25] **Now this Hagar is Mount Sinai in Arabia, and corresponds to the present Jerusalem, for she is in slavery with her children.** [26] **But the Jerusalem above is free; she is our mother.**

Prophecy teachers today are accustomed to explaining how Hagar and Ishmael are the Arabs, and that therefore they have no right to the city of Jerusalem. Paul says that the old

Jerusalem is Hagar, and her children are Ishmael. Paul is really talking about the Jews who adhere to Judaism. Verses 28-31 says,

> [28] **And you brethren, like Isaac, are children of promise.** [29] **But as at that time he who was born according to the flesh persecuted him *who was born* according to the Spirit, so it is now also.** [30] **But what does the Scripture say? Cast out the bondwoman and her son, For the son of the bondwoman shall not be an heir with the son of the free woman.** [31] **So then, brethren, we are not children of a bondwoman, but of the free woman.**

The old Jerusalem is born after the flesh, not after the Spirit. The leaders of Jerusalem rejected the New Covenant that Jesus had offered them, choosing instead to remain under the old covenant, which had been given at Mount Sinai *in Arabia*. Arabia was the inheritance of Hagar and Ishmael. So when the Jewish leaders made their crucial choice to adhere to the old covenant and reject the Mediator of the New Covenant, they placed themselves and their city under the legal jurisdiction of Mount Sinai *in Arabia*, rather than under the legal jurisdiction of the Jerusalem from above.

For this reason, God sent His armies (the Romans) to destroyed the city and expel the Jews, ultimately banishing them from the land of Palestine. We read of this in the parable Jesus told in Matt. 22:2-7,

> [2] **The kingdom of heaven may be compared to a king** [the Father], **who gave a wedding feast for his son** [Jesus]. [3] **And he sent out his slaves** [the prophets] **to call those who had been invited to the wedding feast, and they were unwilling to come.** [4] **Again he sent out other slaves, saying, Tell those who have been invited, Behold, I have prepared my dinner; my oxen and my fattened livestock are all butchered and everything is ready; come to the wedding feast.** [5] **But they paid no attention and went their way, one to his own farm, another to his business,** [6] **and the rest seized his slaves** [the prophets] **and mistreated them and killed them.** [7] **But the king was enraged and sent his armies** [the Roman armies], **and destroyed those murderers, and set their city** [Jerusalem] **on fire.**

Yet Paul recognized even in his day that the Church itself had a tendency to want to remain under the old covenant and the jurisdiction of "Hagar." For decades the early Christians in Jerusalem continued to offer sacrifices in the temple in Jerusalem, even though they knew that Jesus was the only true Sacrifice for sin. It was not until God hired the Roman army to destroy that city and that temple that the early Church finally began to get the picture. Somewhere around that time, God inspired someone to write the book of Hebrews in order to make it clear to the Hebrew Christians that Christianity was not simply a sect of Judaism.

The Stone that the Jewish builders rejected had become the Head of the Corner of the new way called Christianity.

Unfortunately, in our day much of the Church has once again reverted back to Judaistic thinking. They think that Hagar-Jerusalem is somehow going to bring in the promised Kingdom. It will not. The old Jerusalem is the bondwoman, not the free. The old Jerusalem persecutes the children of the New Jerusalem--not the other way around, as it is so often claimed. Paul, who had Himself persecuted the Church before his conversion, was well aware that the children of Hagar-Jerusalem persecuted the children of Sarah-New Jerusalem.

[29] **But as at that time he who was born according to the flesh persecuted him *who was born* according to the Spirit, so it is now also.**

One only needs to read the historical record of the book of Acts to see how Judaism persecuted the Church. The solution is NOT to re-unite with the Jews of Judaism, as many today have advocated. To do so is to intermarry with Ishmael, spiritually speaking, and thus disqualify one's self from receiving the full inheritance of Tabernacles. When Christians try to identify with Judaism or convert to Judaism, they are actually becoming the spiritual children of Hagar. Let them not think that they will bring forth the promise, for this can be done only through Sarah, the Jerusalem which is from above.

The solution, Paul says, is to "*cast out the bondwoman and her son*" (Gal. 4:30), even as Abraham cast out Hagar and Ishmael in order to establish Sarah and Isaac. This is done by making a clean break with Judaism, even as the early Church finally did with a little help from God and the Roman armies. Let us no longer think that the glory of God will return to the old Jerusalem, or that a carnal temple there will house the glory of God some day. As Paul says in 2 Thess. 2:3-12, that place can only house an antichrist, a man of sin (lawlessness), a son of perdition, a Judas.

Is this, perhaps, a part of the apostasy that Paul envisioned in 2 Thess. 2:3? Has this man of sin already appeared in the Church? Has the Church already forsaken the heavenly Jerusalem in favor of the old? Is the "deluding influence" in 2 Thess. 2:11 the idea that Hagar and her son will inherit the promise and be the one who brings the Kingdom of God to manifestation?

Selah.

Chapter 9
The Jewish Spirit of Revolt

In our second chapter we showed that Esau's descendants (the nation of Edom, or Idumea) were forcibly converted to Judaism in 126 B.C. when John Hyrcanus conquered them and gave them a choice of conversion or expulsion. From that point on in history, Esau's descendants ceased to be a nation. Better yet, Esau's destiny became intertwined with Judah's, for they became one nation.

Thus, the end-time Bible prophecies regarding Esau-Edom in the book of Obadiah, Isaiah 34 and 63, Ezekiel 35 and 36, and Malachi 1:1-4 are all fulfilled simultaneously with the prophecies regarding the remnant of Judah and Jerusalem. Without understanding this Judah-Edomite merger in past history, one cannot possibly understand modern Zionism and its conflict with Ishmael and Islam.

Why Did Judah Reject Jesus as King?

The Jews were looking for a conquering Messiah on the order of Joshua, who had been instructed to conquer the land of Canaan and put its inhabitants to the sword. They wanted a Messiah who would overthrow the Romans by military force, accompanied by miracles. However, Jesus came as the Prince of Peace, rather than as the conquering warrior. Hence, they rejected Him as Messiah.

The people did not realize that *Joshua himself would not have been a military conqueror either*, if the people had been obedient to God. God was not bloodthirsty. He did not hate the Canaanites any more than Jesus hated Samaritans. The only reason God gave Israel a physical sword to establish that first "Kingdom of God" was because the people had rejected the Sword of the Spirit at Mount Sinai.

They had rejected the voice of God at Mount Sinai, when God spoke to the people verbally, and all of them heard His voice (Deut. 4:12). But they were afraid and hardened their hearts from hearing the voice of God (Ps. 95:8-11; Heb. 3:7-11). They all ran away and told Moses to go up the mount by himself and then return and tell them what God said (Ex. 20:19).

This great event, where everyone had the opportunity to hear the voice of God, was later celebrated as the "*feast of weeks of the first-fruits of wheat harvest*" (Ex. 34:22). Many years later, this was called in the Greek language, "Pentecost."

The point is that the Israelites in Joshua's day rejected Pentecost, and therefore, they refused the Sword of the Spirit by which they could have converted Canaan and the rest of the world. That sword was largely withheld from men until Acts 2, when Pentecost was finally fulfilled.

At the base of Mount Sinai, the people worshipped the golden calf, and as a result, the Levites used their physical swords to kill 3,000 men (Ex. 32:28). What *would have happened*, if those Levites had had the Sword of the Spirit at their disposal?? Look at Acts 2. The 120 disciples in the upper room were willing to hear the voice of God. God gave them the Sword of the Spirit, which is the Word from the mouth that is like a sharp sword (Rev. 19:15). This is the Sword Paul mentioned in Eph. 6:17, saying,

> **17 And take the helmet of salvation and the sword of the Spirit which is the Word of God.**

The disciples took their spiritual swords down from the upper room and used it on 3,000 men in the streets below them. Acts 2:41 tells us the result:

> **41 So then, those who had received his word were baptized; and there were added that day about three thousand souls.**

This is what *would have happened* at the base of Mount Sinai, if the Levites had had better weapons. But their rejection of the voice of Jesus Christ speaking to them from the fire on Sinai deprived them of this better and more effective weapon. This is Jesus' weapon as well, as we read in Rev. 19:15,

> **15 And from His mouth comes a sharp sword, so that with it He may smite the nations; and He will rule them with a rod of iron; and He treads the wine press of the fierce wrath of God, the Almighty.**

All of this shows us why Jesus did not come as a conquering warrior, but as a Prince of Peace. It explains why Jesus (Yashua, or Joshua) did not seem to fit the pattern of the Old Testament Joshua. The reason Joshua was given a physical sword was NOT because God loves bloodshed. It was NOT because God hated Canaanites. It was NOT even because the Canaanite religion was so wicked. It was Israel's fault for refusing to hear the voice of God. Thus, they were left with a very dull weapon that could never divide soul from spirit or discern the thoughts and intents of the heart (Heb. 4:12).

The Jews of Jesus' day could not understand this. So they were looking for another Joshua with a bloody sword with which to kill all their "enemies" and oppressors. They had heard it taught that one should love their neighbors and hate their enemies (Matt. 5:43). The gospel of hating Romans and Samaritans was accepted doctrine.

But those who DID accept Jesus were given the Sword of the Word, and they went forth to conquer the world by faith and truth. Unfortunately, since Pentecost is a leavened feast, they were only partially successful. It remains for the overcomers to finish the job. The overcomers must therefore learn to use the Sword of the Spirit effectively, for this Sword brings people to LIFE.

What if Jesus Had Been Accepted as Messiah?

There is historical evidence that if Judah had accepted Jesus as Messiah, Rome soon would have given them their independence with no bloodshed at all. About the year 200 A.D. the Roman Christian lawyer, Tertullian, presented Christ to the "rulers of the Roman Empire" in a letter called Apology. In chapter 21, he writes,

> "All these things Pilate did to Christ; and now in fact a Christian in his own convictions, he sent word of Him to the reigning Caesar, who was at the time Tiberius. Yes, and the Caesars too would have believed on Christ, if either the Caesars had not been necessary for the world, or if Christians could have been Caesars."

In other words, Tertullian tells us that Pontius Pilate was already a Christian by the time he informed Tiberius Caesar of Jesus' crucifixion and resurrection. (We have reproduced Pilate's entire letter in the appendix of our book, The Laws of the Second Coming.) In chapter five, Tertullian continues,

> "Tiberius accordingly, in whose days the Christian name made its entry into the world, having himself received intelligence from Palestine of events which had clearly shown the truth of Christ's divinity, brought the matter before the Senate, with his own decision in favor of Christ. The Senate, because it had not given the approval itself, rejected the proposal. Caesar held to his opinion, threatening wrath against all accusers of the Christians."

We see here that when Tiberius Caesar read Pilate's letter telling him about Jesus, he became convinced that Jesus was a god. It was common practice in those days for the Roman Empire to recognize various gods and their religious adherents. So Tiberius proposed that the Senate proclaim Jesus to be one of the gods of the Empire. However, Roman law said that only the Senate had the right to present a new god for consideration. Since Tiberius himself had made this proposal, the Senate rejected it.

We know, of course, that this Roman rejection was part of the plan of God. But if Judah had accepted Jesus as the Messiah and King, it is certain that Pilate would have interviewed Jesus under very different circumstances. Pilate still would have become a Christian. He would have written to Tiberius Caesar, as it was his duty to keep the emperor informed of such events.

The emperor no doubt would have wanted to interview Jesus in person, at the recommendation of Pilate. Jesus would have made the trip to Rome, addressed the Senate, and I believe they would have been very impressed with His wisdom, love, humility, and miraculous signs. They would have realized very quickly that Jesus was not merely "one of the gods" that ought to be recognized officially.

I believe that soon Rome would have been proclaimed as a Christian nation, and that the pagan people would have forsaken their false gods. I believe that Judah would have been set free, along with all other nations. Or rather, all the nations that Rome ruled would have been given to Jesus Christ, the King of Kings.

We know, of course, that none of this was actually in the plan of God. God had foreordained a Pentecostal Age that would fail to manifest the Kingdom in its fullness. It was also necessary that Jesus be betrayed and killed as the Sacrifice for sin. Yet by looking at what might have been, we can see how Jesus' peaceful method of conquering the world is applicable today.

This is how the overcomers will overcome the world in our day under the anointing of the Feast of Tabernacles. The manifested sons of God (Rom. 8:19) will reflect the will and character of Jesus Christ to the world. This will spark a world-wide "revival," and it will not take long to bring the entire world under the feet of Jesus Christ. But it will be done by love, not by bloodshed, for we have a better sword. There will be bloodshed, of course, during this time, but it will be done by those who do not possess such a sword as ours.

The Jewish Revolt Against Rome (and God)

In Jesus' day there were again both good figs and evil figs. The evil figs chafed under the rule of Rome, even as they had rebelled against the rule of Babylon. The more these figs rebelled, the more Rome oppressed them. The more Rome oppressed them, the more they rebelled. The situation spiraled downward until finally open revolt broke out in 66 A.D. The people of Judah destroyed Rome's 12th Legion at the Feast of Tabernacles that year.

Rome put down the revolt decisively. They were delayed a bit by the death of the emperor Nero in 68 A.D. But finally, at Passover of 70 A.D. the Roman armies surrounded Jerusalem and began the siege. This was precisely 40 years after John the Baptist had been executed at Passover of 30 A.D.

The city was destroyed within a few months, but the final stronghold at Masada still had to be taken. The Romans built a huge ramp of rock and earth to the top of the mountain where the fortress of Masada was located. They finished this ramp on the day before Passover of 73 A.D. That night all the evil figs at Masada committed suicide to avoid capture by the Romans. This occurred 40 years after Jesus' crucifixion at Passover of 33 A.D. The evil figs had been given 40 years of grace in which to repent of their rejection of the Messiah. Instead of repenting, they decided to do the work of the Messiah themselves and in their own violent way.

This method did not work. Jerusalem was destroyed. The temple was destroyed. Over a million were killed and others put into slavery. In the decades that followed, there were other uprisings in Mesopotamia, Egypt, Cyrene, and Cyprus. Abram Leon Sachar writes on page 121, 122 of his book, A History of the Jews,

> "Trajan [the Roman Emperor from 98-116 A.D.] was compelled to send one of his ablest generals to cope with the fury of the Jews. The devastation was complete; when the last embers of the rebellion had been extinguished, it was necessary to rebuild Cyprus from its foundations. No Jew was thereafter permitted to set foot on the island, and even shipwrecked Jewish merchants who sought temporary refuge were done to death when found."

When Trajan died, Hadrian succeeded him. He was known as a man of peace, and the Jews hailed him as a second Cyrus. But Hadrian wanted to put an end to the practice of mutilation that many people practiced, so he passed a law forbidding it. This included circumcision, and this again infuriated the Jews. Secondly, Trajan made plans to rebuild Jerusalem as a Roman city, calling it Aelia Capitolina in honor of the patron god of Rome. This, too, infuriated the Jews and brought about the final revolt. Sachar writes on page 122,

> "The soul of the revolt was the venerable rabbi Akiba, one of the ablest of Israel's spiritual leaders . . . The Roman oppression roused the peaceful rabbi to active conflict. He centred all his hopes on a brilliant young warrior, Bar Kokba, who became the brain and sword of the revolt. . . Apparently, he claimed to be divinely inspired, and to his loyal followers he seemed the long-awaited Messiah.
>
> "Everywhere throughout the country the word was heard that the end of suffering was at hand; the tyrant who had dared to desecrate the house of God would be swept away like chaff; the country would again belong to the people that had made it sacred. Every village, every hamlet, was stirred. Only the newly-formed sect of Christians rejected the authority of the Jewish leaders. . . The Jews believed that this last stand against the Roman eagle was like no other. It was the prelude to the establishment of God's kingdom on earth."

The revolt at first succeeded, and the altar in Jerusalem was rededicated. But Rome brought its general Severus from Britain and reconquered Judea. Sachar tells us on page 123,

> "Bar Kokba and Akiba were both executed, along with all their followers . . . Their casualties were much greater than attended the destruction of the State in 70. . . Jews were forbidden on pain of death ever again to set foot in Jerusalem. Only on the ninth of Ab—the traditional anniversary of the destruction of the Temple—could Jews pay for the right to weep on the site of the old sanctuary. For centuries thereafter they 'bought their tears' weeping over the lost glories of the past, yet never abandoning the hope that some day, in God's own way, a restoration would come and the Holy Land would once again rise from the ruins, tenderly built up by Jewish hands."

This was how the revolt ended. They did not and still do not understand why this tragedy befell them. They do not understand why God did not help them win the wars. This made them bitter against God, instead of repenting of their rejection of the true Messiah. In fact, the fourth-century bishop, Eusebius, quotes Justin Martyr in his Ecclesiastical History, Book 4, viii,

> "In the recent war, Bar Cochba, leader of the Jewish insurrection, ordered the Christians alone to be sentenced to terrible punishments if they did not deny Jesus Christ and blaspheme Him."

The Jews did not understand why God allowed their Roman enemies to succeed in destroying their nation and the second temple. But the explanation is simple. God had released them from an iron yoke of Babylon to a lighter, wooden yoke under Medo-Persia, Greece, and finally Rome. But they were not content with submitting for the duration of their sentence for the sins of their fathers (the evil figs). So they revolted again in 66-73 A.D., trying to throw off the wooden yoke.

They failed, because their revolt was a violation of the law itself, as explained fully by the prophet Jeremiah. In rejecting the Word of the Lord, their hearts were hardened, and this blinded them to the Messiah Himself. They rejected Him because they rejected His peaceful methods of conquering the earth.

So in this revolt against God's judgment, they again found themselves under the iron yoke, forbidden to set foot in Jerusalem, cast off among the nations as captive slaves. This condition continued until the 1940's, when the evil figs among the Jews again staged a revolt to gain possession of the land of Palestine.

Zionism is a movement among Jews who decided that God would never set them free, and that they had to do it themselves. Without repenting, of course.

CHAPTER 10
Zionism's Beginnings

We showed in our previous chapter how the divine law clearly states that Israel's right to be in the Promised Land was contingent upon their obedience to God and His law. Because they continually refused to be obedient, God Himself "sold" Israel into the hands of foreign nations all through the book of Judges. Yet because they were allowed to remain in the land, it was merely a wooden yoke put upon them.

Only centuries later did God finally begin to impose upon them the "yoke of iron" mentioned in Deut. 28:48. This yoke was defined in the law as the removal of Israel from the land and their deportation and scattering into all nations. This actually occurred first with the northern ten tribes of the House of Israel in 745-721 B.C. Judah escaped the iron yoke for another century. But then the people refused to hear the Word of the Lord from the prophet Jeremiah. So God hired the Babylonians to bring the House of Judah under the yoke of iron. This iron yoke lasted for just 70 years, after which time God reduced their sentence to a wooden yoke, where they remained under the yoke of Medo-Persia, Greece, and Rome until the time of Christ.

Jesus then came to give them the Word, and the people once again rejected Him and His Word. He came as the Prince of Peace, but the people preferred a more violent method of establishing the Kingdom. Hence, they chose Barabbas, the murderer guilty of sedition—leading a revolt against Rome—rather than choosing the Messiah (Luke 23:18; Acts 3:14).

They were given a grace period of 40 years in which to change their minds. But in 66-73 A.D. the nation of Judah (Judea) decided to fight the Romans and attempt to throw off the wooden yoke by the arm of flesh. The Barabbas tactic failed, and once again they found themselves under the yoke of iron, scattered among the nations—this time, for a much longer period of time.

In the late 1800's a new Jewish movement arose, which called itself "Zionism." The purpose of this movement was to reverse the iron yoke that God had imposed upon the adherents of Judaism. Its method was carnal and often violent. Its main problem was that it assumed that Jews had a divine right to reverse that captivity without addressing the original reasons that God had imposed the iron yoke upon them in the first century. And so we must study the divine law to see the lawful manner by which such an iron yoke ought to be removed. Then we will compare the lawful method with those methods actually being employed by the Zionists today.

How to Reverse the Captivity

The divine law specified that He would release them from their captivity only under certain conditions. The primary condition was that they repent of their hostility against Jesus Christ, who gave them this law while in His pre-incarnate existence. Lev. 26:40-42 (NASB) says,

> [40] **If they confess their iniquity and the iniquity of their forefathers, in their unfaithfulness which they committed against Me** [Jesus Christ], **and also in their acting with hostility against Me** [Jesus Christ]— [41] **I also was acting with hostility against them, to bring them into the land of their enemies—or if their uncircumcised heart becomes humbled, so that they then make amends for their iniquity,** [42] **then I will remember My covenant with Jacob, and I will remember also My covenant with Isaac, and My covenant with Abraham as well, and I will remember the land.**

The iron yoke came upon them because of their "hostility" against Jesus Christ and because of their preference for the violent methods of Barabbas.

Most people are unaccustomed to thinking of Jesus Christ as the One who gave the law to Moses. But this teaching is clear in both the Old Testament and the New. In Exodus 15:3 and again in Isaiah 12:2, we read that "*The Lord*" (that is, YAHWEH, the God of the Old Testament) "*has become my salvation*" (that is, YASHUA). The word, Yashua, means salvation. This was also the Hebrew name for Jesus. Hence, the Scriptures tell us that Yahweh has become our Yashua, prophesying the incarnation of the Lawgiver in the form of Jesus Christ. Jesus, then, was the One who revealed Himself to Moses by the name of Yahweh (Ex. 6:2, 3). Jesus was the Covenanter and Lawgiver who spoke the Ten Commandments to the people and taught Moses the rest of the law.

The Hebrew word for the divine law is Torah. The first letter, *tav*, was originally written as a *cross*. It literally means "a sign" and is used in Ez. 9:4, where it is translated as a "mark" to be put on the foreheads of the divinely protected ones. This is the ancient origin of the practice of writing the sign of the cross on one's forehead.

The second letter in Torah is the *vav*, which literally means "a nail."

The third letter in Torah is the *resh*, which means "a head" or "the head" in the sense of the leader.

The final letter in Torah is the *hey*, which, when it appears at the end of the word, means "what comes from."

Putting these letters together spells the Hebrew word, Torah, and it literally means "**What comes from the Leader nailed to the Cross**." It is a prophecy that identifies the giver of the Torah as Jesus Christ, the Head or King, the Crucified One, who gave the law to Moses many years before He was born of Mary.

For this reason, the Jews' hostility against Jesus Christ, the Lawgiver, was the reason for their dispersion under the yoke of iron. God used Rome to do this, but one cannot merely blame the Romans for doing bad things to the Jews. Jesus Himself said plainly in Matt. 22:7 that God hired the Roman army as His mercenaries.

But instead of repenting, the Jewish leaders become quite angry when anyone implies that they did something wrong in crucifying Jesus. In fact, they often try to blame the Romans, whereas the New Testament never puts the blame on their shoulders. Pilate was forced to allow the crucifixion against his will. Peter testifies in Acts 3:13-15,

> [13] **The God of Abraham, Isaac, and Jacob, the God of our fathers, has glorified His servant, Jesus, the one whom you delivered up and disowned in the**

presence of Pilate, when he had decided to release him. [14] But you disowned the Holy and Righteous One, and asked for a murderer to be granted unto you, [15] and put to death the Prince of Life, the one whom God raised from the dead, a fact to which we are witnesses.

This is repeated in Acts 5:30, 7:51, 52, 10:39, 40, and 13:28. The apostles did not hesitate to call the Jews to repentance for their "hostility" against Jesus Christ. In fact, it *was required* of them. It is no different today, unless we are prepared to amend the New Testament in the attempt to make Christianity more palatable to Jews or to be more politically correct.

I say this, not in hatred, but in love, for only by such repentance can they hope to reverse the sentence of the law against them, as written in Lev. 26:40-42. No Jew can be saved apart from Jesus Christ. Nor can any Jew obtain God's blessing by moving to the nation called "Israel." As we said earlier, Zionism is a movement among Jews who decided that God would never set them free, and so they felt that they had to set themselves free. They have not repented, and yet they want the blessings of God while yet remaining hostile to Jesus Christ. This is not the way to fulfill Bible prophecy.

By returning to the land apart from Christ and without accepting His peaceful methods of conquest, they have had to resort to the violence and bloodshed advocated by Barabbas. This is the attitude and method used by this Zealot leader in Jesus' day. The people's choice ultimately brought utter disaster upon all of the people.

Jerusalem: The Bloody City

Jerusalem was so named, because it was supposed to be a City of Peace. That was its original calling when it was named by its builder and founder, Melchizedek (Shem), king of "Salem" (Gen. 14:18). The Temple in Jerusalem was built by Solomon, whose name also means "Peace." The temple was to be a house of prayer for ALL people. Unfortunately, however, the people of Judah converted the City of Peace into "the bloody city." Ez. 24:9-13 says,

[9] Therefore, thus says the Lord God, Woe to the bloody city! I also shall make the pile great. . . [13] Because I would have cleansed you, yet you are not clean, you will not be cleansed from your filthiness again until I have spent My wrath on you.

The fact is, the old Jerusalem is a bloody city, while the New Jerusalem is the true City of Peace. This has never been so apparent as today. The physical city of Jerusalem is identified with Hagar, Paul says in Gal. 4:25. As Hagar, that city cannot and will not bring forth the promises of the Kingdom of God—in spite of what Jewish leaders and many Christian ministers may teach.

The Scriptures teach that Hagar and her children must be "cast out" (Gen. 21:10; Gal. 4:30) before Sarah and her children can fulfill their calling to inherit the promises of God. So long as Hagar-Jerusalem is still a contender for the birthright promises to Abraham and Isaac, the promise will continue to be a future hope. That is why the day is soon coming when Hagar-Jerusalem will be destroyed by nuclear war. Only then will men have to look elsewhere for the fulfillment of the biblical Kingdom of God. But let us return to the history of modern Zionism.

The Beginnings of Modern Zionism

Zionism as a modern movement was really born in 1897 with the book, The Jewish State, written by Theodor Herzl. He was a reporter for an Austrian newspaper, covering the story of the Alfred Dreyfus treason trial. He was so appalled by the anti-Semitism of the trial that he came to believe that a Jewish nation of their own was the only solution. Herzl was able to raise money from wealthy contributors and thus succeeded where those before him had remained insignificant. Many viewed him as the promised Messiah.

The first armed group of Zionists in Jaffa was formed by just ten men in 1907, an organization called the Bar-Giora. In Dan Kurzman's biography of former Israeli Prime Minister, Yizhak Rabin, Soldier of Peace, page 72, he tells us of the Bar-Giora:

> "Named after the last Jewish defender of Jerusalem in 70 A.D., it was a secret underground watchmen's organization whose members took the oath, 'In blood and fire Judea fell and in blood and fire Judea shall arise'!"

So the Bar-Giora was so named to honor a man who symbolized the Jewish revolt against Rome. Their oath manifested no remorse or repentance for deliberately disobeying Jeremiah's injunction against the evil figs. Instead, these first armed Zionists came with an oath to continue their fight in the same manner as in 70 A.D. They came advocating "blood and fire."

In 1909 the Bar-Giora formed a larger organization known as Hashomer ("The Watchman"). Ten years later, in 1919, shortly after the end of World War One, the Haganah was formed, and this remained as the official Jewish "self-defense" organization until it was transformed into the Israeli Defense Force in 1948.

The Balfour Declaration

During World War One, the British received the help of Arabs in the overthrow of the Ottoman Empire, because they promised the Arabs independent states. In 1915 the British sent Col. T. E. Lawrence to convince the Arabs to revolt against the Ottomans.

On May 23, 1915 these Arab leaders agreed to the Damascus Protocol, by which they helped the British defeat the Ottoman Empire in exchange for the independence of all Arab land in Asia (except for Aden, south of Saudi Arabia). Subsequent letters written by General Sir Henry McMahon, the British High Commissioner for Egypt, to Hussein, Sharif of Mecca, make it clear that Palestine fell under this agreement. Alfred Lilienthal wrote in his book, The Zionist Connection II, page 16,

> "For some years, because of the nuances in Sir Henry's drafting, it was contended by certain Zionist academicians, supported by the British government, that the independence pledge was purposely vague and never intended to pertain to Palestine. But the publication in 1964 by scholar Dr. Fayaz Sayegh of two British documents, the twenty-page 'Memorandum on British Commitments to King Hussein' and the twelve-page 'Appendix of Previous Commitments to His Majesty's Government in the Middle East,' clearly revealed that Palestine unmistakably was contained within the McMahan independence promise."

These promises were given two years before the Balfour declaration, by which the Zionists laid claim to a state of their own. Hence, if the Zionists invoke the Balfour Declaration to claim a right to a Jewish State, the Arabs have a prior right to have it as a Palestinian State. The Balfour

Declaration was a letter of intent written by Britain's Foreign Minister to Baron Lionel Rothschild on Nov. 2, 1917, saying,

> "His Majesty's Government view with favour the establishment in Palestine of a national home for the Jewish people and will use their best endeavours to facilitate the achievement of this object, it being clearly understood that nothing shall be done which may prejudice civil and religious rights of existing non-Jewish communities in Palestine, or the rights and political status enjoyed by Jews in any other country."

This Declaration did not establish a Jewish *state*, but rather, a Jewish *national home*. It said nothing about dispossessing Arabs or denying them political or social rights. It was understood that Arabs would continue to remain the majority population, and that the Arab-dominated government would also allow Jews to purchase land and live there with *equal rights* among the Arabs, if they so desired. This is not much different from Jews freely living in America today.

Even so, the Balfour Declaration was not a signed agreement that enjoyed legal status. It was merely a letter of intent. The Zionists either ignored what it said about equal rights for all, or else they read into the letter what they wanted to hear. At any rate, Zionists used this to instill in Jews around the world the hope for a Jewish State. This ignited a fire that soon got out of control.

Hence, the Arabs were indeed promised independence in most of the Middle East—including Palestine—but the Jews were promised the right to immigrate to Palestine and live as equals in that Arab territory.

Conflicting Promises Breed Betrayal

In the time between the Damascus Protocol and the Balfour Declaration, the British made a third set of promises to France and Russia by the Sykes-Picot agreement on May 16, 1916. Sir Mark Sykes of Britain and Charles Francois Georges Picot of France agreed to divide the spoils of the Ottoman Empire among three countries. France was to receive western Syria and the city of Mosul. England was to take control from Baghdad to the Persian Gulf. Russia's share fell outside of the Middle East and is not our concern here.

The French knew nothing of the Hussein-McMahan agreements, and the Arabs knew nothing of the Sykes-Picot arrangement that totally contradicted their promises of Arab independence. Only after the Russian revolution in late 1917 did the revolutionaries discover and publish these secret Tsarist papers, for Russia was part of the Sykes-Picot agreement. This was when the Arabs discovered that they had been betrayed.

On May 5, 1920 the Allied Council of Four partitioned Syria to France and gave Britain the mandate to rule Palestine. T. E. Lawrence ("Lawrence of Arabia"), wrote of the fraud with great bitterness on page 275, 276 of his book, Seven Pillars of Wisdom,

> "The Arab Revolt had begun on false pretences. To gain the Sherif's help our Cabinet had offered, through Sir Henry McMahon, to support the establishment of native governments in parts of Syria and Mesopotamia, 'saving the interests of our ally, France'. The last modest clause concealed a treaty (kept secret, till too late, from McMahon, and therefore from the Sherif) by which France, England, and Russia agreed to annex some of these promised areas, and to establish their respective spheres of influence over all the rest.

"Rumors of the fraud reached Arab ears, from Turkey. In the East persons were more trusted than institutions. So the Arabs, having tested my friendliness and sincerity under fire, asked me, as a free agent, to endorse the promises of the British Government. I had had no previous or inner knowledge of the McMahon pledges and the Sykes-Picot treaty, which were both framed by war-time branches of the Foreign Office. But not being a perfect fool, I could see that if we won the war the promises to the Arabs were dead paper. Had I been an honorable adviser, I would have sent my men home and not let them risk their lives for such stuff. Yet the Arab inspiration was our main tool in winning the Eastern war. So I assured them that England kept her word in letter and spirit. In this comfort they performed their fine things; but, of course, instead of being proud of what we did together, I was continually and bitterly ashamed."

The British then issued the "Churchill White Paper" in June 1922, to clarify their policy:

"It is contemplated that the status of all citizens of Palestine in the eyes of the law shall be Palestinian, and it has never been intended that they or any section of them should possess any other juridical status. . . . It is not as has been represented by the Arab delegation that during this war His Majesty's Government gave an undertaking that an independent national government should be at once established in Palestine."

Statement after statement clarified that the Balfour Declaration never intended to create a Jewish state in Palestine, at least not "*at once*." This raised the blood pressure of the Zionists, who, of course, had every intention of doing just that. At any rate, the Balfour Declaration was abundantly clear on this one issue, saying: "it being clearly understood that nothing shall be done which may prejudice civil and religious rights of existing non-Jewish communities in Palestine." This is clearly one issue over which the British government cannot be accused of doublespeak.

The Zionists, however, objected to this clause and made it clear to all that they intended to force the British into creating a Jewish state at the expense of the Arabs who had lived there for over a thousand years. The Arabs read the Zionist literature and were both appalled and angered by this belligerence and lack of respect for the basic human rights of any non-Jews who got in their way.

National Boundaries Established

In 1922 the British recognized the Kingdom of Egypt that included the Sinai, which the Zionists claimed belonged to them. In 1923 Transjordan was made a sovereign nation. This at least partially fulfilled some of the British promises to the Arabs for their support during World War One. The Zionists, however, were furious, because it "gave away" more of "Greater Israel."

These settled boundaries of Egypt and Jordan brought relative stability in those parts of the Middle East. But Palestine was still a problem, because the British wanted to retain it as a colony because of its strategic position, particularly to protect their interest in the Suez Canal. This put the British and the Zionists into direct conflict. Still, most of the Zionist leadership made some attempt to work within the framework of the British government.

But the Zionist intent was to conquer all of Palestine through immigration and settlement. They believed that a Jewish State could only be accomplished by having a majority population. The immigrants were used as their primary weapon. Arab militants began to fight back, killing these "innocent" civilians who had been enlisted by the Zionists in their designs to conquer by immigration.

This was the beginning of the conflict in the twentieth century.

Non-Zionist Rabbis Speak Out

Modern Zionism began primarily as a nationalistic movement to obtain political power in Palestine. But the 1967 war, when the Israelis took control of Jerusalem and the West Bank, sparked a type of secular messianism that had lingered just under the surface. It is a peculiar belief of messianism that is held by atheistic Jews who dominate the Israeli government even today. It is the belief that the Jewish people collectively are its own messiah.

Jewish opinion is divided on this subject. But this is the political view that has set the course of the modern Israeli state. This means simply that the people got tired of waiting for a savior to come and free them from the iron yoke that God had imposed upon them in the first century. They did not feel that they had to repent of rejecting the Messiah, and so they could not understand why God would allow this yoke to remain upon them for 1,900 years.

They finally concluded that God either did not exist, or, if He existed at all, He expected them to be their own savior. Hence, certain Jewish leaders were able to revive the ancient spirit of revolt, overturning centuries of rabbinic teaching in Judaism that they must await the coming of the Messiah before returning to Palestine.

There are, even today, significant numbers of Jewish rabbis who are hotly anti-Zionist, but most Christians never hear their voices. For example, Dr. Israel Shahak, emeritus professor of organic chemistry at the Hebrew University in Jerusalem until his death last year, had long been an advocate of human rights for Palestinian people. He was the founder of the Israeli League of Human Rights. He wrote a letter published by the London *Times* on Jan. 27, 1973 entitled, "A Jewish Duty or Jewish Apostasy?"

> "I am a Jew living in Israel, and consider myself a law-abiding citizen. I serve in the army every year, in spite of being nearly forty years old. But I am not 'devoted' to the State of Israel or to any other state or human organization. I am devoted to my ideals. I believe in speaking the truth and in doing something for securing justice and equality for all human beings. . .
>
> "But to be devoted to the State? I can well imagine Amos or Isaiah splitting their sides with laughter if somebody had demanded of them to be 'devoted' to the Kingdom of Israel or the Kingdom of Judah. 'Hate evil and love good and establish judgment in the gate,' says Amos (Chapter 5, verse 15), who does not spare a word of devotion to the great-warlike and successful Kingdom of Israel of his times.
>
> "In fact, this new doctrine preached as a Jewish duty, is nothing but Jewish apostasy. All Jews used to believe and say it three times a day, that a Jew should be devoted to God, and God alone. A small minority still believes it. But it seems to me that the majority of my people has left God, and has substituted an idol in its place, exactly as happened when they were so devoted to the Golden Calf in the desert that they gave away their gold to make it. The name of this modern idol is the State of Israel."

Other rabbis are just as outspoken as Dr. Shahak. Rabbi Michael Ber Weissmandel wrote an article May 26, 2000 [http://www.jewsnotzionists.org/tenquestions.html],

". . . We should avoid the untenable position of the robber who prays for Divine help in carrying out his crime. We should pray that Zionism and its fruits vanish from the Earth, and that we be redeemed by the Messiah with dispatch.

"A prisoner is released only when he has served his time, or if he is pardoned by the President for good behavior. If he attempts escape and is apprehended, his term is lengthened, besides the beating he receives when he is caught.

". . . We have been sentenced to exile by the King of Kings because of our sins. The eternal, blessed be he, has decreed that we accept the exile with humble gratitude until the time comes, or until we merit His pardon through repentance. If we seek to end the exile with force, G-d will catch us, as our sages have forewarned, and our sentence becomes longer and more difficult.

"Many times in the past have segments of our people been defrauded by false messiahs—but none of the false messiahs has been as fallacious and delusory as the lie of Zionism. . . . If we wish our exile-sentence commuted, we must appeal through repentance . . . Let it be clearly understood that never in Jewish history (even in the time of Jeroboam or Achav) have such hostile atheists stood at the helm of the Jewish people as today."

Though many rabbis warned the people against the errors of Zionism, the idea of returning to the land proved to be too tantalizing for a great many Jews. It awakened a hope within them long nurtured by Judaism, and Zionism offered them an immediate reward without awaiting for a divine Messiah. Zionism would give them a land without the need for repentance, for they would be their own messiah. They would "redeem" the land themselves by transferring it to Jewish ownership. This would be done at first by purchasing land peacefully; but ultimately, if Arabs refused to sell the land, it would be appropriated by the Land Acquisition Act of 1953, legalizing all seizures of Arab land. The rest of the land would be conquered by military force whenever possible.

Arab Reaction to Zionism

The Jewish Agency was an organization that attempted to work primarily to bring about the conquest of Palestine by political means—that is, by immigration. The Arabs objected to the Zionist objective of establishing a Jewish State, citing earlier British promises that, if anything, there should be an independent Palestinian State. But since Transjordan had already been given statehood, the British gave them assurances that Palestine would be turned into a Palestinian State in which Jews would be allowed to live as equal citizens.

Many Arabs, however, were far-sighted enough to see that the Zionists would never content themselves by living as equals. Zionist literature showed clearly their intent to establish a Jewish state.

The mufti, Haj Amin el-Husseini, religious leader of Jerusalem, was outspokenly militant and periodically urged the Arabs to kill Jews that he believed were taking over their land and threatening even their holy places. In 1920 more than 130 Jews and close to 100 Arabs were killed in the fighting around Jerusalem, Hebron, Haifa, Safed, and other Jewish settlements. The mufti was not far-sighted enough to see that his actions merely legitimized the Zionists, who could then demonize the Arabs and garner world sympathy. Blinded by hatred and vengeance, he forsook the moral high ground and soon expended any world sympathy for Palestinian rights that the world may have had. Taking justice into their own hands, they made it more difficult for the British to defend them in their legitimate grievances.

The British government was caught in the cross-fire of their own making. By this time they knew that they had created a monster that they could not control. Resenting the Jewish insistence upon unlimited immigration rights, the British defended the Jewish Zionists only half-heartedly. They attempted to limit the Jewish immigration to the number that the land could reasonably absorb, but this policy of limited immigration came under fire from the Zionists. It was obvious that they intended to establish a Jewish *state* and would never be content for a mere "homeland."

Arabs, too, soon saw that Britain had no intention of granting them independence. They observed the Zionists putting pressure upon Britain to turn Palestine into a Jewish state with a majority Jewish population with the intent to have Jewish rule over a Palestinian minority. Having felt betrayed by the British already, many Arabs had no confidence in the British government's will to resist the published Zionist intention of establishing a Jewish state.

With each Arab retaliation against Jewish immigrants, and seeing that the British were reluctant or unable to defend them against the Arabs, the Zionists took more and more responsibility for their self-defense. And as time passed, the people became more militant. After all, once they had accepted the basic premise of Zionism and had moved to Palestine, they had no choice but to defend themselves.

This, in turn, led to the era of Jewish terrorist activity against both the Arabs and the British.

CHAPTER 11
The Rise of Jewish Terrorism

In 1936 the mufti of Jerusalem, Haj Amin el-Husseini, called for a general strike among the Arabs. They vowed to close down the economy, but only succeeded in vacating jobs that were quickly filled by new Jewish immigrants, who were in need of employment. Enraged by the failure of the strike, they turned to more violent measures, and Palestine exploded in violence once again. The mufti was short on wisdom and long on hatred.

Vladimir Jabotinsky: Father of Jewish Terrorism

By the mid-1930's the situation was ripe for the next level of violence. The perfect man for the job was a man named Ze'ev Vladimir Jabotinsky. Jabotinsky had been the first commander of the Haganah, the Jewish defense organization founded in 1919 by the World Zionist Organization. In 1923 he founded Betar, named after the fortress where Bar Kokba made his last stand in his revolt against Rome in 135 A.D. Bar Kokba's messianic revolt was the reason Rome banned all Jews from setting foot in Jerusalem. Bar Kokba, a false messiah, was Jabotinsky's role model and the hero of all the Jewish terrorists in the 1940's.

In this context, Jabotinsky founded the Revisionist movement, which soon gave birth to the Irgun Zvai Leumi ("National Military Organization") in April 1937. Shortly afterward, a second terrorist organization was founded—the Lohamei Herut Yisrael ("Fighters for the Freedom of Israel"). Its English acronym was F. F. I, while its Hebrew acronym was Lehi. Named also after its founder, Avraham Stern, it is also known by their friends as the Stern Group and by their adversaries as the Stern Gang.

Jabotinsky himself died in New York in 1940. As for Avraham Stern, he was soon found by British police and immediately executed without trial in 1942. Both Shamir and Begin decried this execution as a "murder." Perhaps it was. But in more recent years, the Israeli government has executed many Arab terrorists in similar fashion without trial. The Arabs also call this murder. The Israelis, however, operate on a double standard and do not consider the execution of Arab terrorists to be murder. It is only murder if the terrorist is a Jew.

Jabotinsky is the father of Jewish terrorism, which sought to continue the messianic nationalism of the past, whose military messiahs always found sympathy among the Jews. In 1935 he left the mainstream Zionist movement and established the radical Zionist Revisionist Organization in opposition to the World Zionist Organization, headed by Chaim Weizmann. Jabotinsky was, in fact, the embodiment of the "bloody city" principle of the old Jerusalem.

Former Israeli Prime Minister, Menachem Begin, wrote in 1951 about Jabotinsky in his book, The Revolt: Story of the Irgun, p. 40,

> "The revolt sprang from the earth. . . The renewed strength which came to us, and especially to our youth, from contact with the soil of our ancient land, is no legend but a fact. The officials of the British Foreign Office had no conception of this when

> they made their plans. . . They could not gauge the character of the Jews who came to Eretz Israel. They assumed that in Eretz Israel, too, the Jews would continue to be timid suppliants for protection. . . But those unseen forces, which have ever saved the Jewish people from obliteration, demolished the British assumption. Vladimir Jabotinsky appeared, educating a whole generation to resist, to be ready for sacrifice, for revolt and for war. David Raziel appeared, the greatest Jewish military mind of our generation, to carry out the decisive act; the *first attack* by Jewish arms."

Mr. Begin later became the head of the Irgun Zvai Leumi, the most important and effective Jewish terrorist organization in the 1940's. Another former Israeli Prime Minister, Yitzhak Shamir, lauds Jabotinsky enthusiastically as well on page 9 of his book, Summing Up,

> "Without doubt, Jabotinsky was the most dynamic and controversial of the many gifted men who left their mark on the Zionist movement and, subsequently, on the State of Israel. . . . For ever the target of strong feelings, he was at once hated, worshipped, feared and admired; accepted as a supreme leader by some, he was rejected by others as a dangerous extremist whose concepts and supporters, if allowed to prevail, would degrade and destroy the essence of the Zionist cause. . .
>
> "Today Jabotinsky's name and spirit are kept alive mostly through the Likud Party, which, to a significant degree, represents and articulates his basic philosophy and is, so to speak, executor of his political testament."

The Likud Party has become the most powerful political party in Israeli politics in recent years. It was the party conceived by Ariel Sharon and formed primarily by Menachem Begin. It is the party to which Yitzhak Shamir belongs. Because this party carries on the philosophy of Vladimir Jabotinsky, it is the party of Jewish terrorism. On page 11 Shamir sums up by saying of him,

> "Essentially, Jabotinsky's vision of Zionism achieved can be compressed into one sentence: a Jewish majority in a Jewish state in the whole of the biblical Land of Israel."

Mr. Shamir was the second most important Jewish terrorist leader in the 1940's, heading the Lehi (the Stern Gang). Jabotinsky was the spiritual inspiration behind the Jewish terrorism waged against the British by both Mr. Begin and Mr. Shamir during the 1940's. From 1943 to 1948 the Irgun terrorists were led by Menachem Begin, the man who became the Likud Party's first Prime Minister of Israel in 1977.

Jewish Pawns in their Leaders' Hands

During the British Mandate government in Palestine (1922-1948), the average Jew was caught in the middle, for he was being used as a pawn in a bigger game than he realized. In 1941 and 1942 the German Gestapo offered to transport all Jews to Spain for $1,000 for each family, on condition that these Jews not move to Palestine. The Jewish Agency declined the offer—they must move to Palestine or suffer in their own countries.

In 1944 a similar offer was made in regard to Hungarian Jews. Again, the Jewish Agency declined the offer—they must move to Palestine or suffer in their own countries to put propaganda pressure upon the European governments. Germany and Britain, during World War II, even agreed to evacuate 500,000 Jews from Europe and resettle them in British colonies. It was the Jewish Agency that refused the offer—they must move to Palestine or suffer in their own countries.

The British government granted to 300 rabbis and their families visas to the Colony of Mauritius, with passage through Turkey. The Jewish Agency stopped this plan, too, saying that the 300 rabbis and their families ought to be "gassed" for their disloyalty to Zionism. Presumably it was more acceptable to the Jewish Agency that their Jewish pawns be "gassed" in order to put more pressure on Britain.

Throughout the early 1900's, thousands of Jews were convinced to move to Palestine illegally in order to force a change in British policy. When stopped at the border (or harbor), then the game turned bloody and grim. When the *S.S. Patria* arrived at the Haifa harbor in Palestine filled with Jewish immigrants, the British authorities refused to allow them to enter the country. They ordered the ship to leave the harbor, and at that point the Jewish Agency in Palestine ordered the ship to be dynamited in order to make the British government look bad. Jewish author, Alfred Lilienthal writes on page 359 of his book, The Zionist Connection II,

> "Violence was often used against their own, as on November 25, 1940, when the *S.S. Patria* was blown up in the Haifa harbor, killing 276 illegal Jewish immigrant passengers. At the time of the incident these deaths were attributed to the British, and it was not until ten years later that the responsibility for this disaster was placed at the door of the Zionists. David Flinker, Israeli correspondent of the Jewish *Morning Journal* (the largest Yiddish daily) described what had happened:
>
> ". . . 'It was then that the Haganah General Staff took a decision at which their leaders shuddered. The decision was not to permit the *Patria* to leave Jaffa. The English must be given to understand that Jews could not be driven away from their own country. The *Patria* must be blown up. . . . The number of victims was officially placed at 276. The survivors were permitted by the High Commissioner to land.'
>
> "Fifteen months later the *S.S. Struma* exploded in the Black Sea, killing 769 illegal Jewish immigrants. The Jewish Agency described it as an act of 'mass-protest and mass-suicide,' and the U.S. media once more placed the responsibility for these deaths at the door of the British and their Palestinian immigration policy."

The Haganah ("Defense") was the official defense organization of the Jewish Agency in Palestine. Though it operated as an underground military group, the British allowed it to operate somewhat freely, as long as it did not attack British targets. It is apparent from the blowing up of the *Patria* (and perhaps the *Struma* as well) that the Haganah was fully capable and prepared to sacrifice its own people to put pressure upon the British government to allow more immigration. The Jewish Agency called it "mass-protest and mass-suicide." It is more accurate to view it as "assisted suicide."

Former Prime Minister Menachem Begin writes about the sinking of the *Patria* on pages 35 and 36 of his book, The Revolt, saying,

> "The *Patria* never sailed. Jewish 'terrorists' placed a bomb to prevent its departure. The bomb exploded and more than two hundred Jews were killed or drowned. The British authorities noted the fact that this was not an Irgun Zvai Leumi operation; it was the Haganah which had placed the bomb."

Obviously, the Jewish Agency, headed by David Ben-Gurion, believed that the end justified the means. Even the great Arch-terrorist Menachem Begin would not have deliberately murdered hundreds of Jews to achieve his goal of a Jewish State, though his bombing of the King David Hotel did kill 17 Jews out of a total of 91. But the Jewish Agency needed another "British" atrocity in order to help their cause. The British were apparently not sufficiently ruthless, so the Haganah had to help with the murder of 276 Jews and then blame the British for the atrocity.

But with a Haganah mindset like that, we cannot help but wonder how many other Jews the Haganah murdered in order to generate sympathy and further its cause.

Zionists Assassinate Lord Moyne

The bombing of the *Stuma* had another consequence. Yitshak Shamir, who was later to become one of Israel's Prime Ministers, was at this time a leading Jewish terrorist in the Lehi. In his biography, Summing Up, pages 41 and 52 describe the sinking of the *Struma* and how it affected Lehi's decision to assassinate Britain's Lord Moyne.

Toronto's The Globe and Mail newspaper for Aug. 6, 1994 carried a review of Shamir's Summing Up, stating:

> "Shamir took part in the decision to kill Lord Moyne, and he helped plan the bold and complex operation. The experience was to serve him well later. During his years with the Mossad, Israel's security and intelligence service, he reportedly directed a squad of assassins. Shamir says he also ordered the execution of a Lehi member, a fanatic who threatened to disrupt the organization. How many other killings he ordered, he does not say. Shamir insists he has no regrets about his actions."

Newspapers seldom mention the fact that the Israeli state was founded by Jewish terrorists. The Israelis did not oppose terrorism until after they pardoned themselves and became the statesmen of their newly-created Jewish State. Then, of course, they banned terrorism, because they did not want terrorists to attempt to overthrow the new Israeli government.

On Nov. 6, 1944 two young terrorists from Yitzhak Shamir's Lehi (Stern Gang) assassinated Britain's Minister for Middle East Affairs, Lord Moyne, in Cairo, Egypt. The assassins were caught, tried, and hanged on Mar. 23, 1945.

In a book published in 1963 entitled The Deed, by Gerold Frank, we are given a detailed account of this assassination and those responsible for it. He writes on p. 35,

> "Explaining the nature of individual terrorism, Itzhak Yizernitsky, who as Shamir, the operations commander of the Stern group, planned the death of Moyne, once said: 'A man who goes forth to take the life of another whom he does not know must believe one thing only—that by his act he will change the course of history'."

Of the two young assassins, Frank writes on p. 36,

> "Each made his way by different roads to the same conclusion: that Britain would not give up Palestine unless forced to; that freedom would be won only by fighting for it and that if it was to be won, Jewish zealots patterned after those who twenty centuries ago rose up against the might of Rome must now rise up against the might of Britain."

Menachem Begin was upset with Shamir, not because of the act of terrorism, but because Shamir had not warned Begin beforehand, which would have allowed Begin to prepare for the British reaction and their crackdowns on terrorists. In his book, The Revolt, on pages 150, 151, Begin chided the Stern Gang, saying:

> "As comrades in revolt and partners in danger, we should have been informed by the F. F. I. chiefs of what was going forward. But they had permitted us to be taken completely by surprise."

The F.F.I. stood for the "Freedom Fighters of Israel," which was Shamir's Stern Gang.

The Jewish Agency, always playing politics, did not care about the assassination either, but they did care about their political position and about the British reprisals that would come. Even so, there were many individual Jews who were outraged by this blatant act of terrorism. Gerold Frank writes in The Deed, p. 32,

> "In Palestine, as the terrible truth was confirmed, the cry rose: excommunicate the terrorists! The Jewish Agency exhorted the population: drive them from their places of hiding, flay them from their jobs, pluck them out of the schools, tear out this cancer which shames us before the world!"

The Jewish Agency should have taken its own words to heart.

The Jewish Agency Unites with the Terrorists

In spite of all his rhetoric, Ben-Gurion soon went to the United States to raise money for arms to fight the British government. He met on July 1, 1945 with seventeen wealthy American Jews, who formed the secret Sonnenborn Institute to secure arms and smuggle them into Palestine. When all was ready, Ben-Gurion sent a letter to Moshe Sneh, the Haganah ("defense") chief in Palestine, telling him to begin the terrorist uprising and to coordinate their operations with the Irgun and the Stern Gang.

This makes it clear that Ben-Gurion and the Jewish Agency itself believed in terrorism against the British. It was not for *moral* reasons that they refrained from terrorism most of the time. Their restraint was based upon *political* considerations, knowing that open terrorism would be detrimental to world opinion and support.

This was the basis of Ben-Gurion's "statesmanship." He both supported and perpetrated terrorism, but usually did so secretly, so as not to let the world know that he too was a terrorist. Once he had raised money for arms in the summer of 1945, the Jewish Agency openly joined with the Stern and Irgun terrorists for about nine months in a reign of terror throughout Palestine. This "United Resistance Movement" lasted from Nov. 1945 to July 1946, ending only with the most spectacular terrorist act: the blowing up of the King David Hotel on July 22, 1946.

The Jewish Agency's shock troops, called the Palmach, was first organized in 1941 but remained relatively inactive for the duration of World War Two. But World War Two had ended in 1945. Twenty-three year old Yitzhak Rabin was appointed second-in-command of the First Battalion. During this time, they coordinated their attacks with the Irgun and with the Stern Gang, as Ben-Gurion had ordered. This was less than one year after the Stern Gang had assassinated Lord Moyne and Ben-Gurion had issued his call to "excommunicate the terrorists."

The Palmach's first action was to free about 200 Jews from the Atlith detention camp, who had been arrested for attempting to enter Palestine illegally. Rabin led his Palmach battalion on

Oct. 10, 1945 and successfully broke them out of the camp and dispersed them throughout various Jewish settlements. The success of this operation encouraged them to engage in an all-out guerilla war against the British, beginning the night of Nov. 1, 1945. Menachem Begin writes of it on page 191 of The Revolt:

> "On the 'night of the railways' the Haganah also sank three British patrol boats. Later they twice attacked the radar station at Haifa. . . One attack was made on the police Observation Post at Givat Olga, which was blown up. . . In February 1946 the Haganah carried out sabotage operations against installations of the Mobile Police. And in June the Haganah brought their armed resistance to a close with the comprehensive and successful attack on the frontier-bridges."

This "night of the railways" was the first major joint operation, which occurred Nov. 1, 1945. Shamir tells us that in their part of the operation against the railway workshops, eleven Lehi members were killed. Toward the end of this united front came the "night of the bridges" in June 1946. On page 203 Begin writes of this:

> "Great steel bridges in the north, the south, and the east, collapsed under the blows of the Haganah men. This was the last military operation of the Resistance Movement."

This proved to be the final terrorist act that brought the British to strike back forcefully on the day known to Jewish historians as "The Black Sabbath." On June 29, 1946 the British forces occupied the headquarters of the Jewish Agency and arrested nearly all of the leaders of their Haganah and Palmach. The ranks of the Palmach (shock troops) were devastated. Yitzhak Rabin was arrested, although he was recovering from a badly broken leg suffered in a motorcycle accident. This turned out to be of benefit to him, because he was taken to a military hospital, where he received good treatment and physical therapy. Kurzman's biography of Rabin, Soldier of Peace, pages 102, 103 says,

> "Actually, the British treated their prisoners quite well. They gave Rabin good medical attention, sending him to the military hospital in Gaza."

One might want to compare the British treatment of Jewish terrorists with today's Jewish treatment of Arab terrorists.

The Jewish Agency loudly proclaimed that the Black Sabbath arrests were nothing short of a British declaration of war upon the Jews themselves. To them, the British had no right to defend themselves against Jewish terrorism. In fact, in their minds, it was the British government's own fault for provoking them to commit terrorist acts by continuing to "occupy" Palestine. Menachem Begin writes on page 205 of his book, The Revolt:

> "Throughout the day the Jewish Agency's *Kol Israel* ["all Israel"—ed.] vociferated: "Britain has declared war on the Jewish people. The Jewish people will fight back. Out with the unclean sons of Titus from our Holy Land! Down with the Nazi-British regime in our country!"

In other words, any time the British defended themselves or attempted to arrest the terrorists who had blown up the bridges, police stations, etc., the British were always said to be the aggressors who had "declared war on the Jewish people." But when Jews declared war, it was always justified in their eyes as a "fight for freedom." Jewish casualties of the fight were the fault of the British "murderers," and any British casualties were also the fault of the British just for being there.

Likewise, when Arabs were killed by these same Zionists, it was their own fault for just being there after they were warned to leave their farms and villages and flee to other Arab nations. The moral blind spot is beyond belief. The double standard has no rational explanation.

At any rate, the Jewish Agency was not nearly as committed to the cause as the Irgun or Lehi. They were too political to accept casualties as a fact of war, and in this way they differed greatly with the Irgun and Stern Gang. With close to half of their fighters in prison, they left the fighting to Begin and Shamir and returned to their official political status. They even issued another public denouncement of terrorism, although they continued to support it secretly. In fact, they decided to take revenge upon the British for arresting their members, and so at that point they approved the bombing of the King David Hotel.

Such was the political duplicity of the Jewish Agency.

Destroying the King David Hotel

A few months before the arrest of the Haganah and Palmach leaders, they had already begun to plan an attack on the King David Hotel, where the military headquarters for the British government was located. In the spring of 1946 the Irgun submitted a plan to the Haganah, but the Haganah thought it was too ambitious.

Then on July 1, 1946, two days after the British had arrested many of their leaders, they approved the plan whereby the Irgun would blow up the hotel. In their way of thinking, this was an appropriate "reprisal" for the Black Sabbath occupation of the headquarters of the Jewish Agency. At least, that was how they justified it later.

In actuality, Mr. Begin makes it very clear that they had planned this action months before the British occupied the Jewish Agency headquarters. The arrests on Black Sabbath caused the Haganah leaders to capitulate to the British and publicly renounce terrorism, but they continued to carry out a secret terrorist war against the British. The only difference was that they now remained in the background and let the Irgun do the dirty work. Begin relates the entire story in Chapter Fifteen of his book.

The operation was led by "Gideon," (Yisrael Levi). They brought milk cans loaded with explosives into the basement through the hotel's Regence Café. When completed, one of them telephoned the hotel and told them to evacuate the building, because bombs had been placed. They were timed to go off in half an hour. However, according to Mr. Begin's account, the hotel was not evacuated, because the British high command refused to "take orders from the Jews." Whatever the reason, 91 people were killed in the explosion.

The explosion was more effective than any of them believed possible, both in its destruction and the high number of casualties. The Haganah panicked again, and asked the Irgun to take public responsibility for this terrorist act. Mr. Begin complied, saving the Haganah any further embarrassment and arrests.

Nonetheless, the Haganah once again became the public adversary of the Irgun, even helping the British arrest Irgun members! Mr. Begin seems largely justified in his contempt for the Haganah and their duplicity. Begin, who calls himself the "Number One Terrorist" on the first page of his book, at least had principles, for he was not a politician, but a military man.

King David Hotel after the explosion

The Haganah not only knew of the operation, but approved of it in advance. It was called "Operation Chick." Begin writes on page 218,

> "Operation 'Chick' was carried out exactly three weeks after we received the Haganah's instructions to execute it. During that time a number of meetings took place between us and the leaders of the Resistance Movement. Once the F. F. I. called for a postponement as they were not yet ready for their task. Twice or thrice we postponed the attack at the request of the Haganah Command."

The blow-up of the King David Hotel brought the "Big Curfew" in Tel Aviv, as Yitzhak Shamir calls it on page 63 of his book, Summing Up. In the British search for terrorists, an officer recognized Yitzhak Shamir in spite of his disguise and imprisoned him. Ultimately, the British court exiled him to the prison camp in Eritrea in Africa, and he was out of the fight until May 1948.

The Deir Yassin Village Massacre

This occurred nine months after the destruction of the King David Hotel, a time when the British government began to give up on keeping the peace in Palestine.

On April 9, 1947 for no good strategic reason Mr. Begin's Irgun Gang teamed up with Shamir's Stern Gang and massacred over 250 men, women, and children in Deir Yassin, a peaceful village outside of Jerusalem. Most of the men were absent, because they were working in Jerusalem. The people were quickly subdued, those who resisted were killed on the spot, and the rest were lined up against a wall in the town square and shot. Many of the women were raped before most of them, too, were killed.

Later apologists tell us that *it was their own fault for not leaving when they were warned.* Surely, such apologists must be a bit insane to think that a few minutes' warning relieves terrorists and murders of all moral responsibility for the massacres! Mr. Begin writes on page 163, 164 of The Revolt,

> "One of our tenders carrying a loud speaker was stationed at the entrance to the village and it exhorted in Arabic all women, children and aged to leave their houses and to take shelter on the slope of the hill. By giving this humane warning our fighters threw away the elements of complete surprise, and thus increased their own risk in the ensuing battle. A substantial number of the inhabitants obeyed the warning and they were unhurt. A few did not leave their stone houses—perhaps because of the confusion. The fire of the enemy was murderous—to which the number of our casualties [four Irgun fighters were killed—ed.] bears eloquent testimony. Our men were compelled to fight for every house; to overcome the enemy they used large numbers of hand grenades. And the civilians who had disregarded our warnings, suffered inevitable casualties."

This "warning" given to the civilians is contradicted by Alfred Lilienthal, who wrote on page 154 of The Zionist Connection II,

> "No warning had been given to the villagers, as was later claimed (Begin has stated that all victims of Irgun attacks had been warned beforehand), because the armored truck with its loudspeaker had tumbled into a ditch and been tossed on its side far short of the first houses of the village. Advised by a night watchman of the approaching Jewish raiders, some inhabitants, with only a robe thrown around them, managed to flee to the west."

> "Jon Kimche, the Zionist writer, calling the incident 'the darkest stain on the Jewish record throughout the fighting,' stated, 'The terrorist justified the massacre of Deir Yassin because it led to the panic flight of the remaining Arabs in the Jewish state area.' Jewish writer Don Peretz described the result of Deir Yassin as a 'mass fear psychosis which grasped the whole Arab community.' Arthur Koestler wrote, this 'bloodbath . . . was the psychologically decisive factor in the spectacular exodus of Arab refugees'." (p. 156)

Menachem Begin also claimed that the town was of strategic military value. He bases this on a letter from Mr. Shaltiel, the Haganah Regional Commander, who had written to Mr. Begin:

> "I learn that you plan an attack on Dir Yassin. I wish to point out that the capture of Dir Yassin and holding it is one stage in our general plan. I have no objection to your carrying out the operation provided you are able to hold the village. If you are unable to do so I warn you against blowing up the village which will result in its inhabitants abandoning it and its ruins and deserted houses being occupied by foreign forces. This situation will increase our difficulties in the general struggle. A second conquest of the place will involve us in heavy sacrifices. Furthermore, if foreign forces enter the place this will upset the plan for establishing an airfield."

So the strategic value of Dir Yassin (or Deir Yassin) was that the Haganah was planning to turn it into an airfield! Certainly that would justify the destruction of the village. And if the people object and fight back, this would certainly justify their massacre. After all, who are they to object to a Jewish airfield? Don't Jews have rights?

The Haganah, as usual, had denied all knowledge of the Irgun's plans to destroy Deir Yassin. But Begin makes it clear that they knew about it and even approved of its operation. Begin says he did the "humane" thing by telling the people to flee from their homes before his attack. It was the Arab villagers' own fault, he thinks, because they did not all flee and leave everything to the Jewish settlers who were soon to occupy the village. When they fought back, then the Irgun invoked its right to "self-defense."

Do Arabs lack the right to fire upon invading Irgun and Lehi attackers? *It was not Deir Yassin that attacked a village of the Irgun.*

The primary goal of this massacre was to terrorize the Arabs into fleeing from their land, for only by their leaving could Jews confiscate it for themselves. Once the Arabs had fled—even if they went to a nearby town to stay with relatives for a time—they would not be allowed to return.

This Zionist definition of self defense is still used today as they confiscate more land and destroy more Arab villages. They come in and tell everyone to leave town, then blow up the town and move Israeli settlers to the land, giving the new settlement an Israeli name. Deir Yassin was no exception. I beg to differ with them on their basic definitions of morality and justice.

This murder was so diabolical that even the Chief Rabbi of Jerusalem, to his credit, excommunicated those who participated in the massacre.

Jacques de Reynier was the Chief Representative of the International Red Cross at the time of the massacre. His report of his inspection of Deir Yassin the day after the massacre may be viewed online at http://www.palestinehistory.com/mass01.htm: It makes grim reading:

> "Suddenly the officer tells me . . . the story of this village populated by 400 Arabs, disarmed since always living on good terms with the Jews who surround them. According to him, the Irgun arrived 24 hours previously and ordered by loudspeaker the whole population to evacuate all the buildings and surrender. There is a 15 minute delay in the execution of the command. Some of the unhappy people came forward and would have been taken prisoners and then turned loose shortly afterwards toward the Arab lines. The rest did not obey the order and suffered the fate they deserved. . .
>
> "Former Haganah officer, Col. Meir Pa'el, upon his retirement from the Israeli army in 1972, made the following public statement about Deir Yassin that was published by Yediot Ahronot (April 4, 1972): 'In the exchange that followed, four [Irgun] men were killed and a dozen were wounded. . . by noon time the battle was over and the shooting had ceased. Although there was calm, the village had not yet surrendered. The Irgun and LEHI men came out of hiding and began to "clean" the houses. They shot whoever they saw, women and children included, the commanders did not try to stop the massacre . . . I pleaded with the commander to order his men to cease fire, but to no avail. In the meantime, 25 Arabs had been loaded on a truck and driven through Mahne Yehuda and Zichron Yousef (like prisoners in a Roman "March of Triumph"). At the end of the drive, they were taken to the quarry between Deir Yassin and Giv'at Shaul, and murdered in cold blood. . . The commanders also

> declined when asked to take their men and bury the 254 Arab bodies. This unpleasant task was performed by two Gadna units brought to the village from Jerusalem.
>
> "Zvi Ankori, who commanded the Haganah unit that occupied Deir Yassin after the massacre, gave this statement in 1982 about the massacre, published by Davar on April 9, 1982: 'I went into 6 to 7 houses. I saw cut off genitals and women's crushed stomachs. According to the shooting signs on the bodies, it was direct murder."

Even today, there are Zionists who deplore this murder. Ami Isseroff, of the Peace Middle East Dialog Group, implores his fellow Zionists,

> "It is long past time for Israeli Zionists, like myself, to apologize. The Israeli government has never apologized for the massacre of Deir Yassin . . . The perpetrators of the massacre at Deir Yassin were never punished."

As you can see, the roots of the present-day conflict go back to the days of Jewish terrorism. *It worked so well for them, the Arabs decided to try the same tactics.* The Jewish state was founded on terrorism by terrorists. This is the true basis of their claim to "the right to exist." This is part of God's reason for prophesying its destruction.

The Violent Take the Kingdom by Force

We have shown from the prophet Jeremiah that there were (and still are) two types of "figs" from the fig tree of Judah. There are good figs and evil figs. The good figs are those that peaceably submit to the judgment of God, and there are those who would rather fight and die (Jer. 24-30). This was true in Jeremiah's day, and it was again true in Jesus' day. Jesus said of these people in Matt. 11:12,

> **[12] And from the days of John the Baptist until now the kingdom of heaven suffers violence, and violent men take it by force.**

Jesus denounced the Jewish belief that the Kingdom of God must be taken by violence and force. Forty years later, God brought judgment and captivity upon Judah, this time at the hand of Rome. It was all for the same reasons that we find in the writings of Jeremiah six centuries earlier. One would think that the people would have learned, since they claimed to believe the writings of Moses and the prophets.

CHAPTER 12
The Israeli State

By the spring of 1947 the British government saw that its presence in Palestine was untenable. The work of the Jewish terrorists had become too successful. It should be noted that it was not Arab terrorism that caused the British to leave Palestine. It was the work of the Jewish terrorists, most notably Menachem Begin and Yitzhak Shamir.

The British government gave the Palestinian problem into the hands of the newly-formed United Nations, which debated the resolution from Nov. 21-29, 1947. The Arab states objected that the Jews would be given any land at all in a partitioned state, but this objection was not feasible, since there were by this time hundreds of thousands of Jews already living along the coast of Palestine and could hardly be expelled at this point.

It was well known that immigration and settlement itself was the most effective means of winning a war. It is difficult to displace that many people who are already living in an area. For this reason, Zionism fought fiercely to bring more Jewish settlers to Palestine. For this reason Zionist leaders were even willing to sacrifice hundreds of lowly Jews for the "greater good" of securing the land.

When the U.N. passed the resolution partitioning the land of Palestine, the conflict escalated. Both sides began a battle to obtain more land. Arabs attacked Jewish settlers, and Jewish settlers began to destroy Arab villages and drive out their citizens. One such example was Deir Yassin, whose story we told in Chapter 11. As of today about 400 Arab villages have been destroyed, and many of the survivors still live in refugee camps.

The British troops finally left Palestine on May 13, 1948, and the Jewish Agency leaders (led by Ben-Gurion) immediately declared a Jewish State. The neighboring Arab countries then declared war. In the attempt to end the fighting, the U.N. sent as its official mediator Count Folke Bernadotte, the nephew of the Swedish king. He was also the head of the Swedish Red Cross.

The Assassination of Count Folke Bernadotte

On Sept. 17, 1948 Bernadotte and his aide, Col. Andre Pierre Serot, were assassinated in Jerusalem for advocating the U.N. plan to partition Palestine and internationalize Jerusalem. Yitzhak Shamir, the head of Lehi (Stern Gang), justified this terrorist assassination on the grounds that the U.N. policy "represented a disaster." On p. 75 of his book, Summing Up, he wrote,

> "The Bernadotte Plan was a development that would have opened the way, without question, to putting an end to the Jewish state within weeks of its birth. . . . Lehi took no responsibility for the deed; the idea was conceived in Jerusalem by Lehi members operating there more or less independently. The assassination was attributed to a splinter group, 'The Fatherland Front'. Israel's Provisional Government acted quickly; it declared Lehi illegal, arrested all the members it could find and broke up the

> Jerusalem units; for a while it both prosecuted and persecuted us. Gera was imprisoned; Eldad and I went into hiding, outlaws again, back in the underground but determined not to fight the State of Israel."

Shamir does not say specifically who was guilty of Bernadotte's assassination, but Alfred Lilienthal writes on page 360 of his book, The Zionist Connection II, about three men who were responsible for this act of terrorism:

> "During a February 1977 press conference marking the publication in Israel of a new book on David Ben-Gurion, The Secret Life of Heinrich Roehm... the late Prime Minister had the names of the three who had carried out the assassination; one of them, Yehoshva Zeitler, was one of Ben Gurion's best friends. Zeitler explained that 'we executed Bernadotte because he was a one-man institution who endangered the status of Jerusalem by his declared intention of turning her into an international city'. . . The decision to kill Count Bernadotte had been taken by three Stern Gang leaders, Nathan Yelin-Mor, Dr. Israel Eldad-Sheib, and Zeitler, commander of activities in Jerusalem and an immediate friend of the first Prime Minister."

At the time, however, the new Israeli government did not know who had actually committed this murder. They did question Shamir in 1948, however, after he had arranged to negotiate with Shaul Avigur, the Deputy Minister of Defense, for a general amnesty. Avigur wanted to know—for the record—who was responsible, but Shamir refused to reveal their names (p. 75, 76, Summing Up). Soon the assassins that had been arrested were freed. After some negotiations,

> ". . . Ben Gurion cut through the tangle to proclaim a 'general amnesty' and the Provisional Government passed a special law so that all Lehi and Irgun members be released, including those already sentenced." (p. 76)

> "Later on, an order was issued which put an end to such judgments by decreeing the destruction of the dossiers of all 'dissidents'—and instructing government offices to treat them like everyone else." (p. 77)

Perhaps the Israeli government was afraid of the Jewish terrorists among them, or Ben Gurion discovered that his friend, Zeitler, was one of the murderers. Whatever the reason, the government decided to assimilate the Lehi and Irgun terrorists into the mainstream of Israeli political and social life, rather than prosecute them for their murderous acts throughout the 1940's. In so doing, they paved the way for the day when these same terrorists, led by Menachem Begin, would form the Likud Party in 1975 and ultimately take over the Israeli government itself.

Zionist Persecution of Iraqi Jews

The Zionists have persecuted their fellow Jews in foreign lands in order to induce them to move to the Jewish State. We have already seen how they were willing to sink the *S.S. Patria* in 1940, killing hundreds of unsuspecting immigrants. But they have done other things as well. Dr. Israel Shahak wrote on page 47 of his book, Jewish Fundamentalism in Israel,

> "The Israeli government induced Jewish immigration from Iraq by bribing the government of Iraq to strip most Iraqi Jews of their citizenship and to confiscate their property."

Alfred Lilienthal writes on page 360 of his book, The Zionist Connection II,

> "In 1950 Zionist agents in Baghdad threw bombs at a synagogue and at other Jewish targets in order to pressure Jews into emigrating to Israel."

Naeim Giladi, an Iraqi Jew, undoubtedly had no idea that his fellow Zionists would do such a thing. He was part of the Zionist underground in his early years, suffering two years of imprisonment and torture in an Iraqi military camp for his Zionist beliefs. He then escaped and went to the Promised Land, arriving in May, 1950. There he soon discovered the reality of Zionism.

I found his story online at http://www.jewsnotzionists.org/iraq.html. He tells how the Labor Office hired him to get Palestinians to sign petitions—written in Hebrew—to the U.N. asking to be transferred out of the Jewish State to Gaza, which was under Egyptian control at the time.

> "I read over the petition. In signing, the Palestinian would be saying that he was of sound mind and body and was making the request for transfer free of pressure or duress. Of course, there was no way that they would leave without being pressured to do so. These families had been there hundreds of years, as farmers, primitive artisans, weavers. The Military Governor prohibited them from pursuing their livelihoods, just penned them up until they lost hope of resuming their normal lives. That's when they signed to leave.
>
> "I was there and heard their grief. 'Our hearts are in pain when we look at the orange trees that we planted with our own hands. Please, let us go, let us give water to those trees. God will not be pleased with us if we leave His trees untended.' I asked the Military Governor to give them relief, but he said, 'No, we want them to leave.'
>
> "I could no longer be part of this oppression, and I left. Those Palestinians who didn't sign up for transfers were taken by force—just put in trucks and dumped in Gaza. About four thousand people were driven from al-Majdal in one way or another. The few who remained were collaborators with the Israeli authorities. . . .
>
> "I was disillusioned at what I found in the Promised Land, disillusioned personally, disillusioned at the institutionalized racism, disillusioned at what I was beginning to learn about Zionism's cruelties.
>
> "And I began to find out about the barbaric methods used to rid the fledgling state of as many Palestinians as possible. The world recoils today at the thought of bacteriological warfare, but Israel was probably the first to actually use it in the Middle East. In the 1948 war, Jewish forces would empty Arab villages of their populations, often by threats, sometimes by just gunning down a half-dozen unarmed Arabs as examples to the rest. To make sure the Arabs couldn't return to make a fresh life for themselves in these villages, the Israelis put typhus and dysentery bacteria into the water wells.
>
> "Uri Mileshtin, an official historian for the Israeli Defense Force, has written and spoken about the use of bacteriological agents. According to Mileshtin, Moshe Dyan, a division commander at the time, gave orders in 1948 to remove Arabs from their

villages, bulldoze their homes, and render water wells unusable with typhus and dysentery bacteria.

"Acre was so situated that it could practically defend itself with one big gun, so the Haganah put bacteria into the spring that fed the town. The spring was called Capri and it ran from the north near a kibbutz. The Haganah put typhus bacteria into the water going to Acre, the people got sick, and the Jewish forces occupied Acre. This worked so well that they sent a Haganah division dressed as Arabs into Gaza, where there were Egyptian forces, and the Egyptians caught them putting two cans of bacteria, typhus and dysentery, into the water supply in wanton disregard of the civilian population. 'In war there is no sentiment,' one the captured Haganah men was quoted as saying."

This is a mere sampling of the things that the Zionists have done to the Palestinians in the name of God and supposedly for the good of all Jews. The extremists cannot understand why dissident Jews do not appreciate them for all the "good" that they have done for their country and for Jews in general. They do not understand that not all Jews condone murder, terror, and biological warfare for the good of the state.

Zealot Attitudes Against Peaceful Zionists

The Likud, along with the increasingly violent and radical settlement movement (called the Gush Emunim), has intimidated many more moderate Israelis into silence for fear of their lives. In fact, if the Israeli government itself should dare to suggest making peace with the Arabs, or to limit the number of new Israeli settlements on Arab land, they run the risk of assassination.

This actually occurred in 1994 when Prime Minister Yitzhak Rabin was assassinated by Yigal Amir. In Dan Kurzman's book about Rabin, Soldier of Peace, page 432, he writes about Rabin's campaign promise in 1992,

"He promised to make peace with the Arabs within nine months and stop building 'political' settlements, while strengthening the army he had built and led to victory."

As early as 1975 while Rabin was Prime Minister for his first time, he was busy negotiating peace with Egypt, laying the foundations for the Peace Accord that was ultimately signed by Egypt's Anwar Sadat and Israel's Menachem Begin in 1978. A main ingredient of this peace was to return the Sinai to Egypt, where the Israelis had already been busy building settlements in order to make such a return impossible. Kurzman writes on page 323 about this peace agreement:

"For most Israelis, the agreement offered the relief of a violent sandstorm dissipating into a tranquil desert wind. But right-wing extremists, especially members of the Gush Emunim, an extremist religious group, were outraged by the accord. When Kissinger had earlier visited Israel, members 'horrified' Rabin and other Israelis by crying anti-Semitic epithets such as 'Jew-boy', while one rabbi referred to Kissinger as 'the husband of a gentile woman.' They demonstrated before the Knesset, and one rightist journalist wrote that the secretary deserved the fate of UN mediator Count Folke Bernadotte, who was assassinated during the 1948 war. Rabin would later rail:

"I felt so thoroughly shocked and ashamed before Kissinger—indeed, before the whole world—that there were no words to express my anguish. I doubt I shall ever witness more deplorable or misguided behavior on the part of my countrymen.

"He was wrong, of course."

When he wrote that Rabin was "wrong," Kurtzman was referring to Rabin's assassination on Nov. 4, 1995. That act was even more deplorable and misguided. Anyone opposing the terrorist policies or the legalized theft of Arab land is immediately demonized as an "anti-Semite" or "self-hating Jew." Those who must resort to name-calling have lost the argument.

This violent suppression of anyone who speaks out against the injustice of Zionists is not a new phenomenon. In an article written May 26, 2000, G. Neuburger tells about the Jewish organization called *Agudath Israel,* "Union of Israel," founded in 1912 . . .

> "to represent the true Jewish people in the world and to unmask the unwarranted and unjust claims of the Zionists. Rabbis everywhere joined Agudath Israel, as did masses of observant Jews.
>
> "Shortly thereafter, Jacob de Haan, a former distinguished Dutch diplomat who was then leader of Agudath Israel in Palestine, initiated talks with Arab leaders with a view toward the eventual establishments of a state there in which Jews and Arabs would have equal rights. In this way he hoped to forestall the creation of a Zionist state. Despite threats to his life, de Haan, fully aware of the ultimate dangers of a Zionist state, continued his talks and negotiations. On the eve of his departure in 1924 for Britain to meet with authorities there, he was assassinated by the Haganah, the Zionist paramilitary force, in the center of Jerusalem as he came from evening prayers . . . .
>
> "The greatest leader of the Neturei Karta [an offshoot of the *Agudath Israel*—ed.] was Rabbi Amram Blau, an inspired and dedicated leader whose compassion equaled his courage. He could not keep silent in the face of injustice, immorality or hypocrisy. He was beloved by Jews and respected by Christians and Muslims. Born in Jerusalem, he never left the Holy Land during his entire life. In his writings he stressed many times that Jews and Arabs had lived in harmony until the advent of political Zionism. Rabbi Blau was imprisoned in Jerusalem, not by the Ottoman authorities, not by the British, and not by the Arabs, but by the Zionists."

Thus we see that Zionism has quite a history of repression and even murder of dissenting Jews as early as 1924. The ultimate goal of this violence is to force all Jews into being Zionists and thus to equate Zionism with Judaism. So it is no great surprise that such murder and persecution would occur as early as 1983 with the murder of Emil Grunzweig, when Jews protested the unjust and murderous policies of Ariel Sharon in Lebanon.

Peace Now organized a rally to protest Sharon's massacre in Lebanon at the camps of Sabra and Shatila, drawing over 400,000 Israelis who demonstrated against Sharon. These advocates for peace were attacked by Sharon's violent supporters. On page 212 of Zealots For Zion, Robert Friedman writes,

> "Several months later, an anti-Lebanon War rally organized by Peace Now in front of the Prime Minister's Office in Jerusalem was violently attacked by right-wing thugs wearing knitted yarmulkes and chanting, 'Begin, Begin, King of Israel.' Women demonstrators were spit upon and told, 'You are Arab women! You should have been in Sabra and Shatila.' Then a grenade was thrown into the crowd, which included many officers from elite combat units. Emil Grunzweig, a young high school math

teacher from Kibbutz Revivim in the Negev, was killed in the blast. Later, at the hospital the injured demonstrators were attacked and beaten, as were the doctors, by Jewish extremists screaming, 'It's a shame that only one was killed!' Not since the clashes between Begin's Irgun and Ben Gurion's Haganah in the 1940's had the danger of serious clashes between Jews in Israel seemed so great.

"In the months following Grunzweig's murder, prominent liberal Israeli academics, artists, and journalists became targets of right-wing violence. Homes and cars were vandalized and firebombed. In one instance, the apartment of a political pollster who reported that a majority of Israelis were ready to trade land for peace was torched. Peace Now founder Dede Zucker was pummeled outside his Jerusalem home by right-wing toughs. Zucker moved to Tel Aviv. The climate of intimidation and fear was encouraged by government officials like Sharon, who publicly labeled members of Peace Now 'defeatists' and 'traitors.' Kahane did the bellicose ex-general one better by calling on his followers to liquidate liberal Jews whose views he found pernicious."

It is apparent that the terrorist mentality of the 1940's is still alive and well, and it has largely taken over Israeli politics today. Those of the Likud Party chanted, "Begin, Begin, King of Israel" as they killed those who objected to the violent side of Zionism.

The terrorists of the 1940's were given full amnesty after establishing their nation, so instead of being brought to justice, they were able eventually to take power and keep all dissenters in line through terror and fear. The terrorists have become statesmen of the Jewish State. They have little moral ground to condemn modern Arab terrorists for doing what they themselves did in the 1940's and 1950's and have continued to do to the present day.

Yitzhak Shamir's definition of a terrorist was given over the radio in 1991, quoted by Jewish author, Robert Friedman, in the introduction to his book, Zealots For Zion, page xxxii,

"Terrorism is a way of fighting that is acceptable under certain conditions and by certain movements," he said, adding that while terrorism was appropriate for Jews fighting for their homeland, it is not for Palestinians who 'are fighting for land that is not theirs. This is the land of the people of Israel'."

This is called a "double standard." In a footnote, it is noted that the Irgun and Stern Gang killed at least 40 Jews to settle personal accounts. Apparently, this too was within Shamir's rights as a "freedom fighter" and does not constitute terrorism or murder.

I suspect that the victims' families might feel differently about this.

CHAPTER 13
The Land War

Zionism, by definition, is a movement that envisions the entire Middle East under Jewish ownership. Many Zionists teach that it is their duty to "redeem the land," and by this they mean the land must come under Jewish ownership. The land is redeemed when it is taken from non-Jews, who are said to have "satanic souls," and transferred—one way or another—into Jewish hands.

Judaism and the Traditions (Precepts) of Men

The underlying problem is that, regardless of their religious claims, these people do not believe either Moses or the prophets. Of course, we write from our Christian perspective. We do not expect adherents of Judaism to agree with Jesus or His followers who wrote the New Testament. Jesus said in John 5:45-47,

> **45 Do not think that I will accuse you before the Father; the one who accuses you is Moses, in whom you have set your hope. 46 For if you believed Moses, you would believe Me; for he wrote of Me. 47 But if you do not believe his writings, how will you believe My words?**

Jesus said that the Jews did not believe Moses, and that this was the reason they would not believe Jesus and accept Him as the Messiah. They believed only the traditions of men, which Jesus severely condemned (Matt. 15:1-8). Jesus concluded in verses 7-9,

> **7 You hypocrites, rightly did Isaiah prophesy of you, saying, 8 This people honors Me with their lips, but their heart is far from Me. 9 But in vain do they worship Me, teaching as doctrines the precepts of men.**

These precepts, or traditions, were written down from about 50 B.C. to about 500 A.D. in a body of Jewish literature called the "Talmud." There are actually two Talmuds: the Jerusalem Talmud and the Babylonian Talmud, each developed in its own area. This is the sacred literature of Judaism. It is NOT the Bible, not even the Old Testament. In Professor Graetz' book, History of the Jews, Vol. 2, page 634, we read that . . .

> ". . . the Babylonian Talmud rather than the Jerusalem Talmud became the fundamental possession of the Jewish race, its life breath, its very soul."

Dr. Israel Shahak writes on page 5 of his very scholarly book, Jewish Fundamentalism in Israel,

> "Jewish fundamentalists believe that the Bible itself is not authoritative unless interpreted correctly by talmudic literature."

Dr. Shahak was an Israeli citizen in Jerusalem for over 40 years until his death on July 2, 2001. He was a professor emeritus of Organic Chemistry at Hebrew University as well as a human rights activist. Dr. Shahak further writes on page 25,

> "The teachings of the biblical prophets, the books of Job and Ecclesiastes and numerous other parts of the Bible are studied neither in the heders [elementary schools] nor the yeshivot [talmudic schools of higher learning] and are therefore unknown to the Haredim [fundamentalists]."

Dr. Shahak is telling us that the religious rabbis do not normally study the Bible itself. They study the traditions of men, which is what men SAY the Bible teaches. The Talmud is often diametrically opposed to the teaching of the prophets themselves.

The Talmudic teachings seldom reflected the real teachings of the Bible. It is often assumed among Christian circles that Jews only need to add Jesus to their Judaism in order to get the perfect religion. This is not true. The Talmud plus Jesus does not equal Christianity.

Jesus, prior to His birth in Bethlehem, was the Lawgiver, the God of the Old Testament. Jesus came to manifest to the world the true meaning of the Scriptures, including the Law. He did this by example and by teaching. His teaching contradicted the chauvinistic teaching of the religious leaders of the day. For this reason, instead of repenting of their false teaching and rebellion against God, they crucified Him.

Classic Judaism's Teaching About Zionism

After the fall of Judea and the cessation of the temple rituals in the first century, the rabbis could not help but understand that God had done this to them because of their sin. However, they never believed that they sinned in crucifying the Messiah. Yet the famous Talmudic passage in *Tractate Ketubot*, page 111, laid the foundation of Jewish thought on the Messiah and the Holy Land. Dr. Shahak writes about this on page 18 of his book,

> ". . . God is said to have imposed three oaths on the Jews. Two of these oaths that clearly contradict Zionist tenets are: 1) Jews should not rebel against non-Jews, and 2) as a group should not massively emigrate to Palestine before the coming of the Messiah. (The third oath, not discussed here, enjoins the Jews not to pray too strongly for the coming of the Messiah, so as not to bring him before his appointed time) . . . During the past 1,500 years, the great majority of traditional Judaism's most important rabbis interpreted the three oaths and the continued existence of the Jews in exile as religious obligations intended to expiate the Jewish sins that caused God to exile them."

Yet there was one dissenting rabbi named Moshe Nachmanides, who died in the year 1270. Speaking of this rabbi, Dr. Shahak says (p. 19) that he . . .

> ". . . opined that Jews should not only emigrate to but should also conquer the land of Israel. Other important rabbis of that time and for many centuries thereafter ignored or strongly disagreed with the view of Nachmanides."

> "In the 1970's, seven centuries after his death, Nachmanides became the patron saint of the NRP {National Religious Party in the Jewish State] and the Gush Emunim settlers."

The Gush Emunim ("Block of Faithful") is the primary settlement movement in the Jewish State that is messianic in its ideology. That is, while they reject Jesus as the Messiah, they are messianic in that they are looking for another messiah that is more to their liking—such as Barabbas, Bar Kokba, or the Eliezar ben Jair, the leader of the Assassins (Sicarii) at Masada.

The Chief Rabbi of Palestine from 1920-1935 was Avracham Yitzhak Hacohen Kook (1865-1935). He was the primary rabbi who developed the most extreme form of Zionism. In 1935 his son, rabbi Tzvi Yehuda Kook succeeded him at his death as head of the NRP until his own death in 1981 at the age of 91.

In 1977 the NRP formed a "holy alliance" with the newly-formed coalition of extreme Zionist parties founded by Ariel Sharon with the help of Menachem Begin. It is called the Likud Party. This was when the Gush Emunim began to exert a huge influence on Israeli policies, particularly in regard to the settlement movement in the occupied territories.

Basic Doctrine of the Gush Emunim

Rabbi Kook was primarily influenced by the ideas of Rabbi Yitzhak Luria, who was the founder of the most influential school of Cabbala (Jewish mysticism) in the 16th century. Luria's book, The Gates of Holiness, taught that all non-Jews have satanic souls. According to Rabbi Hayim Vital, who was Luria's chief interpreter,

> "Souls of non-Jews come entirely from the female part of the satanic sphere. For this reason souls of non-Jews are called evil, not good, and are created without [divine] knowledge." [quoted from Shahak's Jewish Fundamentalism in Israel, p. 58]

This same teaching was echoed by Rabbi Schneerson, who was the head of the Lubovitcher Hassidic movement and lived in New York until his recent death. On page 59, 60 Dr. Shahak quotes from Schneerson's book of recorded messages entitled, Gatherings of Conversations:

> ". . . the body of a Jewish person is of a totally different quality from the body of [members] of all nations of the world . . . An even greater difference exists in regard to the soul. Two contrary types of soul exist, a non-Jewish soul comes from three satanic spheres, while the Jewish soul stems from holiness."

This teaching is not new in the circles of Judaism. The Talmudic writing called Midrasch Talpioth says,

> "Jehovah created the non-Jew in human form so that the Jew would not have to be served by beasts. The non-Jew is consequently an animal in human form, and condemned to serve the Jew day and night."

Since it seems to be insulting to a Jew to equate Zionism with racism, we will not do so. We leave this for the reader to discern. But the basic doctrine of the Gush Emunim is that other people's land belongs to Jews alone. They get this teaching, not from the Bible, but from the Talmud, where we read in Schulchan Aruch,

> "All property of other nations belongs to the Jewish nation, which consequently is entitled to seize upon it without any scruples. An Orthodox Jew is not bound to observe principles of morality towards people of other tribes. He may act contrary to morality, if profitable to himself or to Jews in general."

This Talmudic teaching is their "tradition" of what the Old Testament teaches. As a Christian, I disagree with that tradition, even as I disagree with the Christian tradition that the Jews are to be admired for their Zionistic zeal. In my view, the Bible calls this theft. Later, on page 61 of Dr. Shahak's Jewish Fundamentalism in Israel, he mentions:

> "Ariel Sharon was the Rebbe's favorite Israeli senior politician. Sharon in turn praised the Rebbe publicly and delivered a moving speech about him in the Knesset after the Rebbe's death.

This sheds much light on the personal ideology of Ariel Sharon in his treatment of non-Jews. It explains why the Arabs hate him above all Israelis.

Ariel Sharon

Ariel Sharon's own autobiography, Warrior, tells us much about him, although he omits many things and lies about that which he is forced to admit. He was just 20 years of age in 1948, so he was too young to join the terrorist organizations of Begin and Shamir during the 1940's. But he then joined the military and soon rose to higher ranks.

On October 14, 1953, Ariel Sharon, commander of "101 Unit," was just 25 years of age when he dynamited 56 houses of Kibbiya (or Qibya) one night, killing 67 civilians who were trapped inside and not allowed to leave. Sharon tells the background of this raid in his own words, writing on pages 85 and 86 of Warrior,

> "At times the successes were mixed with tragedy and sometimes controversy, as happened at the village of Kibbiya in mid-October. The raid on Kibbiya was mounted in response to a particularly horrendous incident at the town of Yehud, where terrorists murdered a young mother named Susan Kanias and her two infants, one and three years old, while they were asleep. The police investigation indicated that the killers had infiltrated from the direction of Kibbiya, a Palestinian village near the border . . . .
>
> "The paratroop officer and I were informed that General Headquarters had decided to carry out a retaliatory operation against Kibbiya . . . .
>
> "This would be the first major Israeli reaction to Arab terrorism. . . ."

On page 88, Sharon continues the story:

> "The orders were clear. Kibbiya was to be a lesson. I was to inflict as many casualties as I could on the Arab home guard and on whatever Jordanian army reinforcements showed up. I was also to blow up every major building in the town. A political decision had been made at the highest level."

In Sharon's book he excuses himself, claiming he did not know there were people in the houses. He says on pages 89, 90,

> "According to the radio, sixty-nine people had been killed, mostly civilians and many of them women and children. I couldn't believe my ears. As I went back over each step of the operation, I began to understand what must have happened. For years Israeli reprisal raids had never succeeded in doing more than blowing up a few outlying buildings, if that. Expecting the same, some Arab families must have stayed in their houses rather than running away. In those big stone houses where three generations of a family might live together, some could easily have hidden in the cellars and back rooms, keeping quiet when the paratroopers went in to check and yell out a warning. The result was this tragedy that had happened."

Sharon tries hard to make people think this was just a "tragedy," over which he had no control. And yet he says specifically that his orders were to inflict as many casualties as possible. *Where did he expect those casualties to come from, if not from civilians*? It was, after all, a "reprisal raid" for an attack on a civilian Jewish woman and her two children, killed by an Arab "terrorist" who had no right to oppose Zionist immigration and conquest of his own land.

The incident forced David Ben-Gurion, Israel's first Prime Minister, to make a public apology for Sharon's actions. However, Sharon makes it clear that he was only acting under orders—Ben Gurion's orders! Frankly, I believe he tells the truth here. In fact, Sharon's willingness to murder Arabs is why he rose in the ranks of the military. Sharon writes a very revealing paragraph on page 250 of his book, Warrior,

> "Years before, not too long after I had taken over the paratroopers, Dayan had once said to me, 'Do you know why you're the one who does all the operations? Because you never ask for written orders. Everyone else wants explicit clarifications. But you never need it in writing. You just do it.' Now it was almost twenty years later and absolutely nothing had changed. Anyone other than Dayan would have carefully formulated an order describing what should be done and defining the parameters of the intended action. But from him there was only a signal, the nod of a head. That meant, as it always had, 'Do what you want. If you succeed, fine. If it backfires, don't start looking to me for support'."

So we see the typical way in which Israeli politics was conducted in the years that the Labor Party was in power. They supported terrorism, but did not want to be held liable for their terrorism. So they hired Sharon as their "hit man" to do the dirty work for them. He was happy to do it without written orders, so this would always maintain the fiction that the political leaders were not responsible. It is called "plausible deniability."

Sharon's account of his own innocence is contradicted by Alexander Cockburn's Feb. 6, 2001 article for *Upstream*, entitled "Ariel Sharon—the People's Choice?" where we read,

> "Sharon's order was to penetrate Qibya, blow up houses and inflict heavy casualties on its inhabitants. His success in carrying out the order surpassed all expectations. . . Sharon and his men claimed that they believed that all the inhabitants had run away, and that they had no idea that anyone was hiding inside the houses.
>
> "The UN observer who inspected the scene reached a different conclusion. 'One story was repeated time after time: the bullet splintered door, the body sprawled across the threshold, indicating that the inhabitants had been forced by heavy fire to stay inside until their homes were blown up over them.'
>
> "The U.S. Department of State issued a statement on 18 October 1953, expressing its 'deepest sympathy for the families of those who lost their lives' in the Qibya attack as well as the conviction that those responsible 'should be brought to account and that effective measures should be taken to prevent such incidents in the future'."

Sharon, of course, was never brought to trial, nor was he held accountable in any way. Ultimately, he was elected Prime Minister. Such murders continued unabated, all justified as retaliatory strikes against "Arab terrorism." Sharon himself has never wanted peace and has actively worked against any peace arrangement, believing that the only solution is to drive all

Arabs off the land. This has been the consistent policy of the Gush Emunim's settlement movement, backed by Sharon.

Legalized Theft of Land is Covetousness

Zionism started out as a movement to allow Jews to purchase land in Palestine and live peaceably with their neighbors who may not want to sell their family inheritance. But as time progressed, Zionism became degraded into sheer *covetousness*. To covet another man's land is sin. In fact, covetousness is the most insidious form of idolatry (Col. 3:5). There is nothing wrong with desiring someone else's land, if one abides by the basic laws of humanity. If you want land, then buy it. If you steal it or obtain it by fraud, then it is covetousness and idolatry. Zionists may object to this, but nothing will change this simple fact.

Their main thrust has been to confiscate land and establish Jewish settlements in Gaza and the West Bank territory, while at the same time making laws extremely confining and oppressive in order to "encourage" Arabs to leave the country. These Zionists would like nothing better than to have peace—so long as the Arabs move out of the Jewish state and give their land to the "rightful owners." They have no plans to rule the Arab population with justice and equity. How can you rule them with justice after you have stolen their lands and harshly repressed all who attempt to regain them? True peace is possible only when there is either justice or abject slavery of the victims of injustice.

The settlement movement itself has become the primary successor of the terrorist movements in the 1940's. The settlement of Elon Moreh was built in 1979 upon land expropriated from the Arab town of Rujeb. The Israeli military stole the land on the grounds of "national security," the catch-all phrase that seems to justify all theft. But it was later proven in court that the settlement was actually detrimental to national security, because in case of war, it would tie up troops there to protect the settlers. The high court on October 22, 1979 decided that Elon Moreh had to be dismantled.

Six months later, however, the extremists, led by Ariel Sharon and others, prevailed upon the Israeli Cabinet to expropriate all land that had been previously owned by Jordan, as well as all land that was not officially registered or under cultivation. No longer did the settlement movement have to justify their land theft on the grounds of "national security."

Of course, much of the Arab land had been in their families for generations, extending far back into the days of the Ottoman Empire. Many of them did not have their land officially registered. Thus, April 1980 began the great Arab Land Grab, which is still the single most explosive issue today. It is a policy of legalized theft, and, having no effective legal recourse, those who object violently only give the Israelis more excuses to confiscate more land.

Out of the Elon Moreh case in 1979 the Peace Now movement was formed to counter the extremists in the settlement movement. To their credit, a huge groundswell of Israelis joined their ranks until violent Arab reaction of their own turned many Israelis against Peace Now. Many Israelis recognize that the Palestinians are being abused, but when Arab militants fight Jewish terrorism with terrorism of their own, they lose the propaganda war and expend the moral high ground on the morbid satisfaction of seeing Jewish blood spilt. Not being students of the Scriptures, they do not see that their tactics are of the old Jerusalem, rather than the New Jerusalem. Both sides are convinced that violence and terrorism is the way to resolve the issue.

Neither side looks to Jesus Christ for the answer. And so, more and more blood will be shed until the people are satiated with their bloody religious principles.

By now, with all the violence on both sides, most Americans have long forgotten the original sin that started the conflict. The entire issue has been simplified to a few basic tenets, such as the Zionist claim of "the right to exist." It is not a question of existence—as if the alternative to Zionism is Jewish "nonexistence" (i.e., genocide). It is not even a question of the existence of a state in which Jews may live. The question is whether or not Jews have the right to dispossess the Palestinian population by force and take all the land for themselves.

Shall Jews be given full citizenship, while all others—if allowed to remain at all—should be second-class citizens with fewer rights? Are Jews justified in treating Palestinians as Canaanites, making them "hewers of wood and drawers of water" (Joshua 9:27)? If so, does this also include the thousands of Palestinian Christians?

Consider the case of the village of Birim, a town that has been dead for over fifty years. Israel Shamir [http://www.hoffman-info.com/palestine41.html] wrote about this Christian village in his article, "Exposing the Big Lie About Muslims and Christians":

> "It was not ruined by war. Its Christian inhabitants were expelled from their houses well after the 1948 war. They were told to leave for a week or two for 'security' reasons. They had no option but to believe the Israeli officers and move out. Their village was dynamited, their church surrounded by barbed wire. They went to Israeli court, they went to the government, commissions were appointed and petitions signed. Nothing helped. Ever since, for 50 years, they have lived in the nearby villages and on Sundays they continue to visit their church. Their lands were seized by their Jewish neighbors, but they still bring their dead to be buried in the church graveyard, under the sign of the cross."

It is refreshing to hear from Israelis who are concerned with the basic principles of justice for all people, instead of the narrow nationalistic view that whatever benefits Zionists is always good.

The same situation as in Birim still exists with the now-deserted Christian villages of Kafr Baram and Ikrit. In 1948, when the Israeli army asked them to evacuate for about two weeks, they left eighteen men to guard their property and sought shelter in a nearby village. In 1953 the Land Acquisition Act gave the "uninhabited" land to the government. The army blew up the houses as the villagers watched from a nearby "hill of tears," as the trucks hauled away the ruins. Such has been common practice. Force the inhabitants to move away for a short time, then do not let them return, then finally confiscate "uninhabited" land.

Question: Did the biblical God approve of this? Will Zionist Christians also justify these land thefts in the name of Jesus Christ? Are Christians, too, mere second-class citizens in the eyes of God? Is the Kingdom of God divided into Jewish rulers and Christian hewers of wood and drawers of water? Was "the middle wall of partition" (Eph. 2:14) rebuilt in 1948? If so, who rebuilt it? Certainly not Jesus Christ. But the Church has conspired to help the Zionists rebuild it.

Lilienthal tells of another law that the Israeli government passed in order to "legally" expropriate Arab land. He writes on pages 116-118 of The Zionist Connection II,

"Under the Cultivation of Wastelands ordinance, the government was authorized to take over land not cultivated. Since the declaration of a security zone results in the area not being cultivated, it could then be taken over by the government and given to Jewish settlers, who were permitted to enter and cultivate it. By these and similar means, as early as 1965 some 3,125,000 acres . . . more than 60 percent of the land of Arab Israelis who had never left Israel, had been confiscated.

"Not only did the Palestinians lose their land, they also lost their right to work on the land . . . The minister of Agriculture under Regulation 125 has been permitted to expropriate 'fallow' lands. First, the owner is told he cannot work the land, after a certain period of time the area becomes fallow and the Agricultural Minister can then expropriate it. A former Minister of Defense said regarding this regulation: 'The 125th Paragraph on which the military government bases itself in great measure is a direct continuation of the struggle for Jewish settlement and immigration'."

It was the Zionists who thus took the land from the Palestinians—not the other way around. The Arabs did not drive the Jews out of Palestine. The Arabs did not settle the land until the seventh century A.D. It was the Romans who dispersed the Jews—or rather, it was God who sent His armies to do the job (Matt. 22:7). The Arab population is not at fault and should not be forced to give land to Jews who may covet it for themselves.

Modern Zionism is based upon the assumption that God gave Palestine to the Jews, and that this means the Arabs are living on land that is not theirs. Zionists justify all acts of violence, oppression, and unjust laws against the Arab population by this basic assumption. All Arabs living on land claimed by Israel are treated as if they had stolen land from the Jews. Anyone who disagrees with their claims or their immoral sense of justice is "biased."

Well, let me make a point perfectly clear, in case the reader has not already discovered this: I am totally biased against violent Zionism that, in the name of God, perpetrates injustice upon the Arabs and upon peace-loving Zionists. I am biased by the divine law. I am biased by the prophets of the Bible. I am biased by Jesus and the writings of His disciples. Nothing in this old Jerusalem method reflects the Golden Rule in any shape or form. Nor did Jesus at any time advocate that the Judeans in His day uproot or declare war upon the Samaritans, who had occupied a large portion of the land for seven centuries. Not once did Jesus advocate violence against the Romans. I cannot comment extensively upon the moral principles of Judaism and its various branches, but there is no excuse for Christians to support this violence and theft.

If Christians must support this on the grounds that the Jews are God's chosen people and are privileged to sin with immunity, then what will they say when the Jews lay claim to both Syria and Jordan, as well as Egyptian territory all the way to Nile River? Will they treat the Syrians and Jordanians in the same way they now treat the Palestinians?

Where will it end? When will the bloodshed and injustice cease? Ultimately, these extreme Zionists will demand to rule over the entire world, on the grounds that the God of Israel is to be the God of the whole earth (Is. 54:5). I do not doubt that the Kingdom of God will include the whole earth at some point in time. In fact, I look forward to that day myself. The problem is in the method of achieving that goal. Will it be done by the power of the sword or by the power of the Spirit? Will covetous men rule the world by fear, or will the overcomers rule in love?

CHAPTER 14
Israeli Policy Toward the Palestinians

Jewish author, Robert Friedman, writes in his book, Zealots For Zion, page 73, about the policy of the Likud Party of Begin, Shamir, and Ariel Sharon:

> "Part of Likud's plan was to deny Palestinians residential building permits in an attempt to stem their expansion on land they had resided on from time immemorial and squeeze them into crowded cities."

Israeli government policies have spawned the feeling of hopelessness. An increasing number of Arabs would rather die as martyrs and freedom fighters than live under such conditions. Many of their religious leaders as well have encouraged such martyrdom with their militant brand of Islamic belief. And so there is an increasing supply of suicide bombers, for they have been denied all other methods of obtaining freedom.

They target civilians, because civilians are being used on both sides as soldiers in this war. The Israeli government uses the West Bank settlers as front-line soldiers armed to the teeth. Arab suicide bombers are also civilians, because the Palestinians have no standing army. The success of their missions, of course, solves nothing, but only brings more retaliation and further oppression, as the Israelis forcibly suppress them back into submission. And the cycle of violence spirals higher and higher.

Rabbi Levinger

Rabbi Moshe Levinger is one of the founders of the Settlement Movement and considered by many Israeli settlers to be a hero. His attitude and actions speak for themselves. On pages 6-8 of Zealots For Zion, Jewish author Robert Friedman tells the story of Abdul Rahman Samua, who became the object of Levinger's wrath after the Rabbi's daughter was teased by Arab girls.

> "One afternoon in the spring of 1988, he [Samua] closed the metal shutters on his shop and walked the few blocks home for lunch and a nap. Suddenly, Samua was jolted awake by screams. He came out of his bedroom to find Rabbi Levinger standing in the middle of his living room beating his wife and children while three armed settlers watched. 'Levinger had his hands around the neck of my [seven-year-old] daughter and tried to kill her,' Samua told me matter-of-factly in Hebron. When his nine-year-old son intervened, the rabbi punched the child in the eye, then twisted and broke his arm. Samua's wife, a big woman, scooped up her daughter, holding her tightly. 'Levinger beat my wife on her back with his fists. It all happened in a matter of seconds'. . . .
>
> "By the time a jeepload of Israeli soldiers pulled up in front of Samua's home, Levinger was shouting for someone to fetch his pistol. Levinger's daughter and a pack of her friends, teenage girls in white blouses and black skirts, stood in the front

doorway, egging the rabbi on. The Samuas' television had been kicked in, and the dining-room furniture had been smashed into kindling. Levinger refused to budge, calling one Israeli soldier who tried to shove him outside 'a PLO agent'. '*This is my house!*' screamed Levinger. '*This is my house!*'

"Yisrael Medad, New York-born settlement leader from Shiloh on the West Bank and a friend of Levinger's, explains, 'The fact that an Arab insulted a Jewish child after we've ruled Judea and Samaria for twenty-three years was for Rabbi Levinger simply intolerable. It was an assault on Jewish sovereignty and honor'.

"Palestinians also have a keen sense of honor. But Samua told me that he was afraid to press charges. It was only upon the urging of the Israeli military officers who investigated the incident that he agreed to bring Levinger to trial. 'About eight months later, the Israelis sent a police car to my house and drove me to a Jerusalem court,' recalled Samua. After a brief trial, Judge Yoel Tsur acquitted Levinger on assault charges and on charges that he insulted an Israeli soldier. (The judge dismissed testimony from the Samua family, saying they were 'interested parties.') In dismissing the testimony of the soldier who was the first to enter Samua's home—and who corroborated much of the Arab family's account—the judge ruled that once he left his rooftop post, he was no longer officially on duty. Tsur also acquitted Levinger of trespassing, ruling that when he barged into Samua's home, it was as a neighbor visiting a friend. The state prosecutor appealed to a three-judge appellate court, which, in an extremely rare action, overturned Judge Tsur's ruling. It criticized him for blatantly disregarding evidence and convicted the rabbi of assault.

"Levinger was sentenced to four months in jail on January 14, 1991, the day the world counted down the hours to the Persian Gulf War. When the sentence was read, Levinger bounded over the defense table, shrieking that the court was a tool of Yasir Arafat. His attorney, David Rotem, dragged him outside. The rabbi was sentenced to an additional ten days for the outburst. Sometime later, Samua said, he was closing his shop when three burly settlers wearing knitted yarmulkes and brandishing clubs beat him unconscious.

"There was the time when the rabbi let loose Doberman pinschers on Arab demonstrators. And there was that wild afternoon when he gunned down an Arab shoe-store owner in a fit of hysteria."

Friedman was referring to the time Rabbi Levinger drove to Hebron, parked his car, and walked toward Arab demonstrators, firing his pistol indiscriminately. Friedman writes on page 38 of his book of an incident that occurred in 1988,

". . . Ibrahim Bali, an Arab textile salesman, was buying new shoes for his daughter when he heard the shooting. He was standing outside a shop when a bullet tore through his shoulder. A bullet also ripped into the chest of Khayel Salah, who was about to close the metal shutters of his shoe store. The Israeli Army company commander who witnessed the shooting said that after the rabbi fired his weapon, he walked down the road screaming 'You're dogs' at Arab vendors, kicking over vegetable crates and flower containers. The officer said he grabbed Levinger's trembling hand and told him not to move. Levinger snarled back, 'Leftist! Arab lover'!"

Levinger was finally tried for negligence and sentenced to five months in prison. He was released after serving just ten weeks. Victor Ostrovsky, former Israeli spy for the Mossad, in his book, By Way of Deception, page 335, quotes an Israeli Supreme Court judge who commented upon Levinger's court case:

> "Justice Heim Cohen, a retired judge of Israel's supreme court, said, 'The way the situation is going now, I would be afraid to say where we are going. I never heard of anybody who was tried for negligence after shooting somebody in cold blood. I'm probably getting old'."

Friedman records on page 39 of Zealots For Zion the words of Salah's brother, Khaled:

> "Khaled says the short prison term Levinger received for killing his brother just compounds his family's grief. 'When I see Levinger in the street today with a pistol and a rifle, what shall I do? There is a saying in Arabic, 'If your enemy is the judge, to whom are you going to complain?'"

Friedman also notes on page 4,

> "Ariel Sharon calls Levinger and his wife 'true heroes of our generation'."

This is why the Palestinian people have revolted to the point of giving their lives as suicide bombers. Lack of basic justice has spawned Arab terrorism. There will be no peace, because the Israelis have never ruled Arabs with equal justice for all. Israelis are not overcomers. They are not chosen to rule the world. Zionism is not a godly movement. And God will have no tyrants ruling in His Kingdom.

West Bank Settlements

The greatest obstacle to peace remains the issue of the West Bank Jewish settlements. Jews presently own 42% of the West Bank territory. Yet they want it all and are working feverishly to obtain it all, legally or illegally. Friedman writes on page 118,

> "Rabbi Aviner has put it this way: 'We must settle the whole Land of Israel, and over all of it establish our rule. In the words of [Nachmanides]: "Do not abandon the land to any other nation." If that is possible by peaceful means, wonderful, and if not, we are commanded to make war to accomplish it'."

Gush Emunim ideology teaches that the Messiah will not come if any part of *Eretz Israel* is relinquished. They believe that all Arabs are simply "resident aliens" on Jewish land and therefore have no right to be there at all, much less have their own Palestinian state. From their point of view, the right of a Jewish State to exist means that a Palestinian State has no right to exist.

It is important to them that Jews immigrate and settle the West Bank, because only when all Arabs have been expelled from the West Bank and Gaza Strip can they foment another war with neighboring countries for the purpose of taking more land. Ultimately, their intent is to take all of Jordan, Syria, Cyprus, the Sinai, and even parts of Iraq, Kuwait, and Saudi Arabia. They firmly believe that all of this land belongs to Jews only. The occupation of the West Bank is only the beginning of a long-term strategy to displace millions of Arabs in the region.

This is called "Greater Israel." One of the Gush Emunim's greatest supporters from the start was Sharon.

In the introduction of Jewish author Robert Friedman's Zealots For Zion, written in 1992, he writes:

> "This is a book about the settlers and their controversial enterprise. Whatever its future, the settlement movement has changed the geography and character of Israel. Far more than a massive construction project, it is a marriage of Jabotinsky's militant secular nationalism and Gush Emunim's messianism. Revisionism and militant religious nationalism, both marginal Zionist ideologies for the first two decades of Israel's history, had combined to set the national agenda of the Jewish state. . . . And if Labor falters and Likud returns to power, there may be no turning back. The heirs of Jabotinsky and of the Zealots who fought the Romans will have triumphed over the liberal Zionist idea, the Palestinian Arabs, and the nascent peace process. Four million Jews will then permanently rule two million hostile Palestinian Arabs, and Belfast will seem like Disneyland."

Friedman's greatest fears have now been realized. The Likud Party returned to power under Netanyahu, Barak, and now finally, Ariel Sharon.

One of the earlier West Bank settlements was at Hebron and known by the name Kiryat Arba. It was established in 1970 on land confiscated from Hebron's mayor, Sheikh Humammad Ali Ja'abri. A few years later, in 1973 Rabbis Kook and Levinger formed the Gush Emunim, "Block of the Faithful." Their ideology was that establishing the borders of "Greater Israel," laying claim to the entire land, and filling it with Jewish settlers was the key to Israel's redemption. Rabbi Kook taught vehemently that the Torah forbade them to give up even one inch of land. They call this "redeeming the land." By this they mean that the land is redeemed when ownership is transferred from non-Jews to Jews. Friedman writes on page 75,

> "Indeed, a 1983 report by the Israeli state comptroller said that much of the thirty-one thousand acres of West Bank land bought by Jews had been fraudulently obtained. On August 23, 1985, a *Ha'aretz* editorial strongly criticized unscrupulous Israeli land brokers for conducting business on the West Bank as if it were 'the Wild West.' 'Swindlers must be dealt with in a most forceful manner'. . . .
>
> "*The New York Times* reported on August 20, 1985 that Shamir had ordered the police not to look too deeply into West Bank land-fraud cases, saying, according to the Times reporter, that 'a certain amount of sleight of hand' was needed to obtain land from the Arabs. 'Redeeming land in the Land of Israel often necessitated crafty and tricky devices,' Shamir said in a speech at about the same time."

Consider the case of Moshe Zar, friend of Ariel Sharon, and Iranian Jew who is one of the biggest land dealers on the West Bank. Friedman writes of him on page 25,

> "Residents of the nearby Arab village of Jinsafut say they have lodged hundreds of complaints against him in a Nablus court for fraudulent land deals.
>
> "'When Zar moved here, he was very sweet, very nice, and offered us a lot of money for our land," a Jinsafut resident told me. 'When we said no, he kept persisting. Finally he just showed up in our field with armed men, a bulldozer, and a piece of paper that said the land was his'."

Zar was also a member of a Jewish terrorist organization called the Makhteret, ("underground"). This group was founded primarily to plot the destruction of the Dome of the Rock Mosque. Its chief ideologue was Yehuda Etzion, whose father, Avraham Mintz, fought in the Irgun under Begin in the 1940's. On June 2, 1980 he and his cohorts rigged a bomb to a car owned by Nablus mayor Bassam Shaka. The mayor lost his legs in the explosion. Others in the organization rigged a bomb to the Cadillac of Ramallah mayor Karim Khalif, who lost a foot in the explosion. They also rigged a booby trap at Hebron's soccer field and in a mosque, injuring Arab schoolchildren and adults.

Prime Minister Begin refused to do anything about it, because he had profusely supported the Gush Emunim. But finally, on April 26, 1984 the Jewish terrorists were caught red-handed. Three of them, including Rabbi Levinger's son-in-law, attached bombs to five buses in East Jerusalem. One of the buses had been chartered by a German tour group. Agents of the Shin Bet (Israeli FBI) dismantled the bombs and arrested three dozen of the Makhteret. Friedman writes of this on page 31,

> "In a signed confession, Menachem Livni told Shin Bet that several prominent rabbis, including Levinger, were actively involved in the underground and had 'blessed' the attacks on the mayors."
>
> "After recovering from the shock of the arrests, Gush Emunim sympathizers set up a legal-defense fund—primarily with American Jewish donations collected by Rabbi Weiss, who raised more than $100,000. (About $75,000 of that sum was donated by Charlie Fox, an elderly Jew from Florida who had been mobster Meyer Lansky's bagman.)

Although in 1985 the perpetrators were found guilty, and their sentences ranged from four months to life in prison, the court in Jerusalem also stated for the record that these men should be "praised for their pioneering ethos and war records. The following day Shamir began to press for clemency" (Friedman, p. 32). By 1992 all of these Jewish terrorists were free.

The Jewish Defense League

The JDL was founded in 1968 by Rabbi Meir Kahane and Morton Dolinsky. Friedman tells the story on pages 48, 49,

> "Kahane and Dolinsky met again in 1967 in Laurelton, Queens. Blacks were beginning to move into the quiet, tree-lined, predominantly Jewish, working-class neighborhood. 'Larelton home-owners didn't want blacks in!' Dolinsky said emphatically. 'We knew what would happen to property values.' The prophetic tradition of Judaism teaches Jews to fight social injustice; but as far as Kahane and Dolinsky were concerned, it was Jews who were being mistreated by blacks who were moving into their neighborhoods, taking over their schools, and turning their streets into battle zones of drugs and crime. It was Jewish civil rights, they asserted, that needed to be defended. They created the Jewish Defense League in 1968 to combat these problems. . . . Within a year of its founding, the JDL had evolved into a militant right-wing Zionist organization that used terror violence against its perceived enemies, most notably Arab-Americans and Russian diplomats. Dozens of its members, mostly lower-middle-class Jews from New York's ethnic neighborhoods, fled to Israel, often one step ahead of federal indictments."

Friedman writes further about the founding of the JDL on pages 182, 183,

> "By 1970 the JDL's bombings and shooting attacks against the Soviet embassies in America and Europe were so numerous that, according to confidential State Department documents, President Richard Nixon became concerned that Kahane would wreck the Strategic Arms Limitation Talks...Little did they know that the JDL's guerrilla war against the Soviet Union was orchestrated by right-wing Mossad officers led by Israel's future prime minister, Yitzhak Shamir.
>
> "The secret relationship was forged in December 1969 when Geula Cohen, who had just been elected to the Knesset as a member of Begin's Herut party, visited Kahane in his cramped JDL office on Manhattan's Fifth Avenue. 'Why are you wasting your time fighting the *shvartzers*?' asked Cohen, who had dropped out of Begin's Irgun underground in the 1940's to fight with Shamir's more extreme Stern Gang because she found Begin 'too mild.'
>
> "During the next few months, Cohen, Shamir, and a group of Mossad officers and Jewish businessmen helped lay the groundwork for the JDL's violent campaign to publicize the plight of Soviet Jewry. Cohen and Shamir calculated that the selective use of violence against Soviet targets in America and Europe would inevitably strain U.S.-Soviet relations. They predicted that rather than risk the breakdown of détente, the Soviet Union would be forced to alleviate the crisis by freeing hundreds of thousands of Jews, who would then be herded to the Jewish state. . . .
>
> "Kahane moved to Israel in September 1971, one step ahead of a federal indictment for his role in a number of violent attacks against Russian diplomats based in the United States, and set up the Kach ['This is the way'] party. He frequently returned to America to raise funds, hold demonstrations, and speak at synagogues and on college campuses, where he dispensed a dangerous brew of hatred and violence."

Alfred Lilienthal, writes of Kahane on page 394 of his book, The Zionist Connection II, saying,

> "The five-year suspended sentence given him in 1971 after his admitted manufacture of bombs, harassment of Soviet diplomats, and acts of violence against American and Arab citizens was scarcely believable. Only in a Brooklyn District Court presided over by Judge Jack Weinstein and in an America under Zionist domination could this have happened."

It would appear that Jewish terrorists are treated more sympathetically at least in the New York court system than their Arab counterparts would be treated. And why is it that it is illegal to contribute to an Arab organization that might have terrorist ties, but no one is ever prosecuted for contributing to Jewish terrorist organizations?

In 1982 an American Orthodox Jew, Alan Goodman, went to the Temple Mount and shot two Arabs with an M-16 rifle, killing one and injuring another. Meir Kahane not only paid Goodman's legal fees, but also made him an honorary member of the JDL.

Ariel: Jerusalem Occupied by God's Enemies

The prophetic name of Jerusalem is Ariel. We read in Isaiah 29:1-6,

[1] Woe, O Ariel! Ariel the city where David camped! Add year to year, observe your feasts on schedule. [2] And I will bring distress to Ariel, and she shall be a city of lamenting and mourning; and she shall be like an Ariel to me. [3] And I will camp against you encircling you, and I will set siegeworks against you, and I will raise up battle towers against you. [4] Then you shall be brought low. . . [5] But the multitude of your enemies shall become like fine dust, and the multitude of the ruthless ones like the chaff which blows away; and it shall happen instantly, suddenly. [6] From the Lord of hosts you will be punished with thunder and earthquake and loud noise, with whirlwind and tempest and the flame of a consuming fire.

Who are Jerusalem's "enemies" that have come to camp in the city where David camped? It has been assumed that God was speaking about destroying the non-Jewish enemies who had come against Jerusalem. But that is simply not true. God did not say that He would save the Jews from annihilation at Jerusalem. He was speaking to Jerusalem itself, which would be delivered from God's enemies, the Zionists, who are the avowed enemies of Jesus Christ.

Jesus told a parable about His "enemies" in Luke 19:12-27. The parable is about "a certain nobleman" who obviously was Jesus Himself.

[12] . . . A certain nobleman went to a distant country to receive a kingdom for himself and then return.

Before going to the distant country (heaven) the nobleman gave his servants various amounts of money with the instruction: "*Do business with this until I come back.*" The servants were those that served Him—that is, the good figs, the Christian believers.

Besides the servants in the parable, there are also "citizens." These are the citizens of the kingdom, that is, citizens of the nation of Judea and Galilee in Jesus' day. Of these citizens, Jesus says in verse 14,

[14] But his citizens hated him and sent a delegation after him, saying, We do not want this man to reign over us.

Jesus drew this quote from 1 Sam. 8:7, where the people had demanded a king to rule them. God told Samuel,

[7] . . . Listen to the voice of the people in regard to all that they say to you, for they have not rejected you, but they have rejected Me from being king over them.

When the nobleman in the parable returned from the distant country, he first rewarded his servants to whom the money was entrusted before dealing with the citizens who hated him. Some of the servants had increased his money by lawful trading—that is, buying and selling things of value. One of the servants, of course, was driven by fear, thinking that his master was a hard and unjust man. Verses 20 and 21 reads,

[20] And another came, saying, Master, behold your mina, which I kept put away in a handkerchief; [21] For I was afraid of you, because you are an exacting man; you take up what you did not lay down, and reap what you did not sow.

In other words, the servant thought that the nobleman (Jesus) was a thief. Any man who reaps another man's field is a thief. The nobleman then told this servant in verse 23,

[23] Then why did you not put the money in the bank, and having come, I would have collected it with interest?

Jesus was not teaching us that He had put away the law forbidding interest on money, as many have taught. He was saying to the servant, "*If you really thought I was a thief, then why did you not put my money in the bank, so I could steal from others by collecting interest*?" In other words, Jesus affirmed that collecting interest on money is theft, unless (as the law says) it is a loan to foreigners who are not obedient to the moral principles of the divine law.

Finally, Luke 19:27 turns our attention to the "citizens" who did not want the Messiah to reign over them,

[27] But these enemies of mine, who did not want me to reign over them, bring them here and slay them in my presence.

He was speaking of the Zionists themselves at the end of the age at the return of Jesus Christ. They are the "enemies" of Jesus Christ in the parable, the "citizens" who hated Him and refused to have Him reign over them.

These are also the enemies of Jerusalem itself, "*Ariel, the city where David camped.*" These are the avowed enemies of Jesus Christ who have invaded and conquered Jerusalem today. Jesus said to "*bring them here and slay them in My presence.*" Where is "here"? We are told in the next verse, Luke 19:28,

[28] And after He had said these things, He was going on ahead, ascending to Jerusalem.

It is plain from this prophecy that Jesus prophesied the return of the "citizens" of Judah to the area around Jerusalem. But the purpose of their return is NOT to be blessed, but to be slain for their refusal to have the Messiah reign over them. This is not a tortured interpretation of the passage. This is the plain truth. God Himself said He would bring His enemies to Jerusalem where they would be slain. Most Bible teachers assume that this means the Russians, the Chinese, or the Arabs. But the Bible does not list these nations as God's enemies, except in men's presumptuous interpretations.

Thus, the question arises about the so-called "Russian chapters of Ezekiel." In Ezekiel 38 and 39 the prophet speaks of an invasion of people called "Gog" from the land of Magog. These chapters are commonly interpreted to mean that some day Russia will attack Palestine in alliance with Arab nations for the purpose of destroying "Israel."

Perhaps we need to take a closer look at this.

CHAPTER 15
Gog's Invasion

Most Christians are expecting Russia to invade Israel. They get this from a misunderstanding of Ez. 38 and 39. The invaders are not Russia, but "*Gog, prince of Rosh, Meshech, and Tubal*" (Ez. 39:1). Also included in the list of invaders are Persia, Ethiopia, Put (Libya), Gomer and the house of Togarmah (Ez. 38:5, 6).

Because many theologians have assumed that the Jews are Israel, they first have assumed that Zionism was a movement of Israelites to the old land in fulfillment of Bible prophecy. That was their first grave mistake, for the Jews claim descent from the southern house of Judah, which included only three tribes: Judah, Benjamin, and Levi. While there were certainly a few individuals living among them from other Israelite tribes, such as Anna, who was of the tribe of Asher (Luke 2:36), these other individuals did not constitute other tribal units. The tribal unit resided in the prince of the tribe, and the tribe could properly be said to be where that person was living.

Secondly, many theologians have assumed that the Jews who rejected Jesus as the Messiah continued to carry the tribal name of Judah. But Jesus was the prince of the tribe of Judah, and thus the tribe of Judah itself resided in Him and in those who followed Him. Those who staged a revolt against Him and usurped the throne certainly did take the name of Judah, but it was done so in violation of the law, for by the law (Lev. 17:4) they were cut off from among their people. Hence, non-Christian Jews are not legally of the tribe of Judah—at least not in the sight of God. The only way a Jew can be re-instated into the tribe of Judah is if he quits the revolt and is grafted to Jesus, who is the trunk of the Judah Tree. Those who continue in the revolt are legally defined as God's enemies.

Who is Gog?

Gog literally means "great" or "lifted up." It is spelled *gimel-vav-gimel*. The *gimel* is the third letter of the Hebrew alphabet. The letter *gimel* literally means a camel, but it also carries the symbolic meaning of being lifted up. This is because the camel normally kneels for a rider to mount, and then the camel rises to lift the rider. It can also carry the symbolic meaning of pride—being "lifted up" in one's own eyes. When a camel walks, it holds its head high with its nose in the air. A camel appears to walk with pride.

Hence, the name, Gog, spelled with two *gimels*, literally means "doubly lifted up in pride." The middle letter is the *vav*, which literally means a nail or peg. It also serves as the word "and," because it is a conjunction. A conjunction joins (or nails) two things together. So literally, Gog could be literally rendered "pride and (more) pride."

All nations have national pride, but it seems to be an exaggerated characteristic of Gog in this prophecy. Yet we read in Ezekiel 38 that Gog is "*of the land of Magog, the prince of Rosh, Meshech, and Tubal.*" This is more helpful. The land itself is Magog, who is mentioned in Gen. 10:2 in the genealogy of Japheth:

[2] The sons of Japheth were Gomer and Magog and Madai and Javan and Tubal and Meshech and Tiras. [3] And the sons of Gomer were Ashkenaz and Riphath and Togarmah. [4] And the sons of Javan were Elishah and Tarshish, Kittim and Dodanim.

Madai was the father of the Medes. Javan is Greece, Tubal (Tubolsk) and Meshech (Moscow) are cities in Russia. These places are not often disputed.

Gomer is a bit more difficult to identify. Many theologians identify Gomer with Germany, because the Gimirra migrated from Assyria into Europe, with a large contingent of them going north to the shores of the Baltic Sea about 250 A.D. That history is also beyond dispute. However, the theologians have misidentified Gomer, saying that the Gimirra were from Gomer, son of Japheth and the brother of Magog. They are wrong here. It is a classic case of confusing two people named Gomer.

There was another Gomer in the Bible—the wife of Hosea. This Gomer was a type of Israel, a harlot bride, whom the prophet was told to marry, even as God had married Israel, who had become a harlot in following after false gods.

Gomer (or Ghomri) was the official Assyrian name for the house of Israel, the northern tribes that it conquered and deported to the area south of the Caucasus mountains between the Black Sea and the Caspian Sea. It is there that the historians find the Gimirra. But these people are not descended from Gomer, the son of Japheth. They are Israelites who were called Gomer by the Assyrians. This is proven by all the stone monuments and historical records of the past, including the Black Obelisk of Shalmanezer and the Moabite Stone

Germany, then, certainly represents a large portion of the Gimirra (Gomer), but this does not mean they are descended from Japheth. The Germanic people were largely refugees from Parthia, which fell around 226 A.D. Parthia included the territory of the old Assyrian Empire, and these Gimirra-Israelites had lived there for centuries. When the Persians conquered Parthia, these Gimirra were pushed into Armenia, where they held the line against the advancing Persians. However, that small country was not big enough to house such a huge number of people. Hence, they migrated north through the Caucasus Mountains into Europe, and within 25 years they had settled in northern Europe. They are, therefore, one of the nations formed by the exiles of the northern house of Israel, who migrated into Europe.

Gog represents a people known for their pride, who come from various nations. First, they come out of the land of Magog (the prince of Rosh, or Russia), but they are not the Russians themselves. They come out of Moscow and Tubolsk, cities of Russia. They also come out of Persian (Iran), Ethiopia, Libya, Gomer (Germany), and the house of Togarmah. But they are not Persians, Ethiopians, Libyans, or Germans themselves. They are, in fact, Jewish-Zionist immigrants, who have come out of all of these countries to join a particular struggle and to participate in a war of immigration.

Menachem Begin called it "The Revolt." Nearly everyone called it a "struggle." It was certainly a war, and it was certainly an invasion of "the mountains of Israel." But perhaps the real key is in seeing who Togarmah is today. The house of Togarmah from the north is mentioned in Ez. 38:6 as one of the invaders of the mountains of Israel.

Togarmah in Bible Prophecy

The reason so few people seem to know anything about Togarmah in the modern list of nations is not because of a lack of historical data. It is rather that most theologians are afraid to speak of it above a whisper—if they know anything at all about Togarmah. Yet there is a historical document in Spain that tells us specifically about Togarmah and his descendants.

During the Middle Ages, from about 600 to 1200 A.D., there existed a kingdom in southern Russia all the way south to the Caspian Sea known as Khazaria. It reached its peak about 960 A.D., when the Rus, a Varangian tribe that evolved into the Russian people, began to conquer the Khazars and replace their nation with their own—Russia. According to their own records, the Khazars were descended from Togarmah.

Khazaria was a nation ruled by Jews, or rather, Khazars who had converted to Judaism. Some historians say this occurred around 630 A.D., while others say they were converted around 740 A.D. The precise date of this conversion to Judaism is not important for our purposes. The fact that the Khazar leaders were converted to Judaism is not disputed by any credible historian—Jewish or otherwise. The Jewish Encyclopedia, under the heading of "Chazars," says this about them:

> "A people of Turkish origin whose life and history are interwoven with the very beginnings of the history of the Jews of Russia. The kingdom of the Chazars was firmly established in most of South Russia long before the foundation of the Russian monarchy by the Varangians (855). Jews have lived on the shores of the Black and Caspian seas since the first centuries of the common era. Historical evidence points to the region of the Ural as the home of the Chazars. Among the classical writers of the Middle Ages they were known as the 'Chozars,' 'Khazirs,' 'Akatzirs,' and 'Akatirs,' and in the Russian chronicles as 'Khwalisses' and 'Ugry Byelyye'."

Later, The Jewish Encyclopedia speaks about the Khazar (Chazar) conversion to Judaism:

> "It was probably about that time that the chaghan [king] of the Chazars and his grandees, together with a large number of his heathen people, embraced the Jewish religion. According to A. Harkavy ('Meassef Niddahim,' i.), the conversion took place in 620; according to others, in 740. King Joseph, in his letter to Hasdai ibn Shaprut (about 960), gives the following account of the conversion . . .
>
> "Some centuries ago King Bulan reigned over the Chazars. To him God appeared in a dream and promised him might and glory. Encouraged by this dream, Bulan went by the road of Darlan to the country of Ardebil, where he gained great victories [over the Arabs]. The Byzantine emperor and the calif of the Ishmaelites sent to him envoys with presents, and sages to convert him to their respective religions. Bulan invited also wise men of Israel, and proceeded to examine them all. As each of the champions believed his religion to be the best, Bulan separately questioned the Mohammedans and the Christians as to which of the other two religions they considered the better. When both gave preference to that of the Jews, that king perceived that it must be the true religion. He therefore adopted it."

Interestingly enough, the Khazar Kingdom seems to have been the forerunner of the concept of religious toleration—very much unlike the modern Jewish state, whose laws forbid any attempt to convert Jews to Christianity. In the era of Muslims and Christians persecuting each other in their respective domains, the Khazar Kingdom seems to have had a remarkable religious freedom under Khazar-Jewish rulers. At any rate, according to An Introduction to the History of Khazaria, by Kevin Alan Brook,

> "Under the leadership of kings Bulan and Obadiah, the standard rabbinical form of the Jewish religion spread among the Khazars. Saint Cyril came to Khazaria in 860 in a Byzantine attempt to convert the Khazars to Christianity, but he was unsuccessful, because by that time the Khazars had already adopted a basic level of Judaism. He did, however, convince many of the Slavs to adopt Christianity. . . The Khazar nobility and many of the common people also became Jews. King Obadiah later established synagogues and Jewish schools in Khazaria. Mishnah, Talmud, and Torah thus became important to Khazars. By the 10th century, the Khazars wrote using Hebrew-Aramaic letters. The major Khazar Jewish documents from that period are in Hebrew. The Ukrainian professor Omeljan Pritsak estimated that there were as many as 30,000 Jews in Khazaria by the 10th century."

Mr. Brook's introduction may be viewed online at http://www.khazaria.com along with other items of interest. It is a web site that he calls: "A Resource for Turkic and Jewish History in Russia and Ukraine."

The Khazar Kingdom, ruled by Jews, was conquered, and many of its people scattered. Mr. Brook writes in the same introduction,

> "The Rus inherited most of the former Khazar lands in the late 10th century and early 11th century. One of the most devastating defeats came in 965, when Rus Prince Svyatoslav conquered the Khazar fortress of Sarkel. It is believed that he conquered Itil two years later, after which he campaigned in the Balkans. Despite the loss of their nation, the Khazar people did not disappear. Some of them immigrated westward into Hungary, Romania, and Poland, mixing with other Jewish communities."

In 1976 the well-known Jewish author, Arthur Koestler, brought the Khazar connection to the forefront of modern controversy with the publication of his book, The Thirteenth Tribe. The title of the book was a tongue-in-cheek reference to the addition of the tribe of Khazars to the twelve tribes of Israel. Before that time, American theologians knew little or nothing about the Khazars. Even after this book was published, many went into a state of denial, because of its obvious implications that were detrimental to the Zionist cause that they supported.

Koestler proves the genealogical connection between Togarmah and the Khazarian Jews by quoting from correspondence between King Joseph of the Khazars and Hasdai Ibn Shaprut, the Jewish doctor in the court of Cordova, Spain. Koestler writes on pages 64 and 65 of The Thirteenth Tribe,

> "We now turn from the principal Arab source on the conversion—Masudi and his compilers—to the principal Jewish source. This is the so-called 'Khazar Correspondence': an exchange of letters in Hebrew, between Hasdai Ibn Shaprut, the Jewish chief minister of the Caliph of Cordova, and Joseph, King of the Khazars—or, rather, between their respective scribes. . .
>
> "The exchange of letters apparently took place after 954 and before 961, that is roughly at the time when Masudi wrote. To appreciate its significance a word must be

said about the personality of Hasdai Ibn Shaprut—perhaps the most brilliant figure in the 'Golden Age' (900-1200) of the Jews in Spain. . .

"Hasdai, born 910 in Cordoba into a distinguished Jewish family, first attracted the Caliph's attention as a medical practitioner with some remarkable cures to his credit. Abd-al-Rahman appointed him his court physician and trusted his judgment so completely that Hasdai was called upon, first, to put the state's finances in order, then to act as Foreign Minister and diplomatic trouble-shooter in the new Caliphate's complex dealings with Byzantium, the Christian kingdoms in the north of Spain."

Incidentally, Hasdai lived in Spain during the time that Spain was ruled by Islamic Arabs that had conquered the country in the early 8th century. The Golden Age of Jewry flourished primarily under Islamic rule in Spain. The Caliphate at Cordova (or Cordoba) had been established in 755 A.D. On page 66 of his book, Koestler writes,

"According to his own account, Hasdai first heard of the existence of an independent Jewish kingdom from some merchant traders from Khurasan in Persia; but he doubted the truth of their story. Later he questioned the members of a Byzantine diplomatic mission to Cordoba, and they confirmed the merchants' account, contributing a considerable amount of factual detail about the Khazar kingdom, including the name—Joseph—of its present King. Thereupon Hasdai decided to send couriers with a letter to King Joseph.

"The letter . . . contains a list of questions about the Khazar state, its people, method of government, armed forces, and so on—including an inquiry to which of the twelve tribes Joseph belonged. This seems to indicate that Hasdai thought the Jewish Khazars to hail from Palestine—as the Spanish Jews did—and perhaps even to represent one of the Lost Tribes. Joseph, not being of Jewish descent, belonged, of course, to none of the tribes; in his Reply to Hasdai, he provides, as we shall see, a genealogy of a different kind, but his main concern is to give Hasdai a detailed—if legendary—account of the conversion—which took place two centuries earlier—and the circumstances that led to it."

Koestler devotes many pages to the correspondence, but the most important part of King Joseph's letter for our purposes is recorded on page 72 of his book:

"Joseph then proceeds to provide a genealogy of his people. Though a fierce Jewish nationalist, proud of wielding the 'Sceptre of Judah', he cannot, and does not, claim for them Semitic descent; he traces their ancestry not to Shem, but to Noah's third son, Japheth; or more precisely to Japheth's grandson, Togarma, the ancestor of all Turkish tribes. 'We have found in the family registers of our fathers,' Joseph asserts boldly, 'that Togarma had ten sons, and the names of their offspring are as follows: Uigur, Dursu, Avars, Huns, Basilii, Tarniakh, Khazars, Zagora, Bulgars, Sabir. We are the sons of Khazar, the seventh . . ."

In other words, Togarmah's seventh son was Khazar, the original patriarch of the Khazar tribe and nation that converted to Judaism in the seventh or eighth century A.D. This is, to my knowledge, the only clear reference in history showing the whereabouts of any of the descendants of Togarmah. The family history that King Joseph cites shows that all the descendants of Togarmah moved north into the area of southern Russia and southeastern Europe.

Not all of the Khazars, however, converted to Judaism—nor would we expect this in a nation of religious toleration. No doubt many were Christian, for we see that Saint Cyril had some success in converting people to Christianity. Many were also Muslim. Because of their policy of religious toleration, there were also many Jews who moved to Khazaria to escape persecution in Christian and Muslim territories. So not all Eastern European Jews are necessarily Khazars, but yet there has certainly been an influx of the house of Togarmah into world Jewry, primarily through the Ashkenazi branch.

There seems to be no other identifiable nation in ancient times that carried the banner of Togarmah, other than the Khazars. When their nation was conquered by the Rus, the people were scattered throughout Eastern Europe, with many migrating to Poland, Germany, and Hungary. This branch of Jewry became known as the Ashkenazi Jews. They were—and still are today—distinct from the Sephardim, who claim direct descent from the Jewish survivors of the Roman War in the first century. The Sephardim settled largely in Spain, North Africa, and throughout the Middle East.

Is it not significant, then, that among the relatives of Magog, Togarmah, Meshech, and Tubal are also the people called Ashkenaz? This is the name the Eastern European Jews call themselves. The genealogical table in Genesis 10 looks like this:

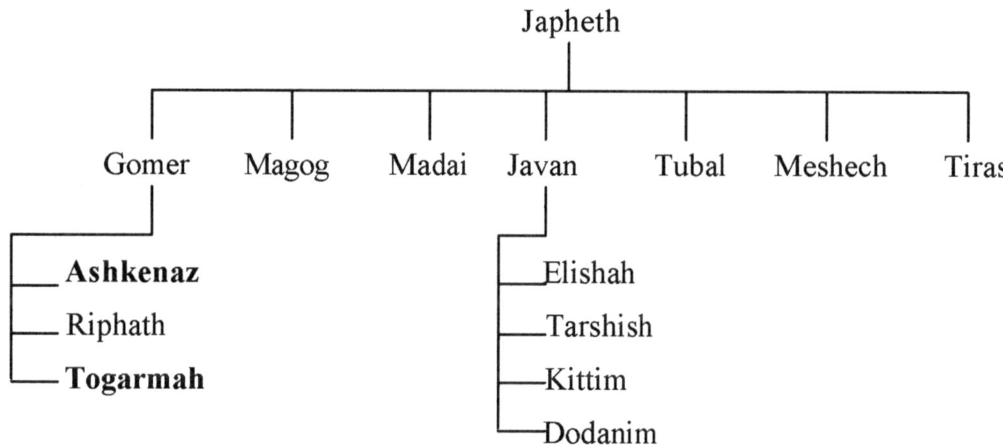

As we can see, Genesis 10 lists Ashkenaz and Togarmah as brothers, two of the sons of Gomer, son of Japheth. Is it then a coincidence that King Joseph traced his own family tree to Khazar, the seventh son of Togarmah—and that this branch of world Jewry is named after Ashkenaz?

The Conquest

Once we begin to see the actual historical proof of the identity of these people, we cannot help but question the teachings of many Bible teachers in regard to the so-called Russian invasion of Israel. While it is no doubt true that Rosh is a reference to the land of Russia, this is not speaking of the Russian people, but to *Russian Jews*, such as Menachem Begin, who immigrated to Palestine as Zionists and conquered that land. They have come from Gomer (Germany) and from Poland, including Yitzhak Shamir. Sephardic Jews came from Persia (Iran) and from North African countries like Libya. Even the Falashis, who are black Jews from Ethiopia, were accepted by the Israeli authorities as authentic Jews.

They came as immigrants to overwhelm the British forces in Palestine and to undermine their authority. They came, not to live under British rule alongside the Arab population, but with the thought of CONQUEST—to establish an independent *Jewish* state, where non-Jews could not have equal rights.

On the other hand, the true descendants of the "lost" house of Israel had long ago migrated out of Assyria and into Europe as Gimirri, or Khumri, Cymri, Cimbri, etc. These people became known as the Celts. Other groups of Israel were called Sakka. The Behistun Rock equates the Gimirri with the Sakka. (See Chapter Fifteen of Secrets of Time.) The Sakka were called Sacae by the Greeks and Saxons by the Romans. These are by no means the only names given to the nations of Israel in the ancient monuments, but they are the main ones. These people became known as the Europeans, called Caucasians, because so many of them crossed the Caucasus Mountains as they left Assyria to migrate into Europe.

These are the true Israelites, according to plain history. These people were never known as Jews, and in fact God caused them to lose their name "Israel" also, for only in this way could they be the "lost sheep" of the house of Israel (Ezekiel 34).

History and archeology have now fully identified where the lost Israelites went. For this reason we are now able to interpret the Scriptures properly, identifying many nations in their prophetic roles in the latter days. The British army under General Allenby had taken Palestine in 1917. The Zionist Jews in their "pride" (Gog) decided to lift themselves up out of the iron yoke that God had imposed upon them for their rebellion and revolt in the first century. And so they came from many nations. They came from the land of Magog, the prince of Rosh. They came from Meshech (Moscow) and from Tubal (Tubolsk). Ashkenazim Jews, descended from Togarmah, came from Eastern Europe, Poland, and Germany. Sephards came from Persia and Libya, and Falashis from Ethiopia.

Zionists came to Palestine at a time when the Israelite nations were living securely (Ez. 38:14), having established themselves in Europe for two millennia. They came in waves of immigrants "*like a cloud to cover the land*" (Ez. 38:16). In fact, Ez. 38:9 makes it clear that they have an initial success in occupying the land. It reads,

> 9 **And you will go up; you will come like a storm; you will be like a cloud covering the land, you and all your troops, and many peoples with you.**

Most prophecy teachers have assumed that this was speaking of soldiers in uniform, perhaps being airlifted as paratroopers. It does not say this. Because of the many wrong assumptions, they have been blinded as to what has actually occurred in the past century. *The invasion has already taken place*! But, like so many prophecies, the invasion took place in a way that few were expecting. Men's assumptions blinded them to the actual fulfillment that was taking place in plain view. And so they missed it.

They assumed the Jews are Israel. They are not. The Zionists are the invaders.

They assumed that Britain was not mentioned in the Bible. They were wrong. Britain is one of the Israel nations. They were in possession of Palestine at the time of the Zionist invasion. While they were, to some extent, victims of their own political policies, they were also the victims of the terrorist activities of the Zionist war against them.

They assumed that Gog was Russia. It is not. It is a people who have a double dose of pride, people who think they are better than others, people who think all others have satanic souls and are therefore not allowed to hinder their aspirations of world dominion.

They assumed that the nations themselves that are listed in Ez. 38, 39 would send their national troops to invade Palestine. They did not. But Zionists came from all of these nations and more to fight in "the struggle."

They assumed that uniformed troops would invade Palestine. This did not happen. They conquered by immigration and by terrorists operating underground.

Ez. 38:10-13 speaks of Gog invading "*a land of unwalled villages*" and coming "*against those who are at rest, that live securely, all of them living without walls, and having no bars or gates.*" Prior to the Zionist invasion, Palestine had relative peace. The Palestinians lived in relative security. One can hardly apply this passage to the Zionists today who are supposedly awaiting an invasion from Russia. The Zionists are armed to the teeth. Their settlements are fortresses, complete with walls, bars, and gates. If we must look for an invasion from Russia in the future, then we ought to see today a Jewish state in relative tranquility and peace. Virtually no one would use these terms to describe the Jewish state today.

During much of the twentieth century, when the Soviet Union posed a super-power threat, it was easier to believe that they were planning an invasion of the Jewish state. But this did not occur, and in the end, the Soviet Union fell. At present, the logistics of a Russian invasion of Palestine is out of the question. The southern republics of the former Soviet Union are now independent of Russia. They have their hands full with their economic problems and do not have the resources to fight a war so far away.

And most of all, the Israelis now have between 150 and 300 nuclear weapons of their own. Being a nuclear power themselves, it is not even conceivable that Russia would attempt to invade the Jewish state. The Jewish state itself is the super power of the Middle East.

All in all, we must conclude that either Ezekiel's prophecy has failed, or it has been fulfilled in an unexpected way. I believe that the latter is true.

The Fall of Zionism and Jerusalem

God makes it clear through the prophet that though they cover the land like a cloud, they will fall there. The invasion will not succeed in the end. Ez. 38:22 says,

> [22] **And with pestilence and with blood I shall enter into judgment with him; and I shall rain on him and on his troops, and on the many peoples who are with him, a torrential rain, with hailstones, fire, and brimstone.**

This terminology was used in Gen. 19:24 about the overthrow of Sodom and Gomorrah,

> [24] **Then the Lord rained on Sodom and Gomorrah brimstone and fire from the Lord out of heaven.**

Moses told Israel that if they violated the covenant and became lawless, that God would judge them like He did with Sodom and Gomorrah. Deut. 29:23-27 says,

> [23] **All its land is brimstone and salt; a burning waste, unsown and unproductive, and no grass grows in it, like the overthrow of Sodom and Gomorrah, Admah and Zeboim, which the Lord overthrew in His anger and in His wrath.** [24] **And all**

the nations shall say, Why has the Lord done this to this land? Why this great outburst of anger? [25] Then men shall say, Because they forsook the covenant of the Lord, the God of their fathers, which He made with them when He brought them out of the land of Egypt. [26] And they went and served other gods and worshiped them, gods whom they have not known and whom He had not allotted to them. [27] Therefore, the anger of the Lord burned against that land, to bring upon it every curse which is written in this book.

In the New Testament, John identifies the city of Jerusalem with Sodom, saying in Rev. 11:8,

[8] And their dead bodies will lie in the street of the great city which mystically [Greek: *pneumatikos*, "spiritually"] **is called Sodom and Egypt, where also their Lord was crucified.**

When God makes the old Jerusalem like Sodom and Gomorrah, then Jer. 19:10, 11 will be fulfilled, where the prophet says of Jerusalem,

[10] Then you are to break the jar in the sight of the men who accompany you [11] and say to them, Thus says the Lord of hosts, Just so shall I break this people and this city, even as one breaks a potter's vessel, which cannot again be repaired. . .

Jerusalem has been destroyed a number of times, particularly in 586 B.C. by the Babylonians and again in 70 A.D. by the Romans. But each time the city was repaired. The day is coming when Jeremiah's prophecy will be fulfilled—the city and its people will be broken like the jar that Jeremiah smashed. It will be broken so badly that it "*cannot again be repaired.*"

The Scriptures are soon to be fulfilled. The destruction of the Jewish state will cause great anxiety and horror, not only among Jews, but also among Christians. Christians have been ill prepared for what is coming, because they have been told that God will destroy the Russian armies with their allies. But because Bible prophecy is going to be fulfilled in a different way from what they expect, they will be at a loss to explain this event.

Worse yet, many Christians have sided with the Jews in their Zionist endeavor, not knowing that the Zionists are violating the law of tribulation. They also do not realize that the Christians supporting Zionism are playing the role of Judas in the second coming of Christ.

Still worse, by not knowing the law or how the prophecy is to be fulfilled, Christians have accepted the enemies of Jesus Christ as brothers in the Lord, treating non-Christian Jews as if they are "almost Christians." In doing this, they have confirmed the Jews in their state of unbelief, and they have helped the Jews immigrate into another holocaust. If they had known the things written in this book, they might have warned them and turned them away from inevitable disaster.

It is our hope, of course, that Jews would come to accept Jesus as the Messiah, for in this way only can they escape the judgment that is coming. The judgment upon Gog is upon the corporate body of people—the nation called "Israel." *It is not directed at every individual Jew.* Any Jew may escape the judgment by refusing to immigrate to the Israeli state. Better yet, he ought to repent of his rejection of Jesus as the Messiah. In so doing, they will not be among those who fulfill the prophecy of Jesus in Luke 19:27 and in Ez. 38, 39.

The day is coming when the city of Jerusalem will be cleansed by a nuclear strike that is clearly described in Isaiah 29:5, 6, quoted earlier. In a nuclear strike, people are vaporized—that is, they "*become like fine dust.*" It happens "instantly" and "suddenly," as the prophet says. It is accompanied by a "loud noise," and the earth shakes as if struck by an "earthquake." The blast creates a huge "*tempest and the flame of a consuming fire.*" Anyone who has seen pictures of a nuclear test know that Isaiah 29:5 and 6 is a perfect description of a nuclear blast.

In this way Jesus' words will be fulfilled in Luke 19, where He says of the Zionists, "*Bring them here and slay them in my presence.*" It is my opinion that Ariel Sharon is the one called to lead the Jewish State to this destruction. It is also possible that the present escalation in the conflict is the beginning of a series of events that will end with this nuclear strike. The Arab nations are very disturbed over Sharon's invasion and reoccupation of the West Bank, the destruction and carnage that he ordered and for which he is personally liable. The U.N. monitors, the Red Cross representatives, and the media were shocked at what they found, and most of the European nations are revolted by Sharon's policies.

Lasting peace is impossible in the Middle East as long as both the Arab people and the Jewish State exist. It is even doubtful if the establishment of a Palestinian State would resolve this problem, because both sides would insist upon having Jerusalem as its capital. Neither side will budge on the issue of Jerusalem. Thus, the war will continue until one side exterminates the other, or until all of them are dead.

As the situation exists today, it is impossible that the Jews would concede defeat and leave the area peacefully. It is just as inconceivable that the Palestinians would accept continued tyrannical rule at the hands of the Israeli government.

Israeli long-term policy has been to make life as miserable for the Arab population as possible in order to encourage them to sell their property to Jews and to emigrate to another country. If they should refuse to leave, the government would simply confiscate the land for "security reasons," that catch-all phrase that justifies all land theft. Some have left, of course, but most of them recognized the policy and dug in their heels, refusing to leave. The pressure on them increased, and the result is continued oppression and tyranny.

CHAPTER 16
The Antichrist

The subject of the antichrist is another of the many biblical themes that is often only partially understood—or misunderstood altogether. Because of this, we must deal with this topic as well.

"Antichrist," is a word used only by one biblical writer. John writes of antichrist five times in two of his epistles. One of these times he writes it as a plural, "antichrists" and another time he refers to "the spirit of antichrist." John seems to speak of antichrist as an end-time individual, but also as a group of people ("antichrists") who have "the spirit of antichrist." But since John himself defines the term for us, let us read 1 John 2:18-23,

> **18 Children, it is the last hour; and just as you heard that antichrist is coming, even now many antichrists have arisen; from this we know that it is the last hour. 19 They went out from us, but they were not really of us; for if they had been of us, they would have remained with us; but they went out in order that it might be shown that they all are not of us. 20 But you have an anointing from the Holy One, and you all know. 21 I have not written to you because you do not know the truth, but because you do know it, and because no lie is of the truth. 22 Who is the liar but the one who denies that Jesus is the Christ? This is the antichrist, the one who denies the Father and the Son. 23 Whoever denies the Son does not have the Father; the one who confesses the Son has the Father also.**

John's primary definition of antichrist is "*the one who denies the Father and the Son*." He explains this, saying that the one who denies that Jesus is the Christ has not only denied the Son but the Father as well. One cannot claim to worship the Father if he rejects the Son. Jesus was the incarnation of the God of the Old Testament.

This statement appears to be specifically directed at the followers of Judaism who had rejected Jesus as the Messiah, and yet claimed to be worshipping the God of the Old Testament. John disagrees with this, saying, "*whoever denies the Son does not have the Father*."

John also gives us certain evidences that help us to put the subject of antichrist into context. He tells us plainly in verse 18 that the fact that "*many antichrists have arisen*" is proof that "*it is the last hour*." John understood that in the "last hour" there would be the rise of antichrist (singular) and antichrists (plural). If there were antichrists already in John's day, how much more today—for we, too, believe that we are now living in the last hour (of the Pentecostal Age).

John further says that these antichrists had at one time been "of us." This can mean one of two things: (1) they used to be part of the fig tree nation of Judah that was under God's covenant, but that by rejecting Jesus as Messiah, they left the covenant and are no longer

Judahites in the sight of God; or (2) they were Judahites who at one time accepted Jesus as Messiah, but later rejected Him and presumably returned to Judaism.

Either way, John's definition of the term "antichrist" would have been understood in his day to be directed at those who called themselves Judahites ("Jews"), claiming to worship the Father, but who had actually rejected the Father by rejecting the Son. John apparently had some revelation that this would occur "at the last hour." Of course, by this broad understanding of timing, "the last hour" would have begun with the rejection of Jesus and His crucifixion.

But the way John describes it, it is as though he expected to see a greater manifestation of this return to Judaism in the last days. John says that "*from this we know that it is the last hour*." He does not cite the rejection of Jesus at the time of His crucifixion, but rather by Christians returning to Judaism after having first accepted Him. The rejection of Jesus and His crucifixion was really the last hour of the previous age, the Passover Age. A second rejection surrounding His second coming would signal the last hour of the Pentecostal Age.

Ignatius, bishop of Antioch in the first century, lived from 30-107 A.D. This makes him a contemporary of all the apostles, though he outlived John by about ten years. It was said that as a small child, he was one of the 500 who witnessed the risen Christ. He wrote a number of epistles, including one to the Church in the town of Magnesia. His Epistle to the Magnesians, Chapter 10, reads,

> "It is absurd to profess Christ Jesus and to Judaize, for Christianity did not embrace Judaism, but Judaism Christianity, so that every tongue which believeth might be gathered together to God."

There is a second, longer version of Ignatius' letter, where this passage reads,

> "It is absurd to speak of Jesus Christ with the tongue, and to cherish in the mind a Judaism which has now come to an end. For where there is Christianity there cannot be Judaism."

Again, Ignatius writes in Chapter 6 of his Epistle to the Philadelphians,

> "If anyone preaches the one God of the law and the prophets, but denies Christ to be the Son of God, he is a liar, even as also is his father the devil, and is a Jew falsely so-called, being possessed of mere carnal circumcision."

Ignatius shows his acquaintance with John's teachings, not only about Judaism, but also he refers to John 8:44, where Jesus said to the Jews who rejected Him, "*You are of your father, the devil*." Likewise, when Ignatius refers to "a Jew falsely so-called," it is apparent that he is referring to Rev. 2:9, where the angel tells John,

> [9] **I know . . . the blasphemy of those who say they are Jews and are not, but are a synagogue of Satan.**

This is essentially repeated in Rev. 3:9, where we read,

> [9] **Behold, I will cause those of the synagogue of Satan, who say that they are Jews, and are not, but lie—behold, I will make them to come and bow down at your feet, and to know that I have loved YOU."**

So we see that Ignatius not only rejects Judaism, but he also puts a great gulf between Judaism and Christianity. He calls Judaism "the synagogue of Satan." He also plainly believes that those who rejected Jesus, for all their claims, are not the true Judahites (Jews) at all. They are only Jews "falsely so-called." These are strong words, and they make manifest the great wedge between the good figs and the evil figs.

Justin Martyr (70-155 A.D.), in his "Dialogue with Trypho," gives us the normal, recommended attitude of Christians toward the evil figs. Justin had met Trypho in Greece some time after the end of the Bar Kokba revolt (135 A.D.) in which Trypho had fought. Justin shows that Jonah, the type of Christ, was in the earth until the third day, and then he preached the warning to Nineveh that after forty days Nineveh would be overthrown. Justin relates this to Jesus and to Jerusalem, saying that after Jesus was in the grave three days, He taught the disciples forty days, and the disciples bore witness forty YEARS until Jerusalem ("Nineveh") was overthrown. Justin then tells Trypho in Chapter 108,

> "Yet you not only have not repented, after you learned that He rose from the dead, but, as I said before, you have sent chosen and ordained men throughout all the world to proclaim that a godless and lawless heresy had sprung from one Jesus, a Galilean deceiver, whom we crucified, but His disciples stole Him by night from the tomb, where He was laid when unfastened from the cross, and now deceive men by asserting that He has risen from the dead and ascended to heaven. . . . Besides this, even when your city is captured, and your land ravaged, you do not repent, but dare to utter imprecations on Him and all who believe in Him. <u>Yet we do not hate you</u>, or those who, by your means, have conceived such prejudices against us; <u>but we pray that even now all of you may repent and obtain mercy from God</u>, the compassionate and long-suffering Father of all."

1 John 2:19 gives us the reason why these antichrists left the faith. It was God's purpose to make manifest their hearts. They had to leave in order that it might be clear to all that they really did not have faith in Jesus Christ from the beginning. Perhaps we can say that they had been persuaded in their minds to follow Christ, but they did not really have faith. Faith and persuasion are two different things. To be persuaded is to be convinced by external evidence, such as reading the Bible. Faith comes by hearing the Word. Persuasion is in one's head; faith is in one's heart. It is often difficult to tell the difference and one must simply await the harvest to see if the people bear fruit or not.

John says to the believers in his letter,

> **20 But <u>you</u> have an anointing from the Holy One, and <u>you</u> all know. 21 I have not written to you because you do not know the truth, but because you do know it, and because no lie is of the truth.**

John was writing to people who did know the truth and who would not depart from it and return to Judaism. John was not writing out of a motive of hatred for those who had rejected Jesus—but neither did he shrink from speaking the plain truth, for only by making the choice clear can men choose to belong to the evil fig tree or the good fig tree.

Christian Judaism in the Last Hour

In the past few decades the delineation between these two trees has become fuzzy once again. More Christians are converting to Judaism than Jews are converting to Christ. Many of those Christians who convert to Judaism think that they can carry Jesus into Judaism. They think that Judaism would be the true religion if only Jesus could be placed on top of all the rabbinic traditions of men.

One prime example of a Jewish convert is Pat Boone. On Dec. 21, 1977 Pat Boone published a letter for the Copley News Service entitled, "Why I Became a Jew." It reads:

> Dear Pat Boone,
>
> More and more I hear you talking about Jewish things on television. My question is, have you converted to Judaism?
>
> Dear Myron:
>
> In a very real way, you could say that I've become Jewish.
>
> This is true of my whole family. Obviously, none of us has been born in a racially Jewish family—but we do strongly identify with the ancient heritage of the people of Israel and feel that we have been adopted into that "chosen" family.
>
> My oldest daughter, Cherry, reads and writes Hebrew, and is married to Dan O'Neill, who not only is fluent in Hebrew, but who lived and worked on two Israeli kibbutzim during the time surrounding the Yom Kippur war.
>
> Occasionally, we have special Hanukkah parties in our home, and attend services at a nearby conservative temple.
>
> Why?
>
> Aren't we Christians? Yes, we are. And that's why we're feeling so Jewish!
>
> What so few people realize these days is that Christianity is a Jewish religion! In fact, as I have explained to a number of rabbis (who have most frequently agreed with me), I see Judaism as divided into four main branches: Orthodox, Conservative, Reformed, and Christian.
>
> <u>We're members of the Christian branch of Judaism</u>.
>
> Abraham is the father of the Arab, the Jew—and the true Christian. God told him that through his offspring, he would bless all the people of the world. And he's done it.
>
> <u>Yes, I have become a Jew</u>. <u>My whole family have become Jews, following the Rabbi and Messiah Yeshua</u>. We have placed our lives and destinies in the hands of the Carpenter from Nazareth who gave His life for us and about whom John proclaimed: "Behold, the Lamb of God, who taketh away the sins of the world."
>
> When my family and I were in Israel a couple of years ago, we discovered that Jews everywhere in that land acknowledged that there was a historical Yeshua who lived around the Sea of Galilee, who performed wonderful miracles, who was crucified outside the city of Jerusalem, and who was a "wonderful teacher." Their faith in the reality of the man Jesus was stronger in most cases than many Christians in this country. But how could a man be a "wonderful teacher" and a demented egomaniac at the same time?

Pat Boone is a classic proof that we are living in "the last hour," when men think there is life in the evil fig tree. Pat Boone is a product of modern evangelical and pentecostal teaching, which supports the evil fig tree, thinking that this tree will some day bear fruit. Is Christianity really just one of four branches of Judaism? No, this is antichrist.

We are living in the last hour, the time of the second appearance of Christ. The evil figs rejected Jesus as King of Judah, denying Him the throne and dominion mandate that was rightfully His. In His second appearance He is rejected again—this time, as the Prince of the tribes of Joseph (Ephraim and Manasseh). In this appearance, His robe is "dipped in blood" (Rev. 19:13), even as Joseph's coat of many colors was dipped in blood (Gen. 37:31). In this second appearance, the conflict is not over the dominion mandate, but over the fruitfulness mandate. It is a question of who is the inheritor of Joseph's birthright (1 Chron. 5:1, 2). It is a question of who has the right to be called by the birthright name of ISRAEL (Gen. 48:16). Does the evil fig tree have the right to be called Israel, or does that name belong to Jesus Christ and to those who accept Him in His second appearance? This is the real issue that faces the Church today. Those who support the right of the evil figs to usurp the name Israel are (unwittingly) betraying Christ in His second appearance, even as Judas supported the usurpers of the throne in Christ's first appearance.

The Literal Meaning of Antichrist

The Greek term, "antichrist," is composed of two Greek words: *anti* and *christos*. In Matt. 2:22 we have an illustration of the meaning of *anti*. It reads,

> [22] **But when he heard that Archelaus was reigning over Judea <u>in place of</u>** [Greek: *anti*] **his father Herod, he was afraid to go there.**

The word *anti* means "in place of" in the sense of someone replacing another. It is more than just acting on behalf of another, such as a vice president who acts on behalf of the president during his absence. The vice president would not dare to do anything that the absent president would not do, for if he presumed to do so, then the vice president would actually be a usurper. The word *anti*, as applied in Matt. 2:22 above, means that Archelaus replaced his father Herod, who had died. If, on the other hand, Archelaus had overthrown his father Herod and then ruled Judea "in place of" his father Herod, men would say that he had usurped the throne unlawfully.

John uses the term "antichrist" in the latter sense. The people had usurped the throne of the true King, Jesus Christ. They were ruling "in place of" or *anti* Christ. This is why John describes the antichrist in terms of those who reject the King, denying that Jesus is the Messiah that the Father had sent to rule the earth.

Judas supported the Jewish leaders and betrayed Jesus. Judas is thus called "the son of perdition" in John 17:12. Paul says in 2 Thess. 2:3, 4,

> [3] **Let no man in any way deceive you; for it will not come unless the apostasy** [*apostasia*, "casting away'] **comes first, and the man of lawlessness** [*anomia*] **be revealed** [*apokaluphthe*, "unveiled"], **the son of destruction** [i.e., perdition], [4] **who opposes and exalts himself above every so-called god or object of worship, so that he takes his seat in the temple of God, displaying himself as being God.**

Paul spoke of this event as taking place in the future. He links it to the "day of the Lord," which, Paul says, will not take place until the "apostasy" first takes place and the unveiling of the man of lawlessness. We know from this that the "day of the Lord" had not yet occurred when Paul wrote his epistle. The "day of the Lord" was the time that the enemies of Christ would be overthrown, and Christ would be given His rightful place as Heir of all things. That is, He would be given both the dominion mandate of Judah and the fruitfulness mandate of Joseph.

But for this to take place, the usurper must be exposed, overthrown, and cast away. It is self-evident that in all this there is "apostasy." But the word *apostasia* literally means "a casting away," not a "falling away," as if someone passively fell. The word *apostasia* is used again in Acts 21:21, where Paul was accused of teaching the people to "forsake" Moses. The word literally means to "cast away" Moses. In that sense, the word can refer to an apostasy FROM the law of Moses. But it literally means to cast away Moses.

So in 2 Thess. 2:3 Paul uses the term again. Something must first be cast aside before the day of the Lord can come. What is it that must be cast away? Paul seems to be saying that the "man of lawlessness" and "son of destruction" must be cast away first. The man of lawlessness is not the same as the son of destruction. The son of destruction is obviously a reference to Judas (John 17:12). The man of lawlessness seems to refer to the Jewish leaders themselves, who had usurped the throne in a lawless manner.

In Acts 2:23 Peter says in his pentecostal sermon,

> [23] **this man** [Jesus]**, delivered up by the predetermined plan and foreknowledge of God, you nailed to a cross by the hands of godless** [*anomos*, "LAWLESS"] **men and put Him to death.**

This same Greek word *anomos* ("lawless") is used again in 2 Thess. 2:8, where Paul says that "*the lawless one will be revealed*" or unveiled by Christ's coming. I do not know why the NASB (quoted above) used the term "godless" instead of lawless. Their mistranslation makes little sense. The Greek word for "godless" is *atheos*. This word is used in Eph. 2:12, where it speaks of the "gentiles" as "*having no hope and without God* [*atheos*, "godless"] *in the world*." On the other hand, the Greek word *anomos* comes from the word *nomos*, which means law. The "a" makes it negative, "lawless."

The fulfillment of the role of "man of lawlessness" and "son of destruction" is no longer a role played by a single individual such as Judas. In the second appearance of Christ, the role is played by a company of people. The man of lawlessness is to be thought of as a collective noun.

So Paul was drawing upon his knowledge of the events in Jerusalem surrounding Jesus' betrayal and crucifixion when he penned the letter to the Thessalonian Church. He saw the man of lawlessness as a corporate body of evil figs led by the chief priests of the temple. Paul saw the son of destruction, or son of perdition, as Judas, the betrayer who helped them usurp the throne and the dominion mandate from Jesus, the rightful King.

Paul says that this "man of sin," in usurping the throne of God in His temple, had replaced Jesus Christ as King. This "man of sin" then "*takes his seat in the temple of God, displaying himself as being God*" (2 Thess. 2:4). Verses 7, 8 continue,

> [7] **The mystery of lawlessness is already at work, only He** [God] **who now restrains** [the evil figs] **will do so until he is taken out of the way.** [8] **And then that lawless one will be revealed** ["unveiled"] **whom the Lord will slay with the breath of His mouth and bring to an end by the appearance of His coming.**

Paul is saying that the evil figs who have usurped the throne of God in His temple will be exposed, revealed, or unveiled at the time of Christ's second appearance. Is this the antichrist?

Yes, of course it is, but it refers specifically to the leaders of Zionist Jewry and also to the leaders of Judaism in general, all of whom are lawless by biblical definition. These rabbinic leaders have blinded the eyes of the common Jews into supporting the revolt of Absalom against David—that is, the Jewish leaders against Jesus.

Likewise, most Christian prophecy teachers today see the rise of antichrist as really a new thing, with very little biblical precedent. They generally do not see (or choose to ignore) the story of Absalom and Ahithophel and how this was a prophetic allegory of the New Testament events. Very few understand how these things have been repeated in the twentieth century with the rise of Zionism and the "State of Israel." For this reason, much of Church teaching has misled the people into becoming one with Judas, betraying their Friend and Master.

It is God, though, who has blinded the eyes of His people in order that the Scriptures might be fulfilled. Even as Israel's eyes were blinded during the entire forty years that Moses led them in the wilderness (Deut. 29:4), so also has the "church in the wilderness" (Acts 7:38) of the New Testament been blinded during its forty Jubilees of wandering under the anointing of Pentecost. None of this could have happened if God had opened the eyes of His people.

Many are expecting a "rapture" to remove the Church from the earth at the beginning, middle, or end of a seven-year tribulation. During this tribulation, they say, the Antichrist will appear as a world leader and will set up his headquarters in a newly-rebuilt temple in Jerusalem. We show in our book, The Laws of the Second Coming, that the concept of the "rapture" needs to be re-defined in terms of the Feast of Tabernacles. It is NOT an escape from the earth, but a transformation of the body. The overcomers who fulfill this feast will have the ability to do as Jesus did after His resurrection. They will be able to "travel" freely between heaven and earth, first teaching people on earth and then ministering to the Father in heaven.

Whether or not a single Jewish leader will emerge as the Antichrist or not, we will wait and see. It makes little difference, though. The important thing to know is that the entire evil fig tree deserves no Christian support, either financial or political. It must be that the lawless ones must usurp the dominion and fruitfulness mandates, but we ought to remain faithful disciples of Jesus Christ and be willing, if necessary, to live with David in the wilderness, rather than in the palace under Absalom.

As for the idea of the tribulation and its duration, we must reserve this topic for another book explaining the Book of Revelation. It is unfortunate that almost never is a topic complete in itself. But this much is written that you may know and not be taken by surprise when events happen in a way different from what Christian prophecy teachers are saying.

The Spirit of Antichrist in the Church

There are, of course, other applications of this term. ANYONE who usurps the throne reserved for Jesus Christ is antichrist. All who support the usurpation are under a "spirit of the antichrist" (1 John 4:3).

We saw earlier that the term "antichrist" literally means "in place of Christ." In the rise of the Roman Catholic Church in the fourth, fifth, and sixth centuries, historians speak of the consolidation of power under one head—Rome. The Bishops of Rome soon came to be called "the Vicar of Christ." A Vicar means one who rules in place of Christ.

Now the term "vicar" can be a rather benign term, so long as the vicar sees himself as "under Christ" and having authority only to dispense rulings and judgments that Christ Himself would have dispensed if He had been ruling on earth in person. Thus also, when David ruled Jerusalem, He was in that sense a "vicar," for he ruled in God's throne but considered himself to be under the authority of God. David dispensed justice as God saw it, not as he himself necessarily saw it. David sought to know the mind of God, so that he would know precisely how to rule the people as God would rule.

But the Roman Bishops have become "vicars" in the other sense of the word. They consider themselves to be above Christ and the apostles and above the divine law. Pope Boniface VIII, who became pope in 1294 A.D. wrote in his Unam Sanctum,

> "All the earth is my diocese, and I am the ordinary [the one who ordains or gives authority] of all men, having the authority of the King of all kings upon subjects. I am all in all and above all, so that God Himself and I, the vicar of God, have but one consistory, and I am able to do almost all that God can do. In all that I list **my will** is to stand for reason, for I am able by the law to dispense **above the law**, and of wrong to make justice in correcting laws and changing them....
>
> "Wherefore, if those things that I do be said not to be done of men, but of God, what can you make me but God? Again, if prelates of the Church be called and counted of Constantine [the pope, not the emperor by that name—ed.] for gods, I then, being above prelates, seem by this reason to be above all gods.
>
> "Wherefore, no marvel if it be in my power to change times and times, to alter and abrogate laws, **to dispense with all things, yea, with the precepts of Christ**; for where Christ biddeth Peter put up his sword, and admonishes His disciples not to use any outward force in revenging themselves, do not I, Pope Nicolas [using another past pope's decree as a precedent to prove his authority] writing to the bishops of France, exhort them to draw out their material swords? And whereas Christ was present Himself at the marriage in Cana of Galilee, do not I, Pope Martin, in my distinction, inhibit the spiritual clergy to be present at marriage feasts, and also to marry? Moreover, where Christ biddeth us lend without hope of gain, do not I, Pope Martin, give dispensation to do the same? What should I speak of murder, making it to be no murder or homicide to slay them that be excommunicated?
>
> "Likewise against the law of nature, item against **the apostles**, also against the canons of the apostles, I can and do dispense; for where they in their canon command a priest for fornication to be deposed, I through the authority of Sylvester, do alter the rigour of their constitution, considering the minds and bodies also of men to be weaker than they were then."

This quote comes from Guinness' book, Romanism and the Reformation, pages 30 and 31. Pope Boniface appeals to the decrees of past popes, claiming the papal right, as Vicar of Christ, to dispense with the laws of Christ and of the apostles. He is saying, in other words, that he is ANTICHRIST. That is, he rules in place of Christ, but has usurped the throne of Christ. The fact that past popes issued such decrees—and he gives examples of such decrees—are themselves the proof of his right to do so! I suppose he claims this right on the grounds that God let him get away with it.

What the Jews did in the Passover Age—making void the law through their traditions of men—the Roman Church did in the Pentecostal Age. Both, in their own way, usurped the authority of Christ. In this way, the spirit of Judas continued to thrive in the Church, and the spirit of antichrist began very early, even in the days of the apostles. In fact, this is not simply a problem of Judaism or Roman Catholicism. The spirit of antichrist is in nearly every denomination of Christianity in the form of the doctrine of "submission to men."

Church members are told that they are in rebellion against God if they are not in submission to a pastor or "recognized" denominational Church. While this is a less extreme manifestation of the spirit of antichrist than that found in the Roman Church, it is there nonetheless. People are taught that there must be a priest between them and Jesus. In effect, they are not allowed to have a personal relationship with Jesus Christ unless it conforms to the doctrines of the denomination. They are often discouraged from hearing the voice of God for themselves, lest they hear something different from what the denomination teaches. Anything God speaks to them must be subject to a veto by the priest or pastor.

This, too, is antichrist. God has not given the five-fold ministry as vicars, but as servants to teach the people how to hear God for themselves, to teach and counsel the people as they grow in Christ and learn His mind. But to usurp authority over them is to rape the bride of Christ, even as Absalom did to David's concubines.

Now, as of August 12, 2002, this is the official theological position of the United States Conference of Roman Catholic Church.

Jews Saved Apart from Christ?

Given the similarity between Judaism and Roman Catholicism—each usurping the throne of God, and each having their traditions of men that nullify the law of God—it is not surprising that these two religions should finally kiss.

From 1948-1993, while the evangelical churches were exulting in the "prophecies of Israel" being fulfilled, the Roman Catholic Church at first refused to recognize the Jewish state as "Israel" and the inheritors of the Covenant with God. But on December 30, 1993 the Vatican finally established diplomatic relations with the Israeli state and recognized them as "Israel." In so doing, they agreed with the Zionists and with evangelical Christianity that the Jews were the lawful inheritors of the fruitfulness mandate given to the sons of Joseph.

Then in March 2000 Pope Paul II visited Jerusalem, proclaiming to the world that the Jews were "Israel" and "the people of the Covenant." Thirty-six years earlier, in 1964, a past pope also visited Jerusalem, but it was not an "official" visit, and he had refrained from calling them "Israel." And so this new policy represented a departure from previous thinking.

The Jews may certainly be the people of the old covenant, but that covenant has been abolished, because the people broke that covenant. That covenant is no covenant at all. It has been nullified for a long time. The only way that ANYONE can be in a covenant relationship with God is through the New Covenant. This comes only by means of Jesus Christ. The Jews of Judaism who reject Jesus Christ are NOT the people of this Covenant. If they will accept the terms of the New Covenant and accept Jesus Christ as its Mediator, then they are welcome to be engrafted into this Kingdom Fig Tree. But Christians have no business becoming Jews and trying to be engrafted into a cursed fig tree. One cannot do so without becoming part of the body of Judas Iscariot.

The ultimate kiss of Judas occurred on August 12, 2002 when the American Bishops of the Roman Church issued their official statement recognizing Judaism as a second true religion that has the power to save Jews apart from accepting Jesus as Messiah.

Their entire statement is online at: http://www.usccb.org/, which is the website of the "United States Conference of Catholic Bishops." The document is entitled: *Reflections on Covenant and Mission.*" This article was issued by the National Council of Synagogues and Delegates of the Bishops' Committee on Ecumenical and Interreligious Affairs. The article gives a history since the Second Vatican Council's declaration in 1965 called *Nostra Aetate*. It says,

> "The post-*Nonstra Aetate* Catholic recognition of the permanence of the Jewish people's covenant relationship to God has led to a new positive regard for the post-biblical or rabbinic Jewish tradition that is unprecedented in Christian history."

In other words, this new teaching is "unprecedented." Neither Jesus nor the disciples taught this. It is a climactic example of the "Vicar of Christ" nullifying the words of Jesus and the apostles, including Peter himself, to whom the Church gives feigned reverence.

> "Knowledge of the history of Jewish life in Christendom also causes such biblical texts as Acts 5:33-39 to be read with new eyes. In that passage the Pharisee Gamaliel declares that only undertakings of divine origin can endure. If this New Testament principle is considered by Christians today to be valid for Christianity, then it must logically also hold for post-biblical Judaism. Rabbinic Judaism, which developed after the destruction of the Temple, must also be 'of God'."

Here they say that because Judaism has endured for the past 2,000 years, they must be "of God." It is ironic that they would issue such a statement just before the Israeli state is destroyed! They are challenging God to either destroy Judaism (and the Israeli state) or leave it alone and let it be validated as being "of God." We ought to watch what God does now to answer this challenge. The article continues,

> "From the point of view of the Catholic Church, Judaism is a religion that springs from divine revelation. As Cardinal Kasper noted, 'God's grace, which is the grace of Jesus Christ according to our faith, is available to all. Therefore, the Church believes that Judaism, i.e., the faithful response of the Jewish people to God's irrevocable covenant, is salvific for them, because God is faithful to His promises."

This is saying that if a Jew is merely faithful to Judaism, then he is saved. They reason that God made an "irrevocable covenant" with the Jews, so that regardless of whether or not they accept Christ, they will be saved by that covenant.

Paul makes it clear that all have sinned (Rom. 3:23). Can any man receive justification apart from Christ? Will Jews be justified by their works, while the rest of "us gentiles" have to be saved by faith in Christ? If this is how a Jew is saved, then no Jew has ever been saved in all of history. The "doers of the law" are certainly justified (Rom. 2:13), but because all have sinned, the law must condemn all men without exception (Rom. 3:19).

To say that Jews are saved by the works of the law is to condemn all Jews, not to save them. The Catholic teaching here may placate the Jews, but they are merely confirming them in their unbelief and to certain judgment. I, on the other hand, do my best to warn them of the judgment to come, both at the Great White Throne and also the more immediate judgment that will surely come upon the Israeli state. They may not like to hear this, but it is what they need to hear.

Paul says in Gal. 1:13 how he acted as a member of Judaism in good standing:

> [2] **For you have heard of my former manner of life in Judaism, how I used to persecute the church of God beyond measure, and tried to destroy it.**

In Gal. 4:25, Paul says that the children of the old Jerusalem are in bondage. But apparently the Catholic Church has decided to leave the Jews in their bondage. Paul also said in 1 Thess. 2:14, 15,

> [14] **. . . for you also endured the same sufferings at the hands of your own countrymen, even as they did from the Jews, [15] who both killed the Lord Jesus and the prophets, and drove us out. They are not pleasing to God, but hostile to all men.**

Yes, their "hostility" is the problem (Lev. 26:40, NASB). The Roman Catholic article continues,

> "This statement about God's saving covenant is quite specific to Judaism. Though the Catholic Church respects all religious traditions and through dialogue with them can discern the workings of the Holy Spirit, and though we believe God's infinite grace is surely available to believers of other faiths, it is only about Israel's covenant that the Church can speak with the certainty of the biblical witness. This is because Israel's scriptures form part of our own biblical canon and they have a 'perpetual value . . . that has not been canceled by the later interpretation of the New Testament'.
>
> "According to Roman Catholic teaching, both the Church and the Jewish people abide in covenant with God."

I can understand the Church not knowing the difference between the Jews and Israel, because God was responsible for causing Israel to be "lost sheep." It was necessary in His plan for Israel to be lost, even as Joseph was lost and presumed dead until his revealing in the end. However, to say that God's "saving covenant" was given to the Jews in the ancient past, and that this saves them even if they continue to reject Jesus Christ, is rank heresy.

It is not that this is really a new doctrine. In fact, the same article explains that it has been pushed by Prof. Tommaso Federici for the past 25 years. The article says,

> "He argued on historical and theological grounds that there should be in the Church no organizations of any kind dedicated to the conversion of Jews. This has over the ensuing years been the de facto practice of the Catholic Church."

Really? So for the past 25 years the Catholic Church has considered Jews to be already saved, so long as they are faithful to Judaism, which hates Jesus and rejects Him as Messiah? Well, it is about time that they make this doctrine public. They continue:

> ". . . the Church must bear witness in the world to the Good News of Christ, so as to prepare the world for the fullness of the kingdom of God. However, this evangelizing task no longer includes the wish to absorb the Jewish faith into Christianity and so end the distinctive witness of Jews to God in human history."

Let me see if I understand this correctly. The Roman Church believes that if a Jew accepts Christ, he will lose his status as a Jew and no longer be one of God's "chosen." If all Jews were to accept Christ, then this would "end the distinctive witness of Jews to God in human history."

Perhaps we ought to admonish Jesus' disciples for following Jesus. Perhaps we ought to chastise the 3,000 who were converted on the day of Pentecost. Perhaps the Great Commission did not include Jews at all. Perhaps Paul erred greatly in preaching in the synagogues. Perhaps Peter himself was wrong in being a minister to the circumcision. Was the early Church working against the plan of God by seeking to convert Jews? It must take a team of serious scholars to come to that conclusion. We continue reading:

> "Thus, while the Catholic Church regards the saving act of Christ as central to the process of human salvation for all, it also acknowledges that Jews already dwell in a saving covenant with God. The Catholic Church must always evangelize and will always witness to its faith in the presence of God's kingdom in Jesus Christ to Jews and to all other people. . . .
>
> "However, it now recognizes that Jews are also called by God to prepare the world for God's kingdom. Their witness to the kingdom, which did not originate with the Church's experience of Christ crucified and raised, must not be curtailed by seeking the conversion of the Jewish people to Christianity."

We thank the Catholic Church for clarifying their heresy in public. My opinion, of course, carries no weight. So I will simply quote Peter, whom the Catholics name and claim as their first pope, who said in Acts 4:10-12,

> **10 Let it be known to all of you and to all the people of Israel, that by the name of Jesus Christ, the Nazarene, whom you crucified, whom God raised from the dead—by this name this man stands here before you in good health. 11 He is the Stone which was rejected by you, the builders, but which became the very corner stone. 12 And there is salvation in no one else; for there is no other name under heaven that has been given among men, by which we must be saved.**

Peter spoke these words to the high priest of Judaism (4:6). It is evident that the Roman Church today is NOT the same Church as it was in the book of Acts. What happened to the Roman Church is the same as what happened to the Old Testament Church. In both cases their traditions made void the law of God. Apparently, they have discovered that the Jews had a right to overrule Moses, even as the Roman Church now claims the right to overrule Jesus and the Apostles!

The Church tells us that God has continued His covenant with the evil figs and that the divine law did not really cut them off from among their people for refusing to apply the blood of Jesus Christ to their heart altars.

The Church taught Replacement Theology for a thousand years, where the Church supposedly replaced the Judah tree. But now the Church teaches that the evil figs of Judaism have been growing and flourishing alongside of the good figs—and that BOTH are in a right relationship with God. Those of the good fig tree must have faith in Jesus Christ; those of the evil fig tree may reject Him, as long as they follow the traditions of men in the religion of Judaism.

If the promises to the Fathers in Israel means that Jews are saved apart from obedience and apart from accepting Jesus as the Messiah, then that covenant is far better than the New Covenant under which the Church operates. Under the New Covenant, men are required to follow Jesus to be saved, and therefore, they say, the vast majority of humanity is doomed to hell. But how fortunate is the Jew, who is under a better covenant than we, who can reject and even hate Jesus Christ and still be saved by following the traditions of Judaism!

If that were true, it would have been far better for Jesus to have never come to give us a New Covenant. Judaism should have remained the one true religion, and men should simply have converted to Judaism. One might ask, "What if a person converts from Catholicism to Judaism? Does his conversion grant him a special privilege of salvation that Catholics do not enjoy? Which covenant is REALLY the "better covenant": the old or the new?

The spirit of antichrist is alive and well.

CHAPTER 17
The Conclusion

The historic events occurring in the world today are part of a long chain of events going back to Adam. This means that in order to understand what is happening today, we must go back to the origins and causes of these events in the first chapter of Genesis. Without understanding the link between Genesis and today's events, it is not possible to view the world as God sees it.

Of course, the most basic of all truths is established in Gen. 1:1, where we are told that God was the Creator of all things. If He created all, then He owns all things by right of creation. With ownership comes sovereignty (ultimate dominion) and responsibility for that which He owns. Hence, the Scriptures always give God the credit for the events in history. While He may not have *directly caused* events to happen, He certainly has the right to take the ultimate responsibility for the events happening.

Man's Use and Abuse of Authority

By right of His sovereignty, He gave man the dominion mandate (Gen. 1:26). This created *authority* in the earth. Authority is always authorized by a higher power, and in this case man's authority is derived from God's sovereignty. While there are limits to man's authority, the authority as such is real. Hence, man is said to exercise "free will" to do as he chooses, and yet in the end we find that God exercises His own Will to bring man's will into alignment with the divine plan.

Meanwhile, history is the time allotted to man to mature from his natural selfishness of childhood to the full maturity of the Sons of God. Children at first tend to misuse any authority they are given. Likewise, history is the story of mankind abusing authority. Governments everywhere and in every age of history have mistaken authority for license. Men have coveted authority, because they have seen it as a means of accumulating wealth and servants. They have not understood the biblical definition of authority, as Jesus portrayed to us, which is the power to be a more effective servant to others. Men have defined power as the privilege to do what others are not allowed to do. Privilege is the power to abuse others with immunity from the law.

The single most important lesson that most of mankind has yet to learn is that with all authority comes an equal level of responsibility. Carnal man, however, naturally desires authority without such responsibility. God has thus given man authority, and man has abused it for six thousand years. The plots and schemes of carnal men have been focused largely on how to overthrow the previous tyrant, so that they themselves can become the privileged tyrants for a season.

Men read history, and they learn one of two things: either they learn how to be a more successful tyrant, or they are repulsed by what they see and learn not to be a tyrant at all. Either they learn by the examples of past tyrants, or they learn the different way that Jesus Christ manifested in His few years of personal ministry on earth. Which path will you follow: the path of carnal man, or the path of Jesus? The path that a man takes will determine his role in the Kingdom of God. The path of Jesus is a difficult path in the six thousand years of history leading to the first great "rest year," the Creation Sabbath, during which time God sets the earth free of its hard bondage to world tyrants. But the path of Jesus will also lead to being placed in positions of responsibility in the seventh millennium, called by many "The Kingdom Age" or "The Messianic Age." (We generally refer to this age as "The Tabernacles Age.")

Those who rule in The Age to come are the overcomers. They are the ones who have learned to exercise the dominion mandate, not lawlessly, but as under God. They have learned to be obedient and to do only what Jesus would do. In other words, they have learned to overcome the natural desire of the flesh that perceives authority as privilege.

Nimrod and Esau: Rivals in Rebellion

The Scriptures speak of Nimrod in Gen. 10:9, 10, whose name means "we will rebel," as being the first major leader to revolt against God's established government on the earth. He revolted against the authority of Noah and Shem, establishing his own kingdom called Babel. This was the beginnings of Babylon, which ultimately became the symbol of all carnal authority and rebellion against the divine law.

Esau studied Nimrod and coveted his position of privilege. And so, when given the opportunity, Esau killed Nimrod and stole his clothing, the skins that God had given Adam. These skins represented—in the eyes of the people—the divine right to rule. Thus, Esau inherited the authority of Babylon that he coveted, and this became prophetic of the desire of Esau's descendants, the Edomites, to rule the world. The primary difference was that the Edomites had converted to Judaism, and hence they used the Bible to justify their right to rule.

In tracing the history of despotic rule throughout the Bible, we are drawn to the study of Babylon and Edom. In the Old Testament we see the rival city-states as Babylon and Jerusalem. Nimrod was the builder of Babylon, while Shem was the builder of Jerusalem. Shem was the legitimate ruler of the earth, since the dominion mandate was passed to him at the death of his father, Noah. But Nimrod represented those who rebelled against the legitimate rule of Shem, who also appears as Melchizedek to Abram.

Like Nimrod, Esau was ruled by the carnal mind, and so he coveted the position of privilege that Nimrod seemed to enjoy. Both were hunters and it seems that both of their personalities were formed by their talent at hunting. Even as they hunted wild game, they also learned to hunt the souls of men.

Edom, Judah, Jacob, and Joseph

Judah conquered Edom (Idumea) in 126 B.C. and annexed their territory, which bordered them to the south. The Judahites forcibly converted all the Edomites to Judaism, and from that point on, Edom ceased to exist as a distinct nation by the old family name. The importance of this merger cannot be overstressed, because the Old Testament prophets foretold the rise of Edom in the end times and its ultimate destruction at the hands of the House of Joseph.

Some have attempted to argue that the destruction of Edom prophesied in Obadiah has already occurred—that the prophecy was fulfilled in 126 B.C. when Judah conquered Edom. However, a simple reading of Obadiah proves otherwise. Obadiah 10 reads,

> [10] **Because of violence to your brother Jacob, you will be covered with shame, and you will be cut off forever.**

There was, of course, a partial fulfillment of this in the past, but this did not exhaust the prophecy. In 126 B.C. it was Judah that conquered Edom, not the House of Joseph that was still in exile. Obadiah's prophecy in verse 18 could not be fulfilled until the revealing of the House of Joseph in the latter days. In fact, Judah's conquest of Edom in 126 B.C. merely set the stage for the events in the latter days, particularly in the 1940's. The spirit of Esau-Edom is seen in the violent methods of Jabotinski, Menachem Begin, Yitzhak Shamir, and all those who participated in the terrorist acts against Jacob, who is represented by Great Britain.

Because Jacob had taken the dominion mandate from Esau in an unlawful manner in Genesis 27, God forced the modern representative of Jacob—Great Britain—to give it back to Esau in 1948. Even though from the beginning God intended for Jacob to receive the promise, this did not give Jacob a license to take it in an unlawful manner. In the same way, in 1948 God intended for Jacob to give it back to Esau, but this did not give Esau a license to take it back in an unlawful manner either. If they had known the plan of God and had believed that God would make it right in His own time, and if they had submitted to the divine plan, there would have been no judgment against them. But they took the birthright from Jacob by violence and force, by murder and terror that they justified under the banner of "freedom fighters." For this reason, Obadiah says, God will bring judgment upon the house of Esau.

Obadiah 15 then shows us that this is an end-time prophecy that was not fulfilled in the Old Testament times:

> [15] **For <u>the day of the Lord draws near</u> on all the nations. As you have done, it will be done to you. Your dealings will return on your own head.**

Obadiah's prophecy against the House of Esau is linked in this verse to "the day of the Lord." Paul tells us in 2 Thessalonians 2:2, 3 that "the day of the Lord" had not yet come during the middle of the first century A.D., and that this day would not come until other events had taken place. Thus, it is obvious that Judah's conquest of Edom in 126 B.C. did not fulfill this prophecy. Further, we read in Obadiah 18,

> [18] **Then the house of Jacob will be a fire and the house of JOSEPH a flame; but the house of Esau will be as stubble, and they will set them on fire and consume them, so that there will be no survivor of the house of Esau, for the Lord has spoken.**

Esau-Edom was consumed by Judah in 126 B.C., and Judah was one of the tribes of Jacob. But Obadiah says that the final fulfillment of this prophecy would come at the hands of Joseph, not Judah. Joseph was the head of the house of Israel, even as Judah was the leading tribe of the house of Judah. The tribes of Joseph were taken to Assyria from 745-721 B.C. and became the "lost tribes of Israel." *These people were not Jews.* They were Israelites, the inheritors of the birthright. Geographically speaking, I believe that Britain represents Jacob, Europe represents the eleven sons of Jacob, and North America represents Joseph, the son who was "separated from his brethren" (Gen. 49:26).

Even as Joseph became two tribes (Ephraim and Manasseh), so also did North America become two nations: The United States and The Dominion of Canada. The International Peace

Arch at the border in Vancouver, B.C. reads, "Children of a Common Mother" and "Brothers Dwelling Together in Unity."

We must conclude, then, that Obadiah's prophecy can be fulfilled only through the tribes of Joseph in the present time—not in Judah's conquest of Edom in 126 B.C. This will happen in the context of "the day of the Lord."

Israel and the Overcomers

The tribes of Joseph, I believe, are represented in the modern nations of Canada and America. However, this does not mean that these nations are particularly righteous in their present conditions. Nor does it mean that all of their citizens are followers of Jesus Christ. In fact, they are in a rather sorry moral condition as of this writing. In order to truly fulfill their national callings, they must make the Bible their only system of justice, and their judges, administrators, and rulers must have the mind of Christ. Anything short of this will continue the slide into lawlessness, oppression, and bondage.

Just because one may be a direct descendant of Joseph or of Israel does not mean that such a person is qualified to rule in God's Kingdom. The vast majority are not so qualified. Therefore, we ought to study the term "Israel" and view it on a higher level than mere genealogy.

Jacob was the first Israelite. He was not born an Israelite. Israel was the name God gave him at the age of 98 after he had wrestled with the angel in Genesis 32:28. It was more than a name; it was a description of spiritual character. It was a name that reflected the fact that Jacob had finally attained to a more enlightened relationship with God than he had had up to then. It indicated that Jacob had become an overcomer, not just a mere believer.

No one is born an overcomer, for no one is born spiritually mature any more than one is born physically mature. There are individuals from all nations who, like Jacob, were not born Israelites, but who have attained a higher relationship with God through trials and troubles. These are the ones who manifest in their lives what the name "Israel" means. Israel means "God rules." In Dr. Bullinger's notes on Gen. 30:28 he writes:

> **"Israel** = 'God commands, orders, or rules.' Man attempts it but always, in the end, fails. Out of some forty Hebrew names compounded with 'El' or 'Jah', God is always the doer of what the verb means (cp. *Dani*-el, God judges)."

In other words, in the final analysis, an Israelite is one who bears testimony to the sovereignty of God. As long as we are mere believers in Christ, we are only of Jacob, the "heel-catcher, or supplanter," for in that immature condition we fancy ourselves as ruling in place of God, supplanting God by our authority. As Jacobites, we perceive authority in terms of privilege rather than servanthood.

The name of Jacob describes the believer who is still partially blind, the one who still is motivated by a spirit of antichrist, one who thinks God needs help to accomplish His purposes in the earth. Jacob thought God needed help to obtain the blessing from his father, Isaac, and so he lied to his father to help God fulfill His Word in Genesis 25:23, "*the elder shall serve the younger.*" Jacob had not yet learned to rest in God's sovereignty. He did not yet truly believe that God was able to accomplish His purposes without a little help from man. Jacob believed in God, but he did not really know God. This lack of understanding caused Jacob to be a supplanter, rather than an overcomer. He supplanted Esau, rather than overcoming him with good.

Finally, after losing the wrestling match with the angel, Jacob could only hang on and ask for the blessing. In losing, he won. At that moment, Jacob died, and Israel was born. Jacob now acknowledged that God was indeed sovereign, and that was when he was given a new name that reflected this testimony. This knowledge helped Israel the next day when he faced Esau. He knew that Esau had come with 400 men to kill him. But God intervened, and Esau was (temporarily) reconciled to Jacob. When they met, Jacob told Esau one of the most profound truths in the entire Scripture in Gen. 33:10, "*I see your face as one sees the face of God.*"

When Jacob had a face-to-face encounter with God (through the angel), his eyes were opened, and he was suddenly able to recognize God everywhere, even in his brother who hated him intensely. When we are able to see the face of God in our bitterest foes, knowing that God has raised them up to exercise us and give us opportunity to overcome, then we are not far from being an overcomer. When we can see God's hand in all things and realize that God really is totally sovereign, then we are not far from being an overcomer. When God opens our eyes by hard experiences to see Him even as He hides Himself from the bulk of humanity, so that we see that He is no longer anonymous in world affairs, then we may take the name "Israel."

The physical nations of the lost house of Israel will be remembered soon. They will take their place at the head of the nations, as prophesied. However, this will not happen until the Sons of God are manifested—those who have the character and spiritual maturity of Israel. Without these people to administer the divine law by the mind of Christ, it would not be possible for the nations of Israel to lead the world in righteousness.

Jacob-Israel is the classic overcomer, the pattern for all overcomers after him. No one starts out in life or in their Christian walk as an overcomer. This is something to be learned by obedience and by the revelation of His character. Only by learning to be obedient to God and recognizing His total sovereignty can anyone hope to rule with Christ in The Age to come. Thus, the overcomers will inherit the highest portion of the dominion mandate given to Adam. The overcomers are also those who will fulfill the fruitfulness mandate in the most perfect manner, for they will manifest the character and works of Christ Himself, once they are endowed with the bodily change that is promised to those who attain the first resurrection. *They will be Israelites indeed*, not because of their genealogy, but by their mature relationship with God.

The manifestation of the sons of God (the overcomers) will cause the national promises to the Israel nations to be fulfilled as well, for the Israelite nations will form the core of the Kingdom of God upon the earth in The Age to come. When other nations see how God has blessed them with Christ-like rulers and judges, they too will join the federation of Kingdom nations until His Kingdom fills the whole earth as the waters cover the sea.

Daniel 2 tells us of the prophetic dream that King Nebuchadnezzar of Babylon was given of the succession of empires that were to rule the earth. The first was Babylon, the head of gold. Next came Medo-Persia, the arms of silver. Third came Greece, the belly and thighs of bronze. Fourth came Rome, the legs of iron, along with its later manifestation of the feet mixed with iron and clay. The fifth kingdom was to be the Stone Kingdom that would crush all of the previous kingdoms in the climax of history. In Daniel 2:34, 35 we read,

[34] You continued looking until a stone was cut out without hands; and it struck the statue on its feet of iron and clay, and crushed them. [35] Then the iron, the clay, the bronze, the silver and the gold were crushed all at the same time; and became like chaff from the summer threshing floors; and the wind carried them away so that not a trace of them was found. But the stone that struck the statue became a great mountain and filled the whole earth.

The stone becomes a mountain. A mountain is a kingdom in Bible symbolism. This prophecy foretells the day when the Kingdom of God will fill the whole earth. All nations will be ruled by Jesus Christ and His children, the overcomers, who will administer His laws according to His mind and intent. This is the heritage of the true Israelites, the overcomers, regardless of their genealogy.

God's Promise to Esau Fulfilled in 1948

God (through Isaac) made a promise to Esau that he would one day receive the dominion mandate, because Jacob had stolen it from him (Gen. 27:40). God chose Great Britain to fulfill this prophecy. For this reason, Britain had to come into possession of Palestine in 1917. They had to be in possession of it in order to be able to give it back to Esau. The British government was unaware of the plan of God in this matter, and for this reason they struggled to maintain control of Palestine. Most of their policy makers did not understand that the Jews contained the remnants of Esau and that God now intended to right the wrong that Jacob had perpetrated upon Esau thousands of years ago. This is why God allowed the Zionists to win the struggle in 1948.

The success of the Zionist goal was not because the Zionists were so powerful, but because God gave them the power to accomplish His purpose. The defeat of the British was not because the British were so weak or corrupt, but because they were called to represent Jacob. They were called to right an ancient wrong on behalf of all the Israelite nations. But they did not realize this, because God had blinded their eyes so that they would accomplish God's purposes without realizing what they were doing.

Recall that Isaac was blind when Jacob stole the blessing (Gen. 27:1), and Jacob took advantage of Isaac's blindness. The judgment of the law of God decrees, "an eye for an eye" (Exodus 21:24). Hence, God blinded Jacob's descendants, saying of them in Isaiah 42:18-20,

[18] Hear, you deaf! And look, you blind, that you may see. [19] Who is blind but My servant, or so deaf as My messenger whom I send? Who is so blind as he that is at peace with Me, or so blind as the servant of the Lord? [20] You have seen many things, but you do not observe them; your ears are open, but none hears.

In Isaiah 44:18 the prophet tells us that God Himself blinded Israel, saying,

[18] They do not know, nor do they understand, for He [God] **has smeared over their eyes so that they cannot see and their hearts so that they cannot comprehend.**

So God blinded the eyes of Jacob's descendants in order to allow Esau to re-take the blessing by stealth. It was an eye for an eye. God imposed a form of blindness upon them in order to judge Jacob for his deceit. It is a case of mistaken identity caused by blindness. First Jacob was mistaken for being Esau. Now Esau is mistaken for being Jacob.

Without blindness none of this could have happened. The only way that the Zionists representing Esau could re-take dominion over the old land was to take advantage of our blindness and misrepresent themselves as fulfilling the prophecies given to Jacob-Israel. Blindness to the divine law hid from many Christians the judgment of God upon Jacob for his crime against Esau. Blindness to the history of the House of Israel and of the House of Esau-Edom hid from many Christians the true identity of the modern nations in prophecy. All of this was orchestrated by God Himself in order to fulfill the divine plan for the earth.

So God saw to it that the whole world recognized Esau as "Israel," for Israel is the birthright name given to the sons of Joseph. In order for Esau to truly possess the birthright, they had to be given the birthright name, Israel. To accomplish this, God spent many years losing the real Israelites by dispersion. In that way only could carnal men and Christians be blinded and so induced into giving up the birthright. God knew that if it were generally known that Europe and its daughter nations around the world were the true physical descendants of Israel, they would not have given up the birthright. Why? Because so few people understand the divine law and how God would restore the lawful order in the dispute between Jacob and Esau. And so, if God had not "lost" the real tribes of Israel, His purposes never would have been accomplished.

In 1948 God fulfilled this obligation to Esau through their descendants who were absorbed into Judaism. *The Jews were unable to take Palestine under the banner of Judah, but they were able to do so under the banner of Esau.* God did not owe the bad figs of Judah anything, any more than King David owed Absalom anything for usurping his throne. But God did owe Esau an opportunity to own and use the birthright and the dominion mandate. That is why God did this. But that is also why the Zionists took it by violence and theft. That is the character of Esau.

God had a legal obligation to fulfill toward Esau, lest his descendants would have any legal cause against God and be able to accuse Him of injustice at the Great White Throne. In fact, God even gave Esau the best and most prosperous years in all of history.

And yet, while we may view this as a "bad" thing from the earthly perspective, we can only praise God for His wisdom, justice, and mercy toward all. From the divine perspective, we can see that Zionism, for all its carnality, is fulfilling the plan of God. We can see the face of God in Esau and rejoice, for this is a prime example, not of injustice, but of divine justice, giving Esau what is lawfully due to him. If God is so just as to give even Esau true justice in the divine court, then we can know for certain that He will do what is right for all men, regardless of their condition.

For this reason, we do not hate anyone, nor do we preach hatred at all. Hatred is not a Christian virtue, not even when directed at one's perceived enemies. We simply believe that the time has come when God is opening the eyes of the blind. It is the time when God is revealing His true purposes, including His purpose for the Zionist state. We believe that the fruit of Zionism has been tasted and found to be bitter fruit that is unfit for consumption, even as it was in the days of Jeremiah. But until the fruit was ripe, it was not generally known that it would be so bitter. So it is now possible for men to see what they could not see in past years.

It is unfortunate that the Palestinians and the Arab world in general do not have this revelation, nor do they understand why God allowed Zionists to steal their land and to oppress them with unjust laws designed to encourage them to leave. All they understand is that the Zionists have done them injustice. If they had known the mind of God, they might have submitted to it for a season, knowing that in the end God would reward them for submitting to

His judgments. But like most of the Christian world, they did not know, and there was no one to tell them, even if they could have accepted it. And so, many of them fought back with terrorism and violence of their own, not believing that God was able to rectify the situation without their help. This only made the situation worse, as the Israelis responded by increasing the oppression and the bloodshed. In every new war, the Israelis took more land for themselves and expelled or disenfranchised more Palestinians.

Even so, God has used the Arabs to judge the Israelis, blood for blood, even as the prophecy about Edom in Ez. 35:6 tells us,

> 6 **Therefore, as I live, declares the Lord God, I will give you over to bloodshed** [Heb. *dam*, "blood"], **and bloodshed** [*dam*] **will pursue you; since you have not hated bloodshed** [*dam*], **therefore bloodshed** [*dam*] **will pursue you.**

This is a play on words. "Edom" means red, for it comes from the Hebrew word *dam*, which means blood. This is similar to "Adam," which means ruddy, or reddish. The problem began with Adam, but Edom became the prime inheritor of the carnal man, fallen man, and his lawless ways.

Even as Edom has pursued blood as its national pursuit, so also will others do the same to them. Zionism has pursued blood, not only in its 1940's policy of terrorism to achieve its goals, but also in its religious belief that vengeance is a sacred duty. But the Arab policy in Islamic fundamentalism is the same. Vengeance is a sacred duty before God. Hence, God has placed each side in judgment of the other until the day that the Sons of God are manifested. Only then will all men begin to see that the earth must be ruled by Jesus Christ, the Prince of Peace, for they will see His character in His Sons.

Vengeance may be a virtue to many people in the religions of Judaism and Islam—and even in various denominations that call themselves Christian—but it is not a Christian virtue. It is not a virtue either in the Old Testament or the New. The law says in Deuteronomy 32:35,

> 35 **<u>Vengeance is Mine</u>, and retribution, in due time their foot will slip; for the day of their calamity is near, and the impending things are hastening upon them.** 36 **For the Lord will vindicate His people . . . .**

In other words, God says to leave vengeance to Him, because only He knows how to avenge with a perfect attitude and with perfect justice and mercy. Man does not know how to do it, because his emotions get in the way, and his heart does not know the end from the beginning. Furthermore, Solomon himself tells us in Prov. 25:21, 22,

> 21 **If your enemy is hungry, give him food to eat; and if he is thirsty, give him water to drink;** 22 **For you will heap burning coals on his head, and the Lord will reward you.**

To put fire on someone's head was not a bad thing in those days. When a family was away from home for any length of time, their fire would be extinguished. When they returned home, the wife often went to their neighbor's house and asked for a few live coals to make it easier to restart the fire. They had no matches in those days. A generous neighbor would heap coals of fire into her clay jar, which she carried on her head back to her home. A bad neighbor might not give her any at all. Solomon relates this to all of one's enemies. Be good to them, and give them more than they request or deserve.

The Apostle Paul quotes both Deuteronomy and Proverbs in Rom. 12:19-21, with comments, showing how far he had progressed from his early views when he had been a Pharisee in good standing.

[19] Never take your own revenge, beloved, but leave room for the wrath of God, for it is written, Vengeance is Mine, I will repay, says the Lord. [20] But if your enemy is hungry, feed him, and if he is thirsty, give him a drink; for in so doing you will heap burning coals upon his head. [21] Do not be overcome by evil, but overcome evil with good.

Rabbi Moshe Levinger (Chapter Fourteen) and others like him obviously have a different interpretation of Moses and Solomon. Their traditions of men have nullified the word of God. This is because such people do not believe that doing good to the Palestinians would overcome the evil of Arab terrorism. Perhaps at this point they are right. But if, from the beginning, the Zionists had come to Palestine with proper motives, that area would be quite different today.

The Zionists should have listened to Jesus, for He was the One who gave the law to Moses, and He was the only One who could give an accurate interpretation of the law. Jesus said in Matt. 5:43-48,

[43] You have heard that it was said, You shall love your neighbor and hate your enemy. [44] But I say to you, love your enemies, and pray for those who persecute you [45] in order that you may be sons of your Father who is in heaven; for He causes His sun to rise on the evil and the good, and sends rain on the righteous and the unrighteous. [46] For if you love those who love you, what reward have you? Do not even the tax-gatherers do the same? [47] And if you greet your brothers only, what do you do more than others? Do not even the Gentiles do the same? [48] Therefore you are to be perfect, as your heavenly Father is perfect.

Iin other words, the idea that God allows or even demands that they hate their enemies is absolutely wrong. Such an interpretation of Scripture is not according to the mind of Christ.

Let us then observe what our heavenly Father does, and imitate Him as Jesus says. In so doing, we may be the sons and daughters of our Father who is in heaven. It is by studying the law that we are given the missing revelation of what God is doing in the world today to fulfill prophecy. To understand the full plan of God, one must live by "*every word that proceeds out of the mouth of God*" (Matt. 4:4). That word begins in Genesis 1:1. But that word does NOT end with Revelation 22:21, for God speaks to each one of us, as we are led by the Holy Spirit. The word continues each day as God speaks to us, and that word gives life.

The Way of True Freedom

Most of humanity has an innate desire to be free. This is, in fact, the most important motive behind all revolutions. Men struggle against bondage with the power of their own flesh. But history has shown that bondage is often like quicksand; the more one struggles, the deeper one sinks. This is because men almost always fail to obtain their freedom through Jesus Christ. Jesus lived under the oppression of the Roman Empire and under the greater oppression of the Jewish leaders in His day. Yet Jesus led no political or military revolutions, but said to the Jews in John 8:32, "*the truth shall make you free.*"

This was a radical departure from the way in which most people believed, both in that day and today. Jesus knew the real causes of the nation's loss of independence and freedom. The book of Jeremiah showed clearly that God had put them into bondage because the people did not believe the truth of His Word. Hence, to fight Rome was to fight God's judgment that He had imposed upon the nation for their disobedience. The only real path to freedom lay in their belief in the truth—the word of Jesus Christ. For this reason Jesus said in John 8:24,

> [24] **I said therefore to you, that you shall die in your sins; for unless you believe that I am He, you shall die in your sins.**

To those who did believe in Him, He said in verses 31 and 32,

> [31] **Jesus therefore was saying to those Jews who had believed Him, If you abide in My word, then you are truly disciples of Mine; [32] and you shall know the truth, and the truth shall make you free.**

History is full of examples of men who have attempted to gain freedom apart from Christ. None have succeeded. Nimrod thought that freedom meant putting everyone else into bondage to himself, so he formed the original Babylonian Kingdom for that purpose. Though he gained many servants, he himself remained a servant to the bondage of the flesh. Later, Esau wanted to inherit God's Kingdom by the power of his own strength and without submitting to the training of God. But he lost what he desired most and his descendants were finally conquered and absorbed in Jewry.

The Jews themselves wanted to be chosen to rule the world, but most of them desired to do it by the power of military messiahs and by force of arms. They took Joshua and the deliverers in the book of Judges as their examples, not knowing that the physical sword was never God's weapon of choice. If Israel had been willing to hear the Word at Mount Horeb, God would have given them the Sword of the Spirit. But Israel's heart was hardened, and they could not hear the truth. Jesus—the second Joshua—offered them the Sword of the Spirit a second time. Those individuals who believed in Him were led into the experience of Pentecost, where they were given that sharp two-edged sword that can even divide soul from spirit. The Judean nation itself rejected Jesus and later attempted to gain their freedom by the physical sword. They failed utterly and only brought the iron yoke back upon their heads.

As the centuries passed, even the Church itself set aside their Sword of the Spirit and again took up the physical sword, killing heretics and rebellious infidels in the name of Jesus Christ. In the past century Jewish Zionism arose, and once again we have seen the way of bloodshed preached by both Jews and Christians as the means to establishing the Kingdom of God.

No nation—not even the Israeli state—will know freedom apart from Jesus Christ. More than that, one must give more than lip service to Jesus Christ, as the Church has often done. One must "*abide in My word*" (John 8:31) and put His words into practice.

The day is coming when every knee will bow to Jesus Christ and swear allegiance to Him as their King (Isaiah 45:23; Phil. 2:10, 11). They will not be compelled to do so by force, as many have envisioned, but out of a heart of love and accompanied by deep repentance. This is the glory of God, that He is able to win the nations to Himself by the power of the Spirit, rather than by force of arms. He is able to cover the earth with His glory, even as the waters cover the sea (Num. 14:16-21).

BIBLIOGRAPHY

Reference Books:

A History of the Jews, Abram Leon Sachar, Ph.D., Pres. of Brandeis University: New York, Alfred A. Knopf, 5th edition, 1964.

Ante-Nicene Fathers, Vol. I; Transl. by Rev. S. Thelwall, Christ's College, Cantab., Ed. By Alexander Roberts, D.D. and James Donaldson, LL.D.: Peabody, MA, Hendrickson Publishers, Inc., 1994 edition.

Ante-Nicene Fathers, Vol. III; transl. by Rev. S. Thelwall, Christ's College, Cantab., Ed. By Alexander Roberts, D.D. and James Donaldson, LL.D.: Peabody, MA, Hendrickson Publishers, Inc., 1994 edition.

By Way of Deception, Ostrovsky, Victor and Hoy, Claire: New York, NY, St. Martin's Press, 1991 edition.

Eusebius, Ecclesiastical History, Vol. 1 transl. by Kirsopp Lake, D.D., D.Litt., Winn Prof. of Eccl. Hist. in the Univ. of Harvard.: London, William Heinemann LTD and Cambridge, MA, Harvard Univ. Press, 1975 edition.

Eusebius, Ecclesiastical History, Vol. 2 transl. by J.E.L. Oulton, D.D., Regius Prof. of Divinity in the University of Dublin: London, William Heinemann LTD and Cambridge, MA, Harvard Univ. Press, 1973 edition.

History of the Jews, Graetz, Professor H., Vol. 2: Philadelphia, PA, The Jewish Publication Society of America, 1893.

Josephus, Complete Works, incl. Antiquities of the Jews and Wars of the Jews, transl. by William Whiston, A.M., Grand Rapids, MI; Kregel Publications: 1978 edition.

Secrets of Time, Jones, Stephen E., Ph.T., Minn. Grad. School of Theology; Port Austin, MI: Port Austin Bible Center, 2000 edition.

Seven Pillars of Wisdom, T. E. Lawrence: Garden City, NY, Doubleday, Doran & Co., Inc., 1936.

Jewish Fundamentalism in Israel, Dr. Israel Shahak and Norton Mezvinsky: Sterling, VA, Pluto Press, 1999 edition.

Romanism and the Reformation, Guinness.

Soldier of Peace, The Life of Yitzhak Rabin, Dan Kurzman: New York, NY, HarperCollins Publishers, 1998 edition.

Summing Up, Yitzhak Shamir, former Prime Minister of Israel: Boston, MA, Little Brown and Co., 1994 edition.

The Laws of the Second Coming, Jones, Stephen E., Ph.T., Minn. Grad. School of Theology; Port Austin, MI: Port Austin Bible Center, 2001 edition.

The Revolt: Story of the Irgun, Begin, Menachem, former Prime Minister of Israel, transl. by Shmuel Katz: New York, Henry Schuman, Inc., 1951 edition.

The Story of Celt-Saxon Israel, Bennett, W. H., Windsor, Ontario (Canada): Canadian British Israel Association, 2002.

The Thirteenth Tribe, Koestler, Arthur: New York, NY, Random House, Inc., 1976 edition.

The Zionist Connection II, Lilienthal, Alfred M.: Bullsbrook, Western Australia, Veritas Publishing Co. (Pty.) Ltd., 1983 (revised) edition.

The Barley Overcomers, Jones, Stephen E., Ph.T., Minn. Grad. School of Theology; Port Austin, MI: Port Austin Bible Center, 2002 edition.

The Book of Jasher, transl. by M. M. Noah, New York, NY: M. M. Noah & A. S. Gould, 1840.

The Deed, Frank, Gerold: New York, NY, Simon and Schuster, Inc., 1963 edition.

The Jewish Encyclopedia, 1925 ed.

Warrior, Sharon, Ariel, Prime Minister of Israel (2002) with David Chanoff: New York, NY, Simon and Schuster, Inc., 2001 edition.

Zealots For Zion, Inside Israel's West Bank Settlement Movement, Friedman, Robert: New Brunswick, NJ, Rutgers University Press, 1994 edition.

Articles:

Copley News Service, Dec. 21, 1977, Pat Boone column: "Why I Became a Jew."

Reflections on Covenant and Mission, Aug. 12, 2002, under the auspices of the United States Conference of Catholic Bishops, issued by the National Council of Synagogues and Delegates of the Bishops' Committee on Ecumenical and Interreligious Affairs.

Times (London), Jan. 27, 1973, Letter from Dr. Israel Shahak, "A Jewish Duty or Jewish Apostasy?"

The Globe and Mail (Toronto), Aug. 6, 1994 review of Shamir's autobiography, Summing Up.

Upstream, Feb. 6, 2001, Alexander Cockburn, "Ariel Sharon—the People's Choice?"

Bibles:

Concordant Literal New Testament, Concordant Publishing Concern: Canyon Country, CA , 1976.

New American Standard Bible, The Lockman Foundation, La Habra, CA, Thomas Nelson, Inc., 1985 edition.

The Companion Bible, with notes by Dr. E. W. Bullinger: Grand Rapids, MI, Kregel Publications, 1990.

The Interlinear Bible, Edited and Translated by Jay P. Green, Sr.: Peabody, MA, Hendrickson Publishers, Inc., 2nd ed. 1986.